A GLOBAL COMMUNITY

A GLOBAL COMMUNITY

THE JEWS FROM ALEPPO, SYRIA

WALTER P. ZENNER

WAYNE STATE UNIVERSITY PRESS
DETROIT

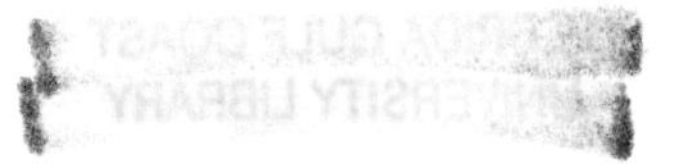

Manufactured in the United States of America.
04 03 02 01 00 5 4 3 2 1

Library of Congress Cataloging-in-Publication Data

Zenner, Walter P.
A global community : the Jews from Aleppo, Syria / Walter P. Zenner.
p. cm. — (Raphael Patai series in Jewish folklore and anthropology)
Includes bibliographical references (p.) and index.
ISBN 0-8143-2791-5 (alk. paper)
1. Jews—Syria—Aleppo—History. 2. Jews, Syrian—New York (State)—New York. 3. Jews, Syrian—England—Manchester. 4. Jews, Syrian—Israel. 5. Jews, Syrian—South America. I. Title. II. Series.

DS135.S95 Z46 2000
956.91'3—dc21
00-026755

To my wife, Linda, and my children, Rachel and Abigail,
who have exercised patience,
assisted me in a wide variety of ways,
and traveled with me in my various forays
in search of this diaspora.

Contents

Preface

My Introduction to Syrian Jewry

My study of the Aleppan diaspora has taken me to several different sites for fieldwork of varying length. It also has required textual research. The experiences that have marked my research over the past forty years have been quite varied. They began when I was a naive and inexperienced graduate student going into the field in outer Brooklyn on the New York subways in the late 1950s, and they have continued to the present, as I talk with the grandchildren of my original interviewees.

In 1958 I chose to study the topic of Syrian Jewry because I knew of no other anthropological work on the topic. Such a motive for research on a topic was reflective of the "butterfly collection" or "salvage ethnographic" tradition that had marked anthropology up to that time. While I began my work in New York, I really wanted to do my research in Israel, which at that time was absorbing masses of Jewish immigrants from all over the Middle East. Syrian Jews were among the less visible and less problematic immigrants, and they had received almost no attention from government agencies or social scientists.

My first experiences in Brooklyn were hit-or-miss. I had no formal training in ethnography. I did not know what to ask or how to ask the questions that I wanted to have answered. I began by arranging interviews with rabbis in the community and with people whom they recommended. I did have the foresight to record the scene in each household or office that I visited, as well as the responses to my queries. In most cases, the interviews with leaders were not very memorable, but I learned much from the experience of visiting each household. At one house, for instance, I met a young female cousin who was visiting from Mexico. In another case, I found out that Rabbi X was a son-in-law of Rabbi Y's. Some of the younger rabbis had been classmates or friends of mine at college or yeshiva.

My trips to the neighborhood often also involved a stop for refreshment on Bay Parkway or thereabouts. I noted businesses such as an "oriental" pastry shop, as well as luncheonettes. I would ask counter staff, "What kind of people live around here?" Their answers to this question introduced me to the complexity of Syrian Jewish identity and the ways such terms were negotiated. Generally, I learned that three kinds of people lived in the neighborhood: Jews, Italians, and Syrians, and that the Syrians were known to be fairly observant of Jewish tradition (see chapter 8).

My original plan had been to compare Syrian Orthodox Christians with Syrian Jews in New York City. This plan was not feasible for a summer project, however, and I had few entrees into the Orthodox community. I quickly found out that the two communities lived apart from one another in the New York Metropolitan area.

My reading and my few forays did, however, have value. For instance, I bought the Arabic-Lebanese-American paper, *al-Hodā*. This was a summer when fighting had broken out between Maronite and non-Maronite militias in Lebanon, which led to an American intervention in that country. This affected the willingness of Syrian Orthodox Christians to speak with a young Jewish ethnographer. I did, however, find an advertisement promoting the services of a belly dancer, whose manager lived on Ocean Parkway, a Syrian-Jewish area, and he bore a Syrian Jewish surname. This showed contact between the two communities, not noted at all in my interviews. I also went to Bradley Beach, New Jersey (near Asbury Park), where many Syrian Jews at that time went during the summer.

I continued my visits to Brooklyn for more than a year. In this period, I made friends with a number of Syrian Jews who lived outside of Brooklyn, including graduate students and professionals in Manhattan, some individuals from Israel, and some from South America. These people gave me the names of relatives in Israel and elsewhere, which helped me begin to make connections overseas. One woman gave me the addresses of her mother in Jerusalem and a sister in Paris. Another helped me to visit her family as well.

At this same time, I was still a graduate student taking classes. I used every appropriate opportunity to write my term and seminar papers on topics relating to Syrian Jewry. For several such exercises, I used previously published material on Jewish communities in Syria. Except for about a dozen articles, very little synthesis had been done on the history of these communities, other than for the topic of the Damascus Affair in 1840.

In order to reconstruct Jewish life in Syria during the nineteenth and twentieth centuries, I examined accounts by European residents, travelers, and missionaries. I also looked into Jewish legal responsa (decisions) written by Syrian rabbis. From my training at the Jewish Theological Seminary, the Conservative rabbinical school, I was familiar with Talmud and Jewish codes of law, but my knowledge of Jewish legal literature was limited. I knew of the responsa literature, in which rabbis answered presumably difficult inquiries, but I had never used it before. I concentrated my attention on the questions to the rabbis, rather than on the decisions reached by these legal scholars. I felt that social reality was more clearly reflected in the question than in the often technical response.

Still, the questions themselves were not as simple as they might appear. For instance, one recurring set of questions involved situations where a man ostensibly forced a woman to betroth him in public. As I considered these questions, I could not figure out what was really happening in these instances. These were cases not of rape, but of forced betrothal. I suspected that some of these cases might be something quite different, such as elopement without parental consent.

Another problem I faced was figuring out the loan-words in the documents. For instance, one word used in several inquiries in nineteenth-century responsa was *polizza,* spelled in a variety of ways, including *būlīṣā.* With the help of a number of professors, I realized that this was some kind of negotiable instrument, like a check. The word is related to *policy,* as in insurance.

There were also certain conventions with which I was unfamiliar. Parties to a case were not referred to as A,B, or C or the Hebrew and Arabic equivalents, "ploni" or "Fulān." Rather, they were given the names of the biblical Jacob's sons—e.g. Reuben, Simeon, Levi, and Judah. This convention was easy to figure out. What I did not know, however, was that references to Tiberias and Safed could also be such conventions—that is, they could be references to City A or City B. Since these Holy Cities are fairly near to Damascus, I reasonably assumed that when Reuben had an agent in "Tiberias," he meant Tiberias literally. I did not learn for a long time that this was a mistaken assumption.

The books of responsa themselves were a kind of puzzle, since they were not organized in ways to which contemporary Westerners are accustomed. Since I had studied Talmud, I knew that pages might be numbered as leafs, with side A and side B (i.e., page 1 would be 1-A and page 2 would be page 1-B), but there were other conventions as well. For instance, several collections of responsa were divided up according to the four divisions of the code of Jewish law, the *Shulḥan Arukh.* The first page of each section was page 1. All of this is child's play for rabbinic scholars and historians, but I did not have that type of training. While the use of responsa was the most difficult textual work I conducted, I have used a variety of other texts. The work on reconstructing the nineteenth-century background included use of travelers' accounts and ethical works. In dealing with communities elsewhere, my texts included synagogue plaques and wall posters, organizational bulletins and city directories, weekly newspapers, and occasional magazines put out by a variety of publishers.

My Personal Introduction to Aleppo Jews in Jerusalem

In Israel, I was not only interested in finding Syrian Jews and their descendants, but I also was engaged in getting a general sense of Israeli society as a whole. As is the case for many ethnographers, this experience was part of my maturation. I had found a fairly cohesive community in New York City. When I went to Israel, however, I found an ethnic group that was dispersed into a variety of social segments.

I visited Israel briefly in 1960, then returned in 1961 to do my fieldwork. Fieldwork in Israel was very different from that in New York. An important difference was that few Israelis had telephones in 1960 and 1961. Anthropological fieldwork involves a bit of stealth. Anthropologists want "backstage" presentations as well as "frontstage" performances. When you call ahead and arrange a meeting, people can prepare themselves. This is less possible when you just drop in. In the early 1960s, anthropologists were interested in spontaneous displays of cultures and were less concerned with issues of empowerment and control by the subjects of their research, which became a concern in later decades. Perhaps the spontaneity we saw was our illusion, rather than a quality of the interaction. What I learned from my experience was not just how to collect data, but also how to act in unfamiliar circumstances.

In Jerusalem, I met a whole range of people, from ultra-Orthodox rabbis to truck drivers who had little more than a grade school education. One of the latter was "Jacques Levi" (a pseudonym). I met him when a graduate student in folklore (now a well-known folklorist, Heda Jason, took me to see Reuven Na'aneh, an Iraqi-born shopkeeper in the Maḥaneh Yehuda marketplace. Na'aneh had self-published collections of pious exempla, including some of Middle Eastern origin. After Heda introduced me, I explained my reason for staying in Jerusalem, which was to study Syrian Jews. A man who was shopping in the store immediately introduced himself to me, saying that he was a Syrian Jew. He invited me to visit him and his family.

I did visit them in their small two-room house with an enclosed courtyard. Here he lived with his wife and five children. I subsequently visited the family several times a week. Jacques introduced me to his brothers and I also became acquainted with his sisters and their families. The Levis represented a completely different type of Aleppan Jew from the ones I had met in New York or among the rabbinic and mercantile families in Jerusalem. My interaction with them was much more informal. They were poor and somewhat rough in their humor, but open and warm. Since they had come to Palestine as children and still spoke Arabic, their culture was much more Arab in some ways than that of those who had been born in Jerusalem. For instance, they regularly listened to Jordanian radio programs because they liked Arabic music (this was before many Israelis had television sets).

My regular visits to the Levis and other families gave me a feel for everyday life in Jerusalem. I rented a room from an Orthodox Jewish family from Europe, but within walking distance of most of the Syrian families I had come to know.

At the beginning of my work in Jerusalem, I scheduled interviews with a rabbi who was knowledgeable about the history and background of Aleppan Jewry. I met with him weekly for about a month. Then I began to set up interviews with people who were knowledgeable about various other aspects of my research project.

At first I floundered. I was not sure where to start. Should I concentrate on the history of the Jews in Aleppo and nearby communities, or should I concentrate exclusively on the present situation of Syrian Jews in Israel? Since I was in Jerusalem, the intellectual center of Israel, I consulted with other anthropologists, sociologists, linguists, folklorists, and musicologists in the city about these problems. As it turned out, I worked on both the history and the contemporary sociology of the community. I probably spent one or two mornings or early afternoons each week either speaking to one of my colleagues or at the Hebrew University.

As my year in Jerusalem went on, I gradually developed a routine. On weekday mornings after breakfast, I would often go into the business district near Jaffa Road, where I would visit some Syrian shopkeepers or go to Maḥane Yehuda. Several afternoons a week were spent arranging interviews with Syrian Jews or others from what seemed to me to be related communities, particularly those from Urfa in southeastern Turkey. Several evenings might be spent visiting families, although I found that evening was not a good time for dropping in. On the Sabbath, I would visit rabbinic families in the evening and have Shabbat dinner with them several times a month, generally going there after the evening prayers. On Shabbat morning, I generally went to services at the ʿAdes Synagogue in Naḥalat Tziyon, a synagogue under the supervision of Aleppan rabbis. On Sabbaths during the winter months, I would try to get up at 2 or 3 A.M. to listen to *baqashot,* the Hebrew hymns sung to traditional Arabic melodies. They were sung in the ʿAdes Synagogue until dawn, followed immediately by the morning prayers. Since I rented a room from a moderate Orthodox family, there were no lights in the apartment after about 10 P.M., so I got up in the dark. It was generally quite chilly. I would make my way through dark streets, although if the moon was full, it was quite light. With the cypress trees, the scene reminded me of Van Gogh's paintings. When I arrived at the synagogue, it also would have few lights. The only source of warmth was cups of *kafé shabbat,* a kind of coffee that did not require cooking. The synagogue was generally half empty, with one or two dozen men sitting toward the front, singing these songs. The experience had a certain mystical quality. If I went to *baqashot,* I would return to my room about 10 A.M. and sleep for a few hours before venturing out either to see friends in the community or elsewhere in Jerusalem. Sometimes I was invited to eat with a family after services.

I visited both Orthodox and nonreligious families on the Sabbath. Among the non-Orthodox, card-playing was a common form of activity, while Orthodox homes, especially those of rabbis, were much more restrictive. I did not attempt to record on the Sabbath, so I often spent Saturday night or Sunday "debriefing" myself by taking notes or writing up my observations on the typewriter. I found that I needed two hours to write up each hour of interviewing or observation.

I left Jerusalem at least once a month. I had relatives in Israel whom I wanted to visit, but I also wanted to find out about Syrian Jews outside of Jerusalem. Among those I visited were individuals in Haifa, Tel Aviv, and on kibbutzim. I made many new friends on these visits. In all, these excursions helped place the people in Jerusalem, who were my primary subjects, into a broader perspective. Through my landlord and landlady, my relatives, and my professional colleagues, I learned about the attitudes of the Ashkenazic Jews, especially secular ones, toward their Middle Eastern neighbors. Through the interviews, I met several Syrians who had made their way into the labor movement, which then was at the height of its power in Israel.

I found that the social circles of these various groups—ordinary middle-class Ashkenazim, the university personnel, the truck drivers, and the rabbis—did not generally intersect, but that there were some overlapping ties. For instance, several children of rabbis had become professors. Folklorists and musicologists who studied Middle Eastern Jews did meet with a wide variety of Middle Easterners, as Heda Jason had. On my suggestion, Rabbi David Laniado sought out photographs of rabbis in a book by a Protestant missionary through Meir Benayahu, the son of a rabbi, who was then director of the Ben Zvi Institute. A civil servant, whose father was a rabbi who was only partially observant, would go to hear the singing of certain hymns (*baqashot*) in a proletarian neighborhood.

Unfortunately, I did not maintain contact with my friends in Jerusalem for very long. I did visit Jacques Levy and his family in Jerusalem in 1967. One of the rabbinic families eventually moved to New York, but they were not particularly open to visits from "nonreligious people" like me. Obviously I could and should have maintained contact with my new friends, but I did not. Except for one brief fortnight, I spent very little time in Israel between 1974 and 1991.

By 1991, even the poorer Israelis had telephones. I was in Israel on the eve of the Gulf War and I searched for the Levis in the phone book. I tried to call the number listed for Jacques Levy, but I got no answer. I was in Israel again in 1992 and I called his brother. I arranged for a visit and was warmly greeted but was berated for my negligence of nearly thirty years. I found out to my dismay that both Jacques and his wife had died. The following year I did see some of his children.

My Underlying Concerns

My first two field experiences, in New York and Jerusalem, were the most intense, but my fieldwork also included brief visits to other communities or individuals. For instance, when I was in Mexico City in 1959 and 1965, I visited the Syrian synagogues and spoke with both Syrian and non-Syrian Jews about Jewish life there, but I was there for other reasons. In Manchester, England (1987, see chapter 4) and Chicago (1988, see chapter 9) also, I spent short periods of time interviewing members of the Sephardic community, both Syrians and non-Syrians. These interviews were for the purpose of obtaining oral testimonies, which complemented library work on these communities.

Underlying all of my investigations were my concerns with interethnic relations, ethnic identity, acculturation, and assimilation. For example, I wanted to know how the Italian Picciotto family accommodated itself to life in eighteenth-century Aleppo, an Arabic-speaking city (see chapters 1 and 2). How separate were the Picciottos and other *signores francos* (Italian Jewish merchants and their descendants) from the rest of the Jews in Aleppo? In settings from Israel to Mexico to New York City, these questions persisted. Why did Syrian Jews in Brooklyn live in Jewish neighborhoods and yet refer to other Jews as *J-dubs* and to themselves as *S-Ys,* thus appearing to deny full identification with other Jews? To what degree were these Arabic-speaking Jews recognized by their neighbors as Jews or as Syrians and Arabs? Thus negotiation of identity, assimilation, and separation were concerns throughout my work.

My Personal Position: Gender, Age, and Other Attributes

In anthropological fieldwork, one's personal attributes matter even more than in history and other fields. When I began doing fieldwork in 1958, I was a single male in my twenties. I was both a graduate student in anthropology and a rabbinical student in a Conservative seminary, not an Orthodox yeshiva. By the time I went to Israel in 1961, I was religiously nonobservant, and I was doing doctoral research in anthropology. I was working with people who observed Judaism in a variety of ways, from nonobservant to strictly Orthodox. I was not in a position of authority. While the fact that I lived on grants made me seem wealthy to some in Israel, I lived on a rather modest stipend.

My status as a single male limited my field contacts with women, although I did have extensive conversations with some married women, especially in Israel, less so in New York City. I did have one encounter, where an unmarried woman sought to use me as a way of escaping an uncomfortable situtation, that could have compromised my fieldwork. After that situation was resolved, I generally kept my personal relationships with women separate from my fieldwork. While I have interviewed many women, I am certain that my work as represented in this volume reflects a distinctly masculine bias.

As one who is identified with the Conservative and Reconstructionist branches of Judaism and one who is not particularly strict in observing Jewish law, I have found working with Orthodox Jews somewhat difficult. While I did have extensive contacts with a wide range of Orthodox Aleppan rabbis in my early fieldwork, there are some with whom I have not been able to renew contact in recent years, whether in Israel or in the United States. Even in my early work, I sometimes found myself the subject of criticism. One boy kidded me about wearing a skullcap in my pocket, rather than on my head. In Mexico, young men who found out that I was single when I was twenty-five asked me why. I was informed by a man a few years older than I that I could not understand the inner meaning of Judaism because I was not sufficiently pious and because I had not studied in a yeshiva atmosphere.

I generally have avoided discussing politics with Aleppan Jews in either Israel or the United States, even when they have raised the topic. This has been especially true in the many instances where my positions have been in opposition to the nationalist point of view that my acquaintances have espoused. In fact, I have generally avoided expressing my own viewpoint even with individuals whose viewpoint on the Arab-Israeli conflict is close to mine.

When I began my study of the Jews of Aleppo, I knew next to nothing about them. I have learned over time that these people share a remarkable story of survival as an ethnic group, though scattered throughout the world. The study of Syrian Jews has also provided me with an angle for viewing Jewish history that is different from the conventional Eurocentric perspective pervading much of Judaic studies. For this and many other reasons, I am grateful for having had the opportunity to do this research.

Note on Transliteration

I have followed the guidelines of the *Encyclopedia Judaica* for transliterating Hebrew and Arabic words into English. With regard to the Hebrew letter *ṣadi*, or *tzadi*, I have transliterated it with ṣ when endeavoring to reproduce the Syrian Jewish pronunciation, while using *tz* in transliterating contemporary Israeli Hebrew. I also use the common spelling of names. For example, the name of the second president of Israel should be transliterated as *Yitzḥaq* Ben-Tzvi, but it is conventionally spelled Yitzhak Ben-Zvi.

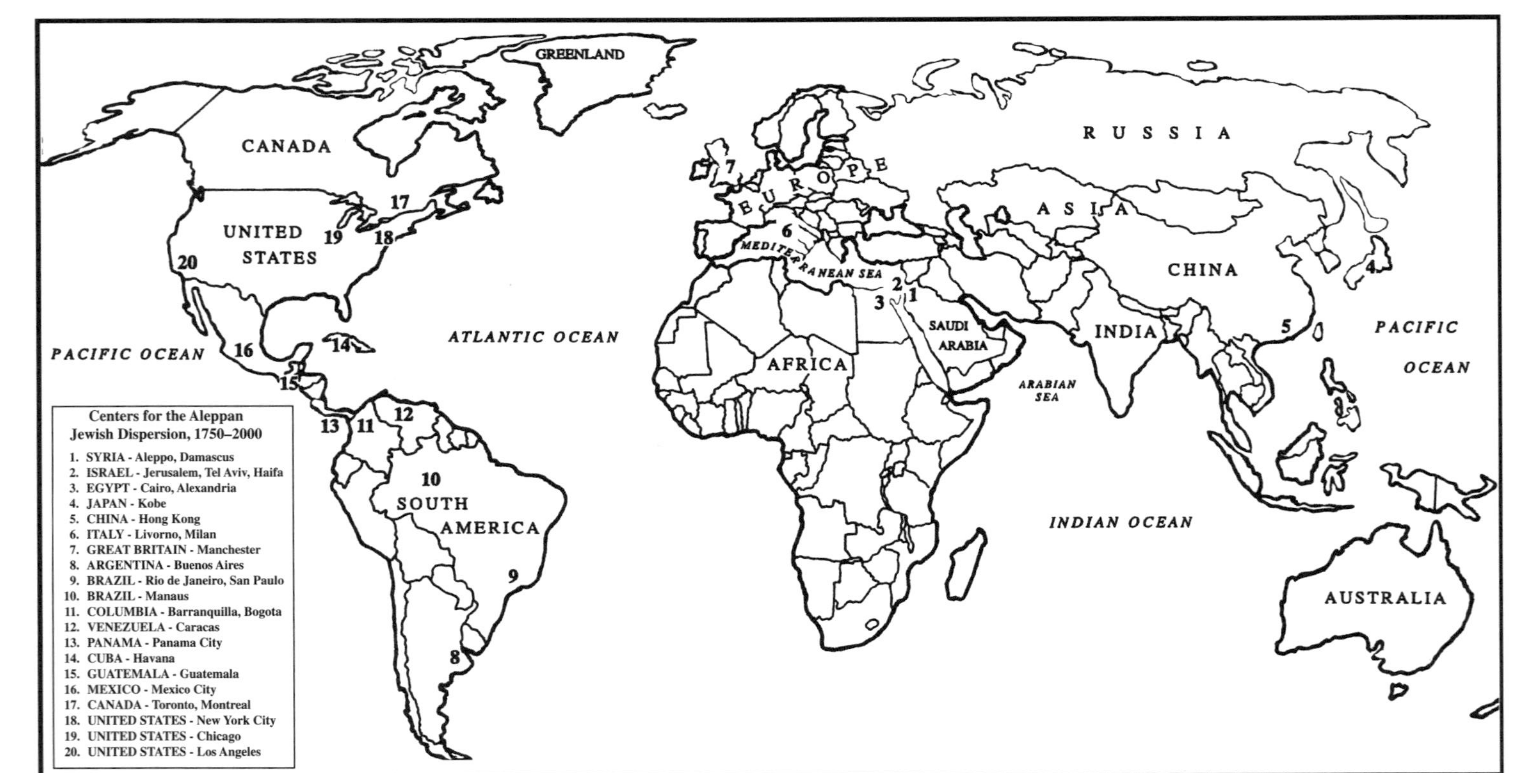
GREENLAND
CANADA
UNITED STATES
RUSSIA
EUROPE
ASIA
CHINA
INDIA
SAUDI ARABIA
AFRICA
SOUTH AMERICA
AUSTRALIA
MEDITERRANEAN SEA
ATLANTIC OCEAN
PACIFIC OCEAN
PACIFIC OCEAN
ARABIAN SEA
INDIAN OCEAN
1
2
3
4
5
6
7
8
9
10
11
12
13
14
15
16
17
18
19
20
Centers for the Aleppan Jewish Dispersion, 1750–2000
1. SYRIA - Aleppo, Damascus
2. ISRAEL - Jerusalem, Tel Aviv, Haifa
3. EGYPT - Cairo, Alexandria
4. JAPAN - Kobe
5. CHINA - Hong Kong
6. ITALY - Livorno, Milan
7. GREAT BRITAIN - Manchester
8. ARGENTINA - Buenos Aires
9. BRAZIL - Rio de Janeiro, San Paulo
10. BRAZIL - Manaus
11. COLUMBIA - Barranquilla, Bogota
12. VENEZUELA - Caracas
13. PANAMA - Panama City
14. CUBA - Havana
15. GUATEMALA - Guatemala
16. MEXICO - Mexico City
17. CANADA - Toronto, Montreal
18. UNITED STATES - New York City
19. UNITED STATES - Chicago
20. UNITED STATES - Los Angeles

Acknowledgments

I want to acknowledge the help that I have received over the past forty years, since this project began. I have received funding from Columbia University, the Ford Foundation Foreign Area Fellowship Program, the National Institute for Mental Health, the Shell Foundation, the Research Foundation of the State University of New York, and the Memorial Foundation for Jewish Culture. I have used the library resources of Columbia University, the Jewish Theological Seminary of America, Union Theological Seminary, Harvard University, the Hebrew University, the Israel Folklore Archives, Ben Zvi Institute, the Center for Jewish Studies of the University of Pennsylvania, the Central Manchester Library, the Manchester Jewish Museum, the Zionist Archives, and the University at Albany.

I have received assistance and hospitality from numerous individuals and families, both Syrian and non-Syrian, in the United States, Israel, Great Britain, and elsewhere. Of particular note are the Laniado family and the family that I have called "Levy," as well as Menahem Yedid, the head of the World Center for the Heritage of Aram Sobah. In recent phases of my work, I have been given assistance and advice from the following: Rabbi Michael Asoze; Kenneth Brown; Robert Chira; Lydia Collins; Judith Laikin Elkin; Rabbi Shimon Ellituv; Morris Eson; Rabbi Dianne Cohler-Esses; Barbara Freed; Samuel Gruber; George Gruen; Fred Halliday; Liz Hamui de Halabe; Yaron Harel; the late Albert Hourani; Basil Jeuda; Ignacio Klich; Jeff Lesser; Daniel Levy; Robert Lyons; Bruce Masters; Diane Matza; Brenda Picciotto

Rosenbaum; Victor, Sylvia and Marianne Sanua; Kay K. Shelemay; Linda Shamah; Daniel Schroeter; Chris Smith; Norman Stillman; the late Yedidah Stillman; the late Sefton Temkin; Rabbi Nathan Weiss; Bill Williams; Yael Zerubavel; and Zvi Zohar; as well as various anonymous reviewers. Over the past twenty years, I have mined the work of Ḥakhām David Laniado and Joseph Sutton, both of blessed memory, and of Amnon Shamosh. My collaboration with Mark Kligman on the last chapter has been of immense value in completing this study.

Several illustrations were first reproduced elsewhere:: photos that first appeared in Alexander Dothan, "On the History of the Ancient Synagogue in Aleppo," *Sefunot* 1 (1957): 25–61, by permission of the Ben Zvi Institute (Jerusalem), in Liz Hamui de Halabe, *Los Judios de Alepo en Mexico* (Mexico, 1987) by permission of Maguen David, A.C. (Mexico City); the catalogue for the exhibit *The Spirit of Aleppo,* by permission of the Sephardic Archives of the Sephardic Community Center (Brooklyn, N.Y.), and the Syrian Synagogue Survey of the World Monument Fund, carried out by Robert Lyons. Portions of chapter 2 are from *Jews among Muslims,* edited by Shlomo Deshen and Walter P. Zenner, and are reprinted here by permission of the publisher, Macmillan of Houndmills, England. Chapter 6 was first published in *Israel Affairs,* 3 (winter 1996): 95–110 and is reprinted here by permission of Frank Cass. Chapter 8 is adapted from the article "Syrian Jews in New York City Twenty Years Ago," first published in *Fields of Offerings: Articles in Honor of Raphael Patai,* Victor D. Sanua, editor (Cranbery, N.J.) and is published here with the permission of Associated Universities Presses. The section on Chicago in chapter 9 is adapted from my article "Chicago's Sephardim: A Historical Exploration," *American Jewish History* 79 (1989/90): 221–41; these portions are reprinted with permission of the Johns Hopkins University Press. Portions of chapters 1 and 2 appeared in "The Ethnography of Diaspora," the 1997 Sklare Memorial Lecture, *Contemporary Jewry* 19 (1998) 151–74 and reprinted by permission of the editors.

I have been assisted in preparation of the text over the years, especially by the late Joann Somich and Betty Kruger. I also want to thank Arthur Evans and Kathryn Wildfong of Wayne State University Press; Sandra Judd, the copy editor; Dan Ben-Amos, the series editor; Edith Leet of EHL Editorial Services; and Sami and Karen Davida of Shutter Speed for preparing this manuscript for press. As always, the final responsibility for the text is mine.

CHAPTER 1

INTRODUCTION: THE JEWS FROM ALEPPO

Until recently in the United States, ordinary people and social scientists alike saw the nation-state as the key determinant of a person's identity. A person born in Germany was a German. Someone born in Brooklyn was an American. If that person's mother came from Warsaw, she was a Pole. A person who declared that he had been born in Egypt but was not an Egyptian was likely to be asked for a lengthy explanation.[1] Nationality and religion also were seen as closely related but separate categories. Not all natives of England were Anglicans, nor were all Italians automatically Catholics.

In this scheme of things, Jews were an anomaly. Although born in a particular country, they were not identified with that country. Their ethnic group was also their religion. Today the word *diaspora,* which originally referred to the dispersion of the Jews across many lands, is applied to many different ethnic groups who are *transnational.* The term *transnational* implies that the group in question resides in several nation-states.

While the old categories remain in common usage, social scientists now use a variety of concepts such as multinational corporations and transnational diasporas. In addition, they now frequently speak of people inventing or negotiating identities, with the understanding that human beings may be described by a variety of terms simultaneously, such as Jew, German, American, doctor, wife, and the like. A person, whether sincerely or manipulatively, may use each identity in a different way, depending on the circumstances. For instance, a person with dual citizenship may use his American passport in one country and his German passport in another.

The problem of establishing the identity of a people has been noteworthy in many periods of human history, but it is particularly troublesome in the modern world. This book looks at one of the older branches of the Jewish people and provides case histories of how one group of people has accommodated itself to a variety of societies. The focus will be on the Jewish community of Aleppo and its outliers. Aleppo is a community that traces its history to the beginnings of the Jewish people.

This introduction to the Jews of Aleppo is divided into five parts. In the first, I will trace one family's immigration to and emigration from Aleppo as an example of the complexity of Aleppan Jewish history. Then I will present the beginning of my own work on this Jewish community, followed by the conceptual framework of this study, a note on terminology, and the plan of the book as a whole.

The Road to and from Aram Ṣōbā

We can look at diasporas in terms of the metaphorical tree with its roots and branches. We can also employ the trope of the pond or lake that is fed by many streams and in turn is the source of other brooks and rivers. The multiplicity of streams and ponds can be seen in the story of the Picciotto family. These many streams and brooks also contribute to the many different identities that apply to Aleppan Jews.

In the early eighteenth century, various Jewish merchants from the Tuscan port of Livorno (Leghorn, Italy) sent representatives of their family firms to different centers of trade in the Mediterranean. One such place in northern Syria was the landlocked city of Aleppo, known to Jews as Aram Ṣōbā. In Aleppo, the traders found an ancient Jewish community, made up of both Jews with deep roots in the Middle East and the descendants of Jews who had settled there a few centuries earlier, after the Expulsion from Spain in 1492.

The Livornese merchants were more European than the locals and became known in Aleppo as *signores francos* (the Frankish or European gentlemen). As subjects of European monarchs, such as the king of France, the grand duke of Tuscany and the Holy Roman Emperor, they were exempted from Ottoman taxes. This exemption was a cause for resentment between them and their fellow Jews. As will be seen in the following, their status gave these Jews great advantages over their coreligionists who were the subjects of the Ottoman sultan. By the end of the century, one of their number, Rafael Picciotto (1742–1827), had become the Austrian consul. As consul, he was the one in charge of giving protection to individuals carrying Austrian passports, regardless of religion.

Rafael Picciotto's grandfather was a Livornese merchant who had sent his son, Hillel, to Aleppo. Hillel married Anna Malki. Hillel, however, returned to Livorno to give his daughter Giudetta (Judith) in marriage to his brother Daniel. Then Daniel settled in Aleppo permanently, though the family kept a branch of the business open in Livorno for many years.

Members of the Picciotto family continued as consuls for Austria and other European powers until nearly the end of the next century. When Rafael became a knight of the Austrian empire in 1806, his branch of the family added the prefix *de* to their family name. As consuls, the Picciottos helped some of their fellow Aleppans gain the rights of foreign nationals in the Ottoman Empire (see chapter 2).

The Picciottos did not all stay in Aleppo. Some went to live in the Holy Cities of Palestine (Jerusalem, Hebron, Tiberias, and Safad); others returned to Italy; still others followed the changing trade routes to Egypt, Britain, and the Western Hemisphere. One of the latter, James Picciotto, gained fame as a pioneer historian of British Jewry in the nineteenth century. Such historical efforts helped Jews, most of whom were descended from recent immigrants, demonstrate that Jews had roots in the British Isles and assisted them in achieving equal rights in that realm.

By the mid-twentieth century, Picciottos could be found throughout the world. Even though they were not originally from Aleppo, Jewish Picciottos came to be associated with that city. Many Picciottos continue to live in places where Jews from Aleppo were concentrated, including Manchester, Milan, New York City, Guatemala, Mexico, and Colombia.

The Picciotto genealogy reveals both centrifugal and centripetal forces. Many Picciottos married cousins, especially during the eighteenth and nineteenth centuries. Surnames of Picciotto spouses well into the twentieth century indicate marriages with members of notable Syrian and Sephardic families. At the same time, family names such as Rothenberg, Rothberg, Rosenbaum, and Fainsylber suggest that Picciottos intermarried with Ashkenazim. Gentile surnames and personal names also appear more and more often in the Picciotto genealogy as time goes on. There is a Christopher, as well as such names as Auclair, Kokinopoulos, and Yoshe Ohiwa. Personal names include those of English, Italian, Hispanic, and modern Hebrew origins. The genealogy provides a roadmap of the family's movement across many geographic, symbolic, and social boundaries.

The family tree also suggests a number of identities that have been assumed by the Picciottos. They have been identified as Sephardic Jews, as Portuguese, as Tuscan and Italian, as Austrian, Syrian, Israeli, and Egyptian. Some branches of the family have become non-Jewish.[2]

The story of the Picciottos is just one of many Jewish Aleppan family histories that move from this city on the edge of the desert to circle the globe. The elements of dispersion, resettlement, and intermarriage with peoples of many origins are not unusual among immigrant and mercantile families, but

Aleppo's Jews have been notable for their maintenance of such ties for long periods of time.

Conceptual Framework: The Social Construction of Status and Identity

A basic assumption in my work is that while there are "objective" material and political constraints, as noted previously, much of what relates to a person's position in society, as well as his or her personal identity, are products of people's mental constructs. These are not simply individual notions that the individual self can change at will, but are the product of interactions that are often long-lasting. Whether we are considered natives or citizens of a particular country or mere sojourners, aliens, or "strangers" is the product of such social constructions. This modified Weberian viewpoint pervades my previous book, *Minorities in the Middle*. As in that book, I see "social construction" as materially grounded and limited by demographic, ecological, economic, and political factors.[3] Such statuses and the identities that people assume are negotiated within various sets of limitations. In the various countries to which Aleppan Jews have emigrated, their statuses and identities have undergone transformations over the years. Their status and their sense of themselves are reflected in the degree to which they are able to and wish to participate in the political affairs of their adopted countries.

For instance, in Muslim states prior to the nineteenth century, Jews were considered *dhimmī*, tolerated subjects who had to maintain a low profile but who had the rights to life, property, and freedom of living under their own religious law. In the nineteenth century, many chose to accept the privileges of foreign citizenship and to live in the Ottoman Empire under the protection of European states. In many countries to which they migrated, Aleppan Jews moved from being alien immigrants to becoming citizens. Many, however, considered their residence in these countries as temporary and did not become involved politically for a long time. These people had, some would argue, a sojourner mentality. In some places and times, political apathy was characteristic of many community members, who did not vote even if they were citizens. In other places, many members of the community became quite active politically, joining radical groups and taking public office.[4] There also were variations in how the majority or dominant population reacted to the Syrian immigrants and in whether or not they encouraged integration as citizens or excluded the newcomers. While this volume places its emphasis on the Syrians' accommodations, the outside perspective should not be forgotten.

Conceptual Framework: The Vocabulary of Acculturation and Assimilation

The sociological and anthropological literature on ethnic identity and group formation before 1970 had generally assumed the reality of societies and cultures as integrated units. Success for individuals and units depended on some form of social solidarity, which would lead to economic development. "Universalistic" goals in Parsonian sociology, for instance, can be identified with those of the society, which is identified with the nation-state. The late Raoul Narroll's effort to define the culture bearing unit had in it several dimensions, but key ones were integration into a unity that had internal peace and made war, as well as having a common language.[5] Immigrants and others not "fully integrated" must come to conform or to transform this unit, but the unit itself is considered ultimately supreme.

Over the years, much has been written about Jewish assimilation in the Western world. Most of this vast body of literature focuses primarily on Ashkenazic Jews. The assimilation of other ethnic groups into North American and other societies has also been studied. In this literature, various pictures of acculturation and assimilation have been produced.

In much of this writing, what is meant by *assimilation* is often unclear. The sociologist Milton M. Gordon clarified the conceptualization of assimilation by making distinctions between different aspects of this phenomenon.[6] The differences between acquiring some of the ways of the dominant group (sometimes called *acculturation*), losing one's former identity and taking on a new identity (*identificational assimilation*), and giving up distinctive group structures (*structural assimilation*) are often confused. Thus sometimes both Jews who have converted to Christianity and Reform Jews may be referred to as "assimilated Jews." The former have renounced Jewish identity (for the most part) and lost special Jewish structures (unless they are "Jews for Jesus"), while Reform Jews for the most part have not given these up. Yet their lifestyle is much closer to that of their Gentile neighbors than it is to that of Hasidic Jews. Gordon's distinctions give us a more precise handle on describing the complex situation.

Groups may also separate themselves from the dominant (or alternative) social groups, maintain a separate identity, build new structures, and preserve or invent distinctive cultural patterns. In the United States, the nineteenth-century Mormons, twentieth-century African-Americans (in developing distinctive names, clothing, and festivals), the Amish, and Hasidim are all examples of such separatist tendencies. Groups may also use a variety of identities in their daily lives, and through the years these identities will change. In current jargon, this constant construction of identities is referred to as manipulation or negotiation of identities.

The word *assimilation* has a very negative tone for those Jews who have fought for the survival and persistence of Jewishness in the modern world. Many such "survivalists" (a word they used before it was co-opted by the militias) were not against "*acculturation*" or acquiring the behaviors necessary to succeed in the dominant culture. The negative attitude toward assimilation has carried over into modern Hebrew. *Hitbollelut* and *temi'ah*, the most common terms used to translate *assimilation* into modern Hebrew imply total dissolution into the larger whole. In Israel, a term such as *mizug* (integration, mixture) is preferred in describing the processes of cultural, structural, and identificational changes.

A different vocabulary developed in anthropology around the terms *acculturation* and *culture contact*. Anthropologists, who studied peoples under colonial rule rather than immigrants and were initially less concerned with identificational change to the majority or dominant population and more interested in behavioral transformations, saw such changes happening in several directions. For example, the Europeans adopted some traits from the natives, while the natives accommodated themselves to the demands of the colonizers in a variety of ways, sometimes resisting them. Even though the anthropological theoretical literature clearly saw *acculturation* as a two-way street, most studies dealt with how the colonized reacted to the demands of the European colonizers. Later critics of the *culture contact* approach criticized it as being essentially biased toward the adoption of Western culture.[7]

The *assimilation* paradigm, the *culture contact* approach, and the whole sociology of minorities has recently come under attack from a new direction, that of "postmodern" anthropology. Recently Barbara Kirshenblatt-Gimblett, commenting on a review of a new body of work that focuses on diasporas, suggested replacing the old sociology (and anthropology) with a new *diasporic discourse* in a wholesale fashion. In the diasporic framework, the stress is on the ethnic group, wherever it appears. One focuses on connections between ethnic communities in different countries, rather than on the changes in the direction of the dominant majority culture.[8] In large part, the diasporic critique has attacked the assumption that territorial nation-states, with their dominant ethnic groupings, are the natural units with which social scientists must deal. Placing the dispersed ethnic group (the diaspora or *transnational community*), rather than the nation-state, at the center gives a perspective different from one that equates the territory of the nation-state with "society."

For historians of the Jews, such an outlook is not particularly novel. It is impossible to write the history of Jews in the late classical world without taking into account communities in Alexandria and Mesopotamia as well as those in Palestine. The great movements and events of modern Jewish history, including the mass migrations, Zionism, and the Holocaust are all transnational in scope. Whereas until recently the Jews were considered an anomaly in the social sciences, they are practically the norm today.

In addition, whereas social scientists formerly saw the centralized state as normal, postmodernists tend to see no permanent center in society. They look at efforts to define such a central focus with any kind of permanence as *essentialistic*, and *essentialism* is the bogey of postmodernists.

Related to this antiessentialism is the view that identities are not permanent entities, but rather are seen as social constructions, which are constantly created, re-created, and negotiated. The categories into which people are placed are similarly in a state of flux and constant redefinition. Jewishness, Americanism, and Christianity are changed in every period of time. Thus instead of speaking about nations or religions that have an essence, many speak today of Judaisms in the plural or of inventing Brazil (as opposed to the 1960s formulation, which would have emphasized "nation-building"). I have referred to this viewpoint as *nominalism.*[9]

This viewpoint has much validity as a critique, but it does neglect continuities, such as those pertaining to religious traditions. Traditional Jews and their Orthodox counterparts did not reinvent the Torah or its injunctions in every generation, nor did Muslims or Christians. But the Jews (and their counterparts in other religions) obviously accommodate their beliefs and the traditional formulations in order to take new situations into account. While there has been constant change, reinterpretation, and varying emphases on different aspects of the tradition, they have not started from scratch.

International Networks and the Diasporic Discourse

The Gordon vocabulary of assimilation can easily be adapted to the diasporic discourse. As the case of the Picciotto family shows, Jewish families could move from place to place and establish themselves in many different Jewish communities, yet they retained characteristics of the previous communities in which they had lived. Among Jews, local subgroups serve the function of providing a "home away from home." Rather than looking on the majority national community as the center into which one assimilates, each nation has many centers with which one may fuse or remain apart. In many though not all places, the Aleppan Jews have had the reputation for maintaining the home away from home.

In my studies of Aleppan Jews over the past four decades, the international familial networks have stood out. Individual after individual have told me about relatives in far off places. In Israel, I was asked several times if I had heard of the speaker's relatives in Buenos Aires or Mexico. In an interview in 1959, I met a man born in Brooklyn who had gone to school in Manchester before his family moved to Colombia. He later married an Israeli woman and lived in both the United States and Colombia. In 1987 I met a woman who was born in Guatemala, spent part of her childhood in Manchester, married an Aleppan-Egyptian, and lived for a time in Milan. Then she returned to Central America. Several of her children live in Mexico and the United States. Another woman who had spent much of her life in upstate New York inquired about an old friend living in Panama.

A retired Israeli civil servant told me of his brothers in New York, his sister who has lived in Argentina, and his vacations in Panama. Several Aleppan rabbis, some Israeli-born, serve congregations in the Western Hemisphere, but spend summers in their apartments in Jerusalem. Using this data, I have formulated a hypothesis that those Aleppan Jews who are part of international networks, whether familial, commercial, or communal-rabbinic, maintain their identity as Aleppans, while those who are not so involved are more likely to assimilate into the local community.

The picture of Syrian Jewish social relations is certainly "transnational" in the sense that Basch, Schiller, and Szanton Blanc describe this phenomenon. They describe *transnationalism* as "the processes by which immigrants forge and sustain multistranded social relations that link together their societies of origin and settlement." Later transnationalism is seen as the way in which migrants in their social, political, and economic relations, as well as in other aspects of their daily lives, forge links across national boundaries. Basch and her associates stress that this is part of the world capitalistic system. By these criteria, Syrian Jews have been a transnational community for centuries.[10]

Syrian Jews as Intermediary Minorities and Trade Diasporas

Important in my consideration has been the relationship of the economic roles adopted by Syrian Jews to their ethnic persistence. This focus on occupations led me to *intermediary minority theory* and the relationship between ethnic identity and class.[11] Early in my research on Syrian Jews in New York, I found that there was a fairly close connection between occupation and active membership in the Syrian Jewish community. Particular lines of trade were dominated by Syrian Jews. This has been particularly true of the Aleppan Jews in New York City and Latin America. Many of these relationships are intercommunal, so that people in Brazil or Panama are in close contact with relatives in New York or Mexico. This does not mean that every businessman in the community was involved in international trade or even in the dominant lines of trade. However, international trade was characteristic of the community over a long period of time and at a number of different sites.[12]

In addition to explaining how occupational specialization reinforces ethnic group persistence, intermediary minority theory also seeks to explain the hostility directed against such minorities by their competitors from the majority group. With regard to Syrian Jews, one can use intermediary minority theory to understand how the economic rivalry of Jewish and Christian merchants in Syria resulted in the ritual murder charges made by Christians against Jews in the nineteenth century.[13]

In addition, the theory can also be used to explain the violence directed at merchants in urban areas of the United States in the late twentieth century. The theory as sometimes presented overstresses economic factors, but when they take cognitive and perceptual factors into account, they become more complete. In much of this book, I do not refer to intermediary minority theories directly, but generally the Syrian Jewish diaspora has been composed of minority intermediaries to whom the generalizations made in my previous book, *Minorities in the Middle,* apply.

Varying Patterns in a Variety of Settings

As social scientists studying ethnic groups have noted, no pattern of relationships or interethnic essence can be applied in all contexts. To paraphrase and conflate a number of generalizations, there is no one-to-one relationship between skin color (race), genotype, mother tongue (language), ethnic identity, and way of life (culture). Syrian Jewish communities are composed of individuals with a wide variety of backgrounds and experiences. To give one example, today in Israel and the United States, some rabbis who most strongly support maintaining a stringently Orthodox Ḥalebi community are indifferent to maintaining a specifically Aleppan pattern of customs, except with regard to some special domains (e.g., liturgical and ceremonial music). In addition, each community is faced with a variety of problems stemming from its immediate social and political environment, which makes it either stronger or weaker internally.

The various countries in which Syrian Jews have lived provide different perspectives on how different groups should relate to the dominant ethnic or religious group of the state. For instance, in Islamic states the relationship between Muslims and their Christian and Jewish neighbors has often been ordered by the toleration of the non-Muslims by Muslims and the agreement of the minorities to acknowledge the superiority of Islam. It has also been marked by what has been called a "mosaic" system, whereby each group maintains its separate structure and keeps itself apart from other groups in a variety of ways.

In contrast, modern European and American states have generally encouraged giving up one's parental heritage for the national culture. Even between Europe and North America there are important differences in this regard. While national school systems in all three areas have encouraged behavioral and identificational assimilation, in North America there is more space for maintaining religious and cultural entities than there is in Western Europe.

Both the older vocabularies of assimilation and acculturation and the new diasporic discourse are useful in describing the changes that occur when peoples with different backgrounds meet. Influencing such interaction are such factors as the economic roles played by members of different ethnic groups, the prevailing attitudes toward minorities, the smaller groups' own self-images, and the legal position of each group. In the analysis offered here both the social construction of identity and objective features, such as occupations, are used.

A Note on Nomenclature

The terms used for the different groups are somewhat confusing to those unfamiliar with different Jewish ethnic nomenclature. Generally Jews are divided into two major groups: Ashkenazim and Sephardim. Ashkenazim are those Jews descended from Central and Eastern European Jews, whose ancestors were Yiddish speakers. The term *Sephardim,* which originally meant Jews from Spain and Portugal, often is used to encompass almost all non-Ashkenazic Jews, especially those from the Mediterranean basin and the Middle East. In the earlier, restricted sense, it applies most particularly to those who are descended from speakers of Judeo-Spanish (Ladino, Judezmo, Hakatia). While most Syrian Jews in recent generations have been Arabic speakers, Syrian Jewry also includes families descended from migrants from Spain. Thus even for those who prefer the older, restricted sense of Sephardi, Syrian Sephardim is not an oxymoron, and some Syrian communities refer to themselves as Sephardim. When we talk about the "negotiation of identities," the changing meanings of a word like *sephardi* are the subject of negotiation. By appropriating this term, Middle Eastern Jews, whose culture is often demeaned by Europeans, have striven to be seen as descendants of a noble European Jewish community that many Gentiles and Central and East European Jews admire. This process took place in Manchester in the nineteenth century, in Chicago in the early decades of this century, and in Palestine/Israel. In Israel today, *Sephardi* may be recovering its original meaning, as Middle Eastern Jews refer to themselves as *mizraḥim* (*mizraḥi,* singular), meaning Easterners.

The term *Syrian* is also problematic. It refers to both more and less than the boundaries of the present Syrian Arab Republic. The main centers of Jewish population in this area have been the cities of Aleppo and Damascus, as well as the hinterlands of these cities. For Aleppo, this included towns that are presently in Turkey, especially south-central Anatolian communities such as Anteb (Gaziantep) and Killiz, and southeastern Anatolian areas around the Euphrates basin such as Urfa (Edessa, Sinilurfa). In Middle Eastern politics, the use of the term is related to the ambitions of various nationalist movements and regimes. For Damascus, it included much of what is now in Lebanon. Jews from the Province of Aleppo were classified by other Jews as *ḥalebi* or *Aleppan,* while those from southern Syria and Lebanon were included in the category of the *shāmī* or *Damascene.* The emphasis in this book will be on Aleppan or North Syrian Jews, but Damascene Jewry and Jews from other places will also be considered. In this book, I use a variety of terms to refer to Aleppan Jews. In writing about Aleppans in Israel, I have always used the term *Ḥalebi*. The predominantly Aleppan community in New York City is usually referred to as Syrian Jewish, although the term *ḥalebi* is known there, too. The problems involved in applying these terms to the subjects of this book are indicative of their and their neighbors' social construction of names and identities.

The Plan of the Book

Chapters 2 and 3 of this book will deal with Jews in the Syrian lands, emphasizing those who lived in Aleppo and its hinterland (some of which is in present-day Turkey). Chapter 2 will take Syrian Jewry from its beginnings to the socioeconomic environment of Late Ottoman Syria. It will concentrate on the status of Jews in the Ottoman Empire, their socioeconomic roles, and their relations with their non-Jewish neighbors. While they were structurally separate from the Muslim majority and from the Christians, who constituted another religious minority, they also shared a common culture with their neighbors. The chapter will also deal with internal aspects of Jewish communal life, including the family, education, religious life, and communal structure. In most of these aspects, the Jews of Aleppo resembled other Jewish communities in the Middle East. The Aleppan rabbinate, however, was remarkable in the way that it resisted certain aspects of Western modernity. This provided one basis for Aleppan separation from other Jewish communities and resistance to assimilation after emigration.

The fate of Jews in the Syrian Republic is the subject of chapter 3. Syrian Jewry's fate was very much tied to internal politics in Syria and the degree to which Syria was involved in the conflict between Israel and its Arab neighbors. Ultimately this resulted in the emigration of Aleppo's Jews.

After a brief overview of Syrian migrations to Egypt and Europe, chapter 4 deals with Syrian Sephardic Jews in Manchester, England. Aleppan Jews became part of an upper-middle-class community of Jews from the Mediterranean and the Middle East. The communal structure was tied in part to the economic role that these immigrants played in the cotton industry and trade that dominated the economy of Lancashire. Aleppan Jews played an important role in this community, which survives despite its economic decline.

In Israel also, Syrian Jewry underwent structural assimilation into larger Jewish entities. The background of this pattern is described in chapter 5, which deals with immigration. In chapter 6, this situation is described in terms of what had developed by the 1960s and how it has continued into the 1990s. While the Aleppan Jews in Jerusalem continue to maintain contacts with their kin and fellow Aleppans abroad, they see themselves as part of a greater Israeli Jewish community.

Chapter 7 turns its attention to the Aleppan Jews who went to the communities of Latin America. Hispanization occurred throughout the area, but

Aleppan Jews have maintained separate congregations in most countries. At the same time, individuals have assimilated. Larger communities, such as Buenos Aires and Mexico City, are stronger, with greater separation and more intense communal activity than in most smaller communities.

The Syrian Jews in the United States are the subject of the next three chapters. Identificational and structural separation are strongest in the enclaves in Brooklyn and Deal, in the New York-New Jersey Metropolitan area. Chapter 8 describes this area in its beginning and as it was around 1960 (1958–63). Chapter 9 deals with individuals of Aleppan and other Syrian origins outside these communities, who either do not wish to maintain their separation from the larger society or find it more difficult to do so. Chapter 10 describes the diversification of these New York/New Jersey communities in the 1990s. The final chapter draws some conclusions about the Aleppan Jewish diaspora and the implications of this book for our view of the Jewish dispersion as a whole and of other transnational communities.

CHAPTER 2

The Jews of the Syrian Lands during the Late Ottoman Empire

Jewish Roots in Syria

Throughout the medieval and early modern periods, the Jews of Aleppo, Damascus, and nearby localities had traditions that associated certain places with biblical personalities. The Book of Genesis associates the Hebrew patriarch Abraham and his kin with the northern Euphrates valley, not far from Aleppo. According to a later legend, Abraham used a spring in Urfa (ancient Edessa) in southeastern Anatolia (recently renamed Sinilurfa), and his flocks were milked in Aleppo. Urfa was identified with Ur of the Chaldees, while Aleppo acquired the name *Ḥaleb* (like *ḥalāv,* milk in Hebrew). Joab, David's general, conquered the biblical Aram Ṣōbā, later identified with Aleppo, and is said to have laid the foundations for the synagogue there (based on 2 Sam. 8:3–8.

Elisha the Prophet healed Naʿaman of Damascus of his leprosy in the Jordan River (2 Kings 5), and the synagogue at Jōbār (a suburb of Damascus) is associated with Flisha. On his return from Babylon to Zion, according to a legend related to me by a native of the place, Ezra stopped in *Tedef al-Yahūd,* a village near Aleppo, and wrote a Torah scroll in a cave there.

Most of these attributions were probably invented long after the events for reasons having more to do with the Byzantine and Islamic regimes under which the Jews lived than with Scripture. Nevertheless, the Jews in Syria and surrounding territories under the Ottoman Empire realized that their ancestors had had a long association with this region.

Language was another link. Hebrew is a Western Semitic language closely related to Canaanite, Amorite, Ugaritic, and Aramaic. The coastal and river plains that lie between the Mediterranean and the Syrian deserts have long been traveled for purposes of trade and conquest by peoples speaking these languages.

Aleppo had existed since the Bronze Age (second millennium B.C.E.), where it appears in various cuneiform and hieroglyphic texts as Halab, Halaba, Halpa, hrp, or their variants. For a time it stood on the border between the West-Semitic peoples and the Hittites who ruled much of Anatolia.[1]

While most archaeologists agree that the original *Aram Ṣōbā*, which was part of the short-lived empire of David and Solomon, lies to the south of Aleppo, nearer to modern Ḥama and Ḥoms, identifying Aleppo with it is not so far off the mark. At the time of Elisha (c. ninth Century B.C.E.), the Kingdoms of Israel and Aram-Damascus were often at war or engaged in short-term alliances. Aleppo is on the old route from southern Mesopotamia to Palestine.

The village of *Tedef al-Yahūd* is not far from Aleppo. Tedef is the site of a shrine to Ezra. Even though Muslims see Ezra in nonheroic terms since he is alleged to have falsified Scripture to make the Hebrew texts differ from the Qur'ān, for many centuries, Muslims protected this shrine from harm.[2]

Certainly in the postbiblical Hellenistic and Roman periods, Jews were living in Syrian lands. Jews probably lived in Antioch, the Seleucid capital, under Antiochus Epiphanes. His policies sparked the Maccabean revolt in Judaea. At this time, an unnamed mother (later called Hannah) and her sons died heroically, probably in Antioch, after refusing to renounce Judaism and suffering cruel tortures (2 Macc. 7; 4 Macc. 8–18). Jews founded a synagogue in Antioch, named *Keneset Ḥashmūnit* (the Hasmonean or Maccabean synagogue) after these martyrs in that northern Syrian city. Eventually this synagogue was converted into a Christian church; the Christians also venerated the Maccabean martyrs. Antioch (now the Turkish town of Antakya) has had a Jewish community from that time to our own day.[3]

From the Roman period on, the Jewish presence throughout Syria is well attested. The quondam Pharisee Saul of Tarsus became a follower of Jesus the Nazarene while Saul was on the road to Damascus, where he was to visit a Jewish congregation.

While Damascus was an important center from at least the Roman period on, several other cities were the centers of trade, administration, and Jewish life in northern Syria and neighboring regions. Throughout the Hellenistic, Roman, and Byzantine periods, Antioch was the preeminent city of the region. Aleppo did not become a major city until well after the Islamic conquest. Aleppo reached the apex of its eminence during the early Ottoman period (1517–1800).

For Jews, however, despite this, Aleppo had long been a sacred center with its own sacred relic of great antiquity. The Great Synagogue of Aleppo, despite a stormy history, has remained a symbol of the venerability of the Jewish community there. As noted previously, its foundation is attributed to David's general, Joab. Most probably the synagogue was built in Byzantine times, after the fifth century of the Christian era. During the Mongol conquest in the thirteenth century, the synagogue was one of six designated places of refuge in the city, but it was destroyed during Tamerlane's subjugation of Aleppo in 1400. Reconstruction of the building was completed in 1418. The synagogue was burned in 1947, when anti-Zionist riots directed at the Jews of Aleppo broke out. In 1995 the building was abandoned, since almost all Jews had left Aleppo and it had fallen into a state of disrepair.[4]

The synagogue contained many objects that attested to its sanctity. Chief among them was the *Keter* or *Keter Torah.* This was the Aleppo Codex, the oldest manuscript of a Torah as well as Prophets and Writings that contained both vocalization and cantillation signs. The Codex is *not* a Torah scroll; Torah scrolls that are central to synagogues contain unvocalized texts of the Torah alone.

The Codex is of great value to scholars, since even minor variations in ancient texts can elucidate difficult passages. While both Christian and Jewish scholars sought access to this important copy of the Hebrew Scriptures (Old Testament), the Jews of Aleppo limited access to the Codex, thus adding to its mystery.

This Codex itself has an eventful history. It evidently was moved from Jerusalem to Egypt in the time of the Crusades, eventually ending up in the Aleppo synagogue. It disappeared in 1947, after the anti-Jewish riots and the burning of the synagogue. Part of the Codex was smuggled out of Syria. Eventually this fragment was brought to Jerusalem, where it is now safeguarded in the Shrine of the Book at the Israel Museum. Various groups still dispute its ownership.[5] We do not know what happened to the remainder of the Aleppo Codex. Since access to the Codex was restricted, trying to study the Aleppo Codex was one of the attractions of Aleppo for scholars and other serious travelers during the nineteenth and early twentieth centuries. Both the synagogue and the Codex were links between Aleppan Jewry's past and its present.

The City of Aleppo in the Ottoman Period

Aleppo was at its peak as the commercial center of northern Syria, southern Anatolia, and northwestern Mesopotamia in the period between the Ottoman conquest in 1517 and the beginning of the nineteenth century.[6] In this period, when Persian silk and Syrian cotton were important commodities exported from the Middle East, Aleppo served as the trading center between Iran and Iraq and Europe. Caravans crossed between east and west and ships to and from Europe docked at ports such as Alexandretta. During this period, Aleppo and all of the hinterlands of Aleppo came under the rule of the Ottoman sultan. This prominence came to an end with the Industrial Revolution (around 1840), which reversed the flow of trade from the Middle East, and with the opening of the Suez Canal, which brought about the end of the caravan trade.

Jews, especially Sephardim, have historically taken part in the textile trade. Many exiles from Spain and southern Italy in the late fifteenth and early sixteenth centuries settled in the Ottoman Empire, including Aleppo and Damascus. The Jewish population of the area up to that point had consisted of *Mustʿaribim* (i.e., Arabic-speaking Jews). The new immigrants traded with other Sephardic Jews in Europe and the rest of the Mediterranean. The Jews of Livorno, such as the Picciotto family, were important participants in this trading diaspora.[7]

Jewish Population in Aleppo

Even though many of the Aleppan Jews were of Spanish origin, Arabic was the language of Aleppo's Jewish community. In addition to European Jews, Jews from elsewhere in the Middle East settled in Aleppo, including those from its Anatolian-Syrian hinterland and from Iran.

According to the Ottoman Census of 1893, there were 10,761 Jews in the Province of Aleppo, most living in the city, while 6,265 Jews lived in Damascus and vicinity. In 1908, there were 9,335 Jews out of a total population of 119,811 in the city. The Jews were concentrated in the northwestern part of the old city, particularly in the Baḥsita and neighboring quarters. Muslims were more likely to be coresidents there than were Christians. Some middle-class and upper-income Jews lived outside the walls in the new *Jamiliya* and *aṣ-Ṣaliba aṣ-Ṣaghir* neighborhoods, which were built at the end of the nineteenth century. Many Christians also lived there.[8]

Common Culture and Separate Groups: Jewish-Gentile Relations

Most Jews of Aleppo, Damascus, and other "Syrian" communities were Arabic-speakers. They shared a common language and many cultural patterns with their non-Jewish neighbors, whether Muslim, Christian, or members of various sects, such as the Nosairis and the Druzes. The common cultural patterns included cuisine; the musical system of *maqāmāt;* the honor-shame code in gender relations; participation in markets; stories and jokes; and popular religious and medical practices. Well into the nineteenth century, members of the various religious communities shared a general religious outlook, including adherence to God and agreement that they should observe the precepts of their respective communities. At the same time, within each community the intensity of observance varied widely.

The different religious communities maintained their distinct identities, sets of rules, and boundaries. Each group had its own laws governing marriage, divorce, and inheritance. The patterns of prayer, meditation, and scriptural reading in the houses of worship of the different sects were also distinctive, as were dietary regulations and the use of music. For instance, the emotional meaning of a particular *maqām* (melody type) used in local music might be different among Jews than among Muslims.[9] *Ma'amul*, a semolina cookie eaten at Purim (a spring Jewish festival), was an Easter sweet for Christians.

The communication networks of each group were also distinctive. Jews and Christians maintained contact with coreligionists in Europe, while Muslims emphasized their relations with Arabia and Istanbul. This made each group open to different avenues of cultural change.

The common language and culture of these peoples provided members of each group with a wide repertoire of elements to use in managing their image vis-à-vis partners and rivals among other groups, as well as in negotiating their own identities for particular circumstances. Thus Jews seeking friendships with Muslims might emphasize the kinship of Isaac and Ishmael, while Druzes might portray the identity of their prophet, Shu'eb, as Jethro, the father-in-law of Moses. Hostility might be illustrated by reference to the Druzes as "Philistines" (as they were labeled in Hebrew). Christians in such contexts would be referred to as the "uncircumcised."

The common knowledge, prejudices, and tensions between the groups were also reflected in jokes and proverbs. For example, once a Jew was eating in the market on the first day of *Ramaḍān,* the Muslim month of fasting (when Muslims fast for thirty days, but eat at night). A Muslim reproved him for eating on a fast day. He put his food away and he did this for two more days. On the fourth day, he took out his bread and again started eating. The Muslim came over to him to bawl him out. The Jew replied, "Muḥammed wrote, Don't eat for 3 days, but as he wrote while the ink was still wet, a fly came along and left a dot next to the number, 3, so why should I not eat on account of a fly?

The anecdote is obviously anachronistic, since Arabic numerals, including the Arabic zero (which is a single dot) were not used in writing the Qur'ān. This joke was related to me by an Aleppo-born Jew in Jerusalem.

A Damascus Jew told me the following: Once a Shiite, of whom there were very few in Damascus, went to a rabbi and asked, "How is it that we will be the donkeys of the Jews when the Messiah comes, since Jews are many and Shiites are few?"

The rabbi replied, using the Quranic chant, that each Shiite would be such a big ass that together they could carry all the Jews.

Beneath this rivalry there is a religious faith, shared by Jews, Christians, and Muslims, that derives from Abrahamic monotheism. Part of it is a fatalism marked by interspersing Arabic phrases, such as "if God wills" (*in sha' allah)* and "thank God"(*al-ḥamdah da-lillah*). This fatalism is balanced by a belief in the efficacy of magical practices. For instance, all groups were concerned about envy of an individual's good fortune, which could be prevented by certain measures against the evil eye. Muslims, Jews, and Druzes all used the color light blue and the number 5, often in the form of a hand, against the evil eye.

People of one religion might resort to holy men or shrines of other religions in times of need. A Jew might call on a *sheikh* to obtain a cure, while Christians might go to a rabbi. At times of intense crisis, such as a severe drought, the leaders of all religions might be called upon to offer prayers.

The graves of saintly men were revered by all. Many stories are told of Muslim attempts to steal the bodies of saintly rabbis because of their inherent magical power. In one legend, Muslims tried to bury the body of Moses Kohen, the first *ḥakhām bāshī* (chief rabbi) of Aleppo, in their cemetery. They were prevented from doing so by the Consuls de Picciotto, who had him interred in their family tomb. The history of the synagogue in Tedef al-Yahūd, at the site where Ezra the Scribe is said to have stopped en route to Jerusalem, shows this shared reverence for saints. It was restored in the 1830s with help from the Muḥammed Ali regime. It was saved from destruction at the time of the anti-Zionist pogrom in November 1947 by a local Arab resident. Despite this effort in 1947, this shrine has since been neglected and is now in ruins.[10]

Visiting in the homes of members of differing religions was limited. It appears to have been most common in those neighborhoods of Aleppo where Jews and Muslims lived on the same street. When Jewish peddlers traveled in rural areas, they had to spend the night in Gentile houses. The relative degree of intimacy, no doubt, depended on the degree of enmity and amity. Gentiles were guests at Jewish weddings. At the end of Passover, on *leil ḥameṣ* (the night of leaven), Muslims would bring their Jewish acquaintances fresh bread and cheese. During the Mandatory period (c. 1919–44), Jewish men would meet their Gentile acquaintances in cafes; Jews were rarely invited into Gentile homes.

In those occupations where there was ethnic specialization, economic interdependence was obvious. In other occupations, Jews, Christians, and Muslims were in competition and this often led to intergroup conflict. Some Jews were employees of non-Jews. One Jew worked as an accountant for a Muslim family firm, and some Jews worked as printers for a Christian during the Mandatory period. Jews generally preferred not to enter into full partnerships with Gentiles. Jews hired Gentiles to do work prohibited to Jews on the Sabbath.

The *Dhimmī* Status

In Islam, Judaism and Christianity are recognized as revealed religions, albeit of a lower status than Islam. The Scriptures of these religions, according to the Muslim viewpoint, are perverted so that they sometimes contradict the true revelation found in the Qur'ān and Muslim tradition. Jews and Christians who accept Muslim rule are to be protected subjects (*dhimmī*) as long they pay special taxes to the Muslim state and demonstrate, by maintaining a low profile, that they are not superior to Muslims. In different places and times, the way in which this low profile was interpreted varied greatly.

Until the nineteenth century, one aspect of this low profile was that new synagogues could not be built. Furthermore, Jews had to justify the existence of older houses of worship by stressing their antiquity, such as attributing the Great Synagogue of Aleppo to Joab the son of Seruya. Ceremonies such as blowing the *shofar* (on the Jewish New Year) and celebrating Purim had to be conducted so as not to disturb their Muslim neighbors. While Jews did serve the Ottoman administration, they did so as contractors, not as direct appointees.

From the 1830s onward, the Ottoman government was under pressure from European powers to grant Christians and Jews equal rights with Muslims, a policy that provoked a Muslim backlash. The old contractual positions in which some Jews had been successful, such as banker to the governor (*ṣarrāf*), disappeared, while new jobs for Jews and Christians as Ottoman civil servants became available. Even the heads of the religious communities, such as the Christian bishops and local chief rabbis (*ḥakhām bāshī*) were now considered governmental appointees. The old discriminatory taxes (*jizya*) on Jews and Christians were now considered substitutions for military service. After 1908, the Ottoman government, under the "Young Turks," instituted military conscription for the *dhimmī*. This accelerated the process of emigration, which was then under way. Some legislative bodies that purported to represent the people were also established in this period, and *dhimmīs* were represented there. In practice, however, the Muslims were reluctant to give equal status to Jews and Christians, and the basic balance of power between the Muslims and the *dhimmīs* remained in force, even though it was under challenge.

In the prereform period, there were both Muslim courts and courts of law within the Jewish community, having wide jurisdiction over many areas of life. Until recently, many scholars stressed the arbitrary and discriminatory practices of Ottoman officials and Muslim courts. New research has shown, however, that Jews in Syria made extensive use of Muslim courts. Probably they manipulated the two court systems for their personal advantage.[11] By the end of the Ottoman period, the divisions between Muslims, Christians, and Jews remained. While some Muslims and *dhimmīs*, especially Christians, envisioned a secular Syria, for most Syrians the society remained divided along sectarian lines. There was jockeying for dominance among the religions.

The separate sets of norms, embodied in several legal codes and enforced by separate judges, whether bishops, *ʿulemā* (Muslim religious specialists), or rabbis, each with their separate social networks, formed the basis of the communal system, sometimes labeled the *millet* (*milla,* nation or ethnic group, Arabic and Turkish). Since the nineteenth century, this term has been applied to formally recognized religious communities who have been granted the right to adjudicate their own sets of personal laws for their adherents. This type of system has long been operative in Islamic lands. While a system of communal pluralism existed before the Ottoman conquest, Ottoman reforms first gave it a formal administrative structure. The appointment of the *ḥakhām bāshī* (chief rabbi) was part of this change. In practice, Ottoman bureaucrats continued to allow local authorities a large measure of autonomy. The informal relations among the various sects and the formal *millet* system established patterns for intergroup relations that led to groups living separately side by side. The late Albert Hourani, an eminent historian of the Arabs and a native of Manchester, England, suggested that Syrians of different religions maintained this pattern of intergroup relations in Manchester,[12] while the Syrian Jews in Brooklyn continued to call their senior rabbi *ḥakhām bāshī* until his death in the 1990s. Thus the patterns of life structured by the Ottoman state have continued to influence emigrants abroad.

Extraterritoriality and Consuls

In its heyday, the Ottoman Empire encouraged trade by granting special privileges to European merchants so that they would not be afraid to travel in its realms. European merchants were granted exemptions from certain taxes and could be tried for offenses before their nation's consuls, rather than in Ottoman courts. By the early nineteenth century, when the Ottoman government's power had weakened, such "extraterritorial" privileges were easily abused. In addition to European residents, many locally born Christians and Jews had acquired passports from European countries, especially Britain, France, and the Austro-Hungarian Empire. They were thus exempt from taxation, and that exemption had a financial impact on the local Jewish community.

The consuls of the European powers, including those of Britain and France, were often prejudiced against Jews, but in the nineteenth century

Jews could sometimes gain the assistance of Jewish organizations and notables in putting pressure on these officials to act on their behalf, as well as on that of local Christians. In Aleppo, for about a century, there was a family of Jewish consuls. In 1788 Rafael Picciotto became the consul for Tuscany and later for the Hapsburg (Austro-Hungarian) Empire. Other members of his family and his descendants represented other European powers until the last decades of the nineteenth century.

The Picciotto consuls were seen as defenders of Jewish interests. By the 1860s, however, they were also seen to be placing their own personal interests and those of the wealthier Jews of Aleppo before those of the community at large. By this time, also, French and British officials, despite their frequently anti-Semitic sentiment, began to seek Jewish clients. For their part, well-to-do Jews welcomed British and French protection.[13] The consular system thus played a role in furthering the estrangement of Jews from their Syrian homes and deepening the conflict between Jews and Christians.

Jewish and Christian Conflict

During the nineteenth century, Muslims feared the growing power of Christians, whom they saw as allied with the hostile European imperialism. The Jews, by comparison, were seen as harmless. Among the *dhimmī* themselves, the old competition between Christians and Jews continued. In the eighteenth and early nineteenth centuries, they had vied for government contracts that would allow them to lend money to the governor and to collect taxes and customs. They also competed for advantages in trade and consular privileges. Thus, relations between the wealthier Jews and Christians included efforts to manipulate the image of self and other and to use such images in negotiating with the Ottoman authorities on the one hand and the European powers on the other.

In the Damascus Affair of 1840, Jews were accused of murdering a Catholic priest in order to use his blood for ritual purposes. The chief public figure accusing the Jews was the French consul, Count Benoit Ratti-Menton. It is hard to gauge the direct involvement of local Greek Catholics in the initiation of these accusations. Undoubtedly Ḥanna Baḥri Bey, the banker to the pasha, was strengthened by the accusations against the Jews, including his rival, Raphael Farḥi. He also took part in interrogating some of the suspects. Some died in prison. Later, when the surviving Jewish defendants were released from prison, their release was seen as a vindication of the Jews and a defeat for Christians. The French consul and the officials who then ruled Damascus (the Egyptian governor, Muhammed Ali, acting as an independent potentate) were aligned with the accusers against the Jewish notables, while Damascus Jewry enlisted the help of Jews in France and Britain, the British and Austrian governments, and the central Ottoman administration.

Christians made similar accusations on other occasions, such as after the Damascus pogrom of 1860. Jews at times reacted to Christian hostility indirectly. For instance, Jews were not unhappy when Muslims rioted against Christians in Aleppo in 1850, even though two hundred Christians had found refuge in the home of Rafael Picciotto, the consul representing Christian Russia.[14]

Jews also had dealings in the nineteenth century with Protestant missionaries, particularly from Britain. The missionaries were usually Jewish converts sent by the London Society for the Promotion of Christianity amongst the Jews. When these missionaries first arrived (around the time of the Damascus Affair), they were seen as friends and allies against the false charges about Judaism made by Catholic and Greek Orthodox Christians. As time went on, however, local rabbis and other Jews saw them as trying to convert Jews to another religion and their attitude became more hostile. Despite this, the Jewish desire for Western education promoted contact with the missionaries, and eventually a modus vivendi was worked out in Damascus, whereby a rabbi would give religious instruction to Jewish children in mission schools. The Protestant missionaries had more of a foothold in Damascus than in Aleppo, where rabbinic authority over the community was more forceful. The Protestants, as outsiders—whether seen as allies or as subverting the Jewish community—were viewed differently than the local Christians.[15]

Occupations

The pervasiveness of ethnic identification in the Middle East is shown in occupational specialization along ethnic lines. Several classic examples of this date from early twentieth-century Damascus. Among shoemakers, Muslims made certain kinds of shoes, while Christians made another kind, and Jews a third variety, although some shoes were produced by shoemakers of each of the three religions. At a Damascus factory, Jews specialized in metalwork, local Christians processed mother of pearl, and Armenians did the woodwork. The picture of a static mosaic of ethnic specialization is the product of observing Syrian society as a series of snapshots, such as those in the previous paragraph. The system was not so static over time, however. Goitein points out that there was less such specialization in the Middle Ages. Even the picture of the division of labor among shoemakers hints at competition.[16]

Competition existed between individuals and groups. The division of labor among shoemakers shows one way around such rivalry while preserving group boundaries. This is exemplified by what happened to a number of young Jews who were interested in converting to Protestantism in Damascus in 1893. As a result of their contact with the missionaries, they were excommunicated and thrown out of work. Since they had worked in "Jewish" lines of trade, Christians would not or could not employ them. They were forced back into the Jewish fold.

In many crafts and lines of trade, however, there was no specialization by religious affiliation. Muslims, Christians, and Jews practiced the same crafts in many cases. In eighteenth-century Aleppo, Muslims, Jews, and Christians could join guilds representing their line of trade. The Jewish butchers were the only group that formed a religiously exclusive guild, because of the Jewish dietary laws. While money changing was a predominantly Jewish occupation, there were some non-Jews in the profession.[17]

Although family names can be misleading, they can give us clues to the past. The surnames of Aleppan and other Syrian Jews indicate that they practiced a variety of occupations. These include the following: dealer in fragrances (*ʿaṭṭār*), dealer in cotton (*qattān*), slaughterer (*dhabbāh*), soldier (*jindī*), blacksmith (*ḥaddād*), greengrocer (*khidāry*), butcher (*qassāb*), baker (*khabbāz*), meatseller (*laḥām*), soap maker (*ṣabbān*), water or beverage carrier (*sakkāh*), jeweler (*ṣayegh*), candlemaker or waxdealer (*shamʿah*), miller (*ṭaḥān*), and olive dealer (*zetūn*). Whether all of these occupations were practiced by Jews is unlikely (for instance, few Jews were soldiers). Still, the list suggests connections with particular economic sectors.[18]

The Jews in Aleppo worked mainly in commercial occupations. It is this characteristic that makes them an intermediary or middleman minority. While some such intermediary minorities are isolated, in societies where engagement in commerce is stigmatized, this is not the case in Syria. Both the minority Christians and many Muslims were engaged in the same or similar occupations. As noted above, competition sometimes takes on the dimensions of intergroup conflict, but not always.

Jewish businesses were generally family firms, though there were partnerships with non-kin, including non-Jews. Partners were often kin: father and sons, uncles and nephews, cousins and brothers. One son might go into business with his father, while another might open a shop with another partner. Failure and bankruptcy were common. Some men emigrated to seek their fortunes abroad; others who had emigrated returned to Aleppo or Damascus. Partnerships were not stable and sometimes led to litigation.

Aleppo had a more even distribution of Jews from poor to rich than Damascus, where a sharp division existed between the very wealthy bankers and the poor peddlers and craftspeople.[19] In late nineteenth-century Aleppo and its north Syrian and southern Anatolian hinterland, Jews continued to be butchers and cheesemakers, as well as soap manufacturers, burlap makers, tinsmiths, and goldsmiths.

The Jewish goldsmiths in Aleppo were a small group of between twenty and fifty craftsmen, several of whom belonged to one family. Children were apprenticed to one or another of the senior individuals. Most had shops in the same market area; they shared this area with Christian silversmiths. The latter sometimes made ritual objects for synagogues.

Jews were also involved in the distribution of agricultural produce, such as meat, dairy products, grains, fruits, and vegetables. In this capacity, some became partners of cultivators and herders. They provided capital to peasants for buying animals, paying taxes, and buying imported and manufactured products. Such partnerships were a form of money lending. The rural retailer or peddler was stocked with goods on consignment from an urban wholesaler. He, in turn, sold these goods to the farmer on credit, sometimes receiving payment in kind. This involved some risk, especially if one lent money before harvest in order to lay claim to the produce. Sometimes such loans were spoken of as partnerships, and interest payment was implicit. These transactions were common in Syria and southern Anatolia. Some Jewish merchants owned sheep and goats, although Muslims were the shepherds.

Jewish slaughterers were ritual functionaries who were ordained by the rabbinate. The proceeds from *sheḥiṭa* (Jewish ritual slaughter) were an important part of Jewish communal income in Syria as elsewhere in the diaspora and served to pay the slaughterers as well as provide welfare for the poor. In the eighteenth century, Jewish slaughterers had their own guild.[20] Much later, in the twentieth century, kosher meat was sold by Muslim butchers after the animal was stamped. Such sale of kosher meat by non-Jewish butchers would seem strange to European Jews. Generally the animal's torso was sold whole, because the legs generally were not stamped, according to rabbinic informants.

In much of the Fertile Crescent, Jews were traders in agricultural produce or in manufactured textiles, which they acquired in commercial centers such as Aleppo. The Jews, like other traders, were intermediaries for the distribution of native and imported goods. The Jewish connections extended from representatives of Aleppan companies in Manchester, Milan, and other centers to peddlers in remote villages in Anatolia or the Anti-Lebanon.

The peddlers were among the poorer Jews of Aleppo, Damascus, and the smaller market towns and villages, such as Killiz, Antakya, and Urfa. They were part of a chain of commercial activity that linked them to the world market. In urban areas, peddlers sold their wares from house to house and to passersby. In rural areas, they made circuits through villages, though many maintained their domicile in cities or market towns, coming home for the Sabbath and for holidays. They might stay away for several months in the summer, but in winter, they returned to the city.

There were also at this time, as at all times, people living on charity or as professional beggars. The gap between rich and poor, while bridged by those with moderate incomes, was still quite sharp. In the nineteenth century, many of the wealthy Jews did not want their children to go to school with the offspring of the poor. In the twentieth century, many of those who were poor remember the rebuffs of the well-to-do.[21]

In Aleppo, only the poorest women worked outside of the home. Some women were seamstresses, while others, especially girls, were domestics in Jewish homes. In the more impoverished community of Damascus, some women worked as copper engravers. Some Jewish women were professional entertainers. This was a profession that was considered akin to prostitution and lacked honor. Most comments about such dancers, however, referred to their poverty and seemed to acquit them of personal immorality[22]

Community and the Rabbinate

The leadership of the community was made up of a self-perpetuating group of wealthy individuals and rabbis. The income of communal organizations was raised from several sources, including the sale of kosher meat, taxes assessed by the communal bodies, and voluntary contributions pledged at the Torah reading in the synagogue or at various ceremonial events during the year. The latter included contributions made on evenings when special songs were sung, such as Lag B'Omer, a minor festival on the thirty-third day between Pesaḥ and Shavu'ot (the Jewish Pentecost). These contributions were generally made to various charitable societies, including the Burial Society, and to funds for study, to dowries (for poor girls), for clothing, and for dealing with the sick.

Rabbis, called *ḥakhāmim,* were generally well respected among Aleppan Jews, both for their learning and for their contact with the divine. They were believed to have the power of clairvoyance, of healing, and of pronouncing curses. Their use of excommunication and of corporal punishment was not unknown.

The Ottoman Empire's decision to appoint provincial chief rabbis caused confusion and conflict within Jewish communities. While the communities played a role in the appointment of these officials, the Ottoman government had the final say. Sometimes unqualified individuals were appointed. At other times, a *ḥakhām bāshī* had the approval of the governor but not of the notables of the community. Members of the community then had to appeal to the central government in Istanbul. Conflicts over these appointments occurred in Aleppo, Damascus, and Sidon, among other places.

Besides the *ḥakhām bāshī,* there was a hierarchy among rabbis. There were those who sat on the *Beit Dīn* (rabbinic court), as well as private scholars (who might work as merchants) and teachers, either in communal institutions or employed as private tutors.

In the 1860s, the rabbis of Aleppo fought a vigorous battle against religious innovation. In 1862, they apparently stamped out an incipient "reform" movement, possibly inspired by European models. Later in that decade, they burnt a commentary on the Bible by a well-known Livorno rabbi that used modern philological techniques to defend Scripture. From its foundation in 1869 up until 1900, however, several key rabbis taught in the Alliance school. In this period, their stance toward modernization was relatively moderate.

After 1900, influenced by Aleppan rabbis who had accepted the "rejectionist" views of Ashkenazi ultra-Orthodox rabbis in Jerusalem, the Aleppan rabbinate again became militantly conservative. In the period before World War I, they excommunicated those who violated the Sabbath and they sought to punish men for watching female performers. They were skeptical of the introduction of secular education by the Alliance Israelite Universelle and they opposed the establishment of a B'nai B'rith lodge and later of Zionist organizations. This led them into an alliance with like-minded Ashkenazi Orthodox Jews in Jerusalem. This pattern set precedents for Aleppan rabbinic actions in Israel and the rest of the diaspora.[23]

Schools

Before the 1860s, the schools for Aleppan Jews were traditional institutions where boys were taught Scripture, rabbinic literature, and some arithmetic by traditional rote methods. The teacher maintained discipline by corporal punishment, and students were accountable to him for behavior outside of school as well as in it. Parents asked teachers to punish their children.

Many students stopped their formal education in adolescence. Those who continued traditional study concentrated on the Talmud. Unlike in Eastern Europe, in Aleppo casuistry was less important in Talmudic study; thorough knowledge of the text received more emphasis.

In the latter half of the nineteenth century, the children of the *signores francos* began receiving instruction either from tutors or in Christian schools for both boys and girls. In 1869, the Alliance Israelite Universelle established a boys' school in Aleppo. In 1889, a girls' school was established. European languages and other modern subjects were stressed in these schools, which can be seen as preparing Aleppan Jews for emigration and for participation in the world economy. Emigration was a particularly desirable solution for those who despaired of any basic change in their situation in Syria, while new horizons to the West had opened up to them.[24]

The Family and Household

The neighborhoods where Jews lived were not closed ghettos. In the walled city, Jews lived on the same streets as Muslims. Christians, Muslims, and Jews all lived in suburban areas, such as Jamiliya. The older houses generally had a courtyard or atrium, and Jews tried to live in all-Jewish courts. People attempted to maintain privacy to the extent that strangers could not look into their houses or courtyards.

Authority in the family was in the hands of the senior males. This prerogative was symbolized by acts of respect, such as receiving one's father's blessing on the Sabbath or not smoking in his presence. When economically feasible, households were joint family affairs, with the married sons and their wives cohabiting with the husband's parents. This was less possible for poorer families. Daughters generally did not inherit property, but they received a dowry at marriage. Property was inherited by sons. Upon divorce or the death of the husband, wives received a payment specified in their marriage contract. There were also provisions for how to deal with this property in the event of the widow's death. While women could not divorce their husbands, they could precipitate a divorce by separating from their husbands and returning to their parents' homes (such a woman was termed a *moredet*, or rebellious woman).

The legal responsa indicate that there were disputes over inheritance and among partners, whether relatives or non-kin. There were also cases involving impotent men and infertile women, levirate marriages (marriage to a husband's brother, when a husband died without offspring), and marriage by some sort of deceit. The Jews of Aleppo were a normally contentious and litigious community.

In the eighteenth century, with the exception of the *signores francos*, most Aleppan Jews wore Middle Eastern-style dress, and the women were veiled. By the early twentieth century, an increasing number of Aleppan Jews, men and women alike, wore European-style clothing.[25]

Creeping Westernization & the Contraction of the Empire

From 1840 onward, Western influence increased in Ottoman Syria and Ottoman power declined. The introduction of Western manufactured goods, the building of the Suez Canal, the waning of the caravan trade, the building of railways, the growth of Western educational institutions, Western fashions, and the bankruptcy of the Ottoman financial regime all contributed to the shift in power. In addition, various Ottoman domains either fell under European colonial rule (e.g., Algeria, Libya, Egypt) or gained independence as Christian states (e.g.. Greece, Serbia, Bulgaria). The Ottoman rulers modeled themselves increasingly on their European counterparts. The Jews, as has been noted, became more and more Europeanized, as well. As the Jews and their neighbors felt the power and attraction of Western ways, their existing social order and regard for tradition were undermined. First in the 1860s and then again after 1900, the Aleppan rabbinate put up a particularly strong fight against religious innovation, although to many this might have seemed futile. Finally, as a result of World War I, the Ottoman empire collapsed.

Interethnic Conflict in Late Ottoman Times

Despite the Westernization that affected all segments of Syrian society, the sectarian boundaries held firm during the Ottoman period. The considerable intergroup conflict during the eighteenth, nineteenth, and twentieth centuries sharpened during and after World War I. Christians had sought to displace the Jewish government contractors in 1840 by using accusations of ritual murder, among other charges. Muslims resented the intervention of European powers on behalf of *dhimmīs*, especially the Christians, and they resented grants of equal rights to them. These tensions were among the causes of the Aleppo riots of 1850 and the Lebanese and Damascus anti-Christian pogroms of 1860. During this period, Jews were in an equivocal position. They tended to view the Muslims as friendlier than their Christian competitors. In turn, the Muslims viewed the Christians as the main beneficiaries of European intervention. Still, Jews also utilized consular intervention when they could. Jews were, however, accused by Christians of helping the Muslims during the 1850 and 1860 pogroms.

The Jews in Aleppo and its hinterland were witnesses to the Armenian massacres during World War I. As with other Christians, the Jews saw the Armenians as rivals. Little love was lost between them and the Jews. This came out in testimonies by old people from southeastern Anatolia and Aleppo who were interviewed in Jerusalem in the 1960s. A man from Cermik (southeastern Anatolia) told of a Jew who had a vision that the Armenians were planning to kill the Turks and the Jews and who warned the Turks. A woman related the story of a Jew who was mistaken for an Armenian but saved himself by displaying his *ṣīṣīt* (fringes of undergarment worn by observant Jews), which proved that he was a Jew.[26] A man from Urfa said that the Turks had ambushed the French after they occupied that town at the end of World War I. After finishing with the French, they massacred the Christian population. One informant claimed that Jews in Ainteb (Gaziantep) had helped Armenians. An Armenian who was born in Aleppo related that he had heard that some Armenian boys had escaped death in this period by hiding in Jewish homes in Anatolia. He himself had witnessed the desecration of Jewish cemeteries in Aleppo by Muslims after 1948.

The picture is thus a mixed one. After the war, there were street fights in Aleppo between Armenian refugees and Jews. This may have been a result of competition between the Armenians, other Anatolian refugees, and the local Arabic-speaking population of Aleppo in this very difficult period.

After World War I, the Jews in southeastern Anatolia felt less secure. This area was now part of the new Turkish republic. With the elimination of the Christian population, they were now the main non-Muslim group. At this time, many Jews left the region for Istanbul or for Aleppo and then for Palestine and the Americas. The last Jews left Urfa in 1946, when a Jewish family was murdered. One member of that family had converted to Islam. According to Jewish sources, he had a dispute over an inheritance with his relatives. When they were killed, other Jews were accused of the murder. The accused Jews believed that the convert had instigated the slaying. The Jews of southeastern Anatolia had come to share the unease of their erstwhile Christian neighbors.

Ottoman religious and ethnic pluralism was a complicated web of individual, group, and international relationships. Economic competition between individuals from different religions had its effect on the Ottoman and European governments and on each of the religious and ethnic groups. The Ottoman communal system was dynamic, and the nature of power and influence was constantly in flux. Individuals might be persecuted as members of corporate religious bodies, but they could also manipulate these relationships for their own benefit. Until the nineteenth century, however, there seems to have been an uneasy equilibrium. Once that balance was upset, waves of violence began that continue to this day, particularly in the strife in Lebanon and between the Azeris and the Armenians in the Caucasus.

The rise of Arab nationalism resulted in a new configuration of ethnic relations in Syria. Christians and members of "heretical" or "secretive" sects, such as Druzes and Alawis, could identify with a secular nationalist movement. After 1920, however, it became increasingly difficult for Jews to join the Arab nationalist movements, because the Arab nationalists regarded the Zionist movement—which sought to establish a Jewish homeland in Palestine—as an obstacle to be overcome. Despite disclaimers by their official leaders, Syrian Jews were increasingly identified with the Zionist enemy. As a result. many Jews emigrated from Syria to Eretz Yisrael. As will be discussed in the following chapter, the Jewish remnant in Syria then underwent a long period of being trapped.

CHAPTER 3

JEWS IN SYRIA FROM 1948 TO 1994: A RESTRICTED REMNANT COMMUNITY

THE MANDATORY AND REPUBLICAN PERIODS

A striking feature of Syrian Jewish history from the breakup of the Ottoman Empire to the present time has been the tying of the destiny of the Jews of Syria with the clash between Zionism and Arab nationalism. While the Westernization of urban Syrians, including the Jews, proceeded apace throughout this period, the Zionist conflict with the Arabs isolated the Jews from their non-Jewish neighbors more than in the past, resulting ultimately in their emigration. While many Syrian Jews were attracted to Zionism and emigrated to Palestine/Israel, the leaders of the community were often forced to affirm their loyalty to the Syrian Arab nation. Syrian Jewry was also affected by the harsh currents of anti-Semitism, which predominated in France and its colonies under the Vichy regime and also influenced Arab nationalists.[1]

After an independent State of Israel was established and as a state of belligerency between Syria and Israel continued, the borders between Israel and Syria remained closed. For much of this time, the emigration of Syrian Jews was severely restricted, if not altogether prohibited. Yet the Jewish communities in Syria continued to decline and to become remnant communities.[2]

In April 1992, the Syrian government removed restrictions on the emigration of Syrian Jews. Between that time and the end of 1994, most of the approximately four thousand Jews who were living in Syria chose to leave the country. Most of the two hundred Jews remaining in Syria at the end of 1994 had travel documents. Some were in the process of selling their property, while others were too old to travel.[3]

This chapter examines the lives of Jews under Syrian regimes from 1948 until 1992. It also attempts to provide some understanding of the condition of one small Jewish community remaining in an Arab country, one of the "confrontation states" maintaining a state of war with Israel. It is based on very sparse sources, most of which are partisan, and has been written without direct interviews or fieldwork. It represents an effort at social scientific interpretation through the use of concepts drawn from qualitative cross-cultural studies. Implicitly, the chapter touches on questions relevant to cultural and ethnic survival, protection of minority rights, and the relationship of ethnic groups to place of birth and to emigration.

Remnant Communities

Communities may grow or decline. Groups of people who live in a particular place and feel that they are bound by common interests and a common destiny may stay together. They may be fruitful and multiply. They may also diminish sharply due to a low birth rate, emigration, disease, famine, or genocide. These declining communities may be farming communities where most of the able-bodied have moved to urban areas, or urban areas where young couples have left for the suburbs. As communities decline, the elderly may be their last remnants. There are many such remnant communities in the world. Whatever their histories, all such communities reveal the sense of loss that comes with change. This is similar to the empty nest syndrome that afflicts parents whose children have moved away. Part of the loss that is felt is the replacement of what was once a familiar landscape, once marked as one's own territory, with something foreign. The transformation of synagogues into churches, of Protestant chapels into Catholic churches, or of Turkish mosques into Greek cinemas are all markers of such change.

So far, the discussion has focused on community changes caused by demographic and economic developments. In many of these cases, family members and friends who have left remain nearby in the same metropolitan area or at least within the same country. Communication is relatively unhampered, especially by telephone. Even in these cases, however, there is a political aspect. Urban housing in the United States is affected by government-supported mortgages, urban redevelopment, and taxation. The Scot Canadians in Quebec have faced a Québécois French national revival and separatism. While these forces help remake one's home into an exile, the people who are in the remnant community can still come and go freely, visiting relatives and the like.[4]

The situation is exacerbated when political conflict and authoritarian rule raise other barriers that prevent those who have left and those who remain from having untrammeled contact. The Jewish communities in certain Middle Eastern countries and those of the Soviet Union up until 1988 are of the restricted variety. In writing about restricted communities, however, one must recognize that there is a continuum of restriction. The Jewish communities of Tunisia and Morocco, while remnant communities, are relatively unrestricted.[5] The Soviet Jewish community until 1988 was among the most restricted. Other communities have gone through a variety of phases. The subjects of this chapter, Jews in Syria from 1948 until 1992, were at the restricted end of the continuum. Yet even there, the restrictiveness changed over the years.

Sources and Biases

Discussion of Jews in contemporary Syria has often been subject to polarization, since each side in the Arab-Israeli conflict has used this example to bolster its own case regarding its opponents. The Syrian/Arab position has been that the continued existence of Jews in Syria, with their functioning synagogues and schools and people who are earning a living and practicing their professions, is prima facie evidence of toleration, if not fully equal status. The Jewish community is held up as an example of an Arab tradition of tolerance toward minorities. Restrictions are seen as necessary in time of crisis and are disregarded. Affirmations of this position by Syrian Jewish spokesmen are used in support of this.[6]

The contrary position focuses on restrictions, discrimination, and crimes committed against Jews, whether by official agencies or by individuals. These actions are seen as an example of traditional Muslim hostility toward non-Muslims. They provide support for a hard-line Israeli policy toward its neighbors.[7] Somewhere in between are those who seek to differentiate between government policies and the unofficial climate. Publications in Jewish sources take either the anti-Muslim or the in-between position. Many of those who agitated on behalf of the free emigration of Syrian Jews focus on the more negative aspects of the situation.

My own bias is more cynical than either. I assume that most governments (especially authoritarian regimes) tend to disregard the welfare of their minorities, and they may not represent the populace either. They are marked by insensitivity at best and unmitigated hostility at worst, with most governments and peoples falling somewhere in between. Obviously, minority members and outsiders may and do manipulate instances of indifference and hostility for their own purposes, just as government supporters use indices of normality.

Sources of information on Syrian Jewry have been hard to come by. Since the Jews are a small and diminishing minority, students of Syrian affairs rarely touch on them. There is more interest in Syrian Jews in Jewish publications than elsewhere. A good continuing source is the *American Jewish Yearbook* (AJYB), published by the American Jewish Committee. It reflects the moderate but generally pro-Israel bias of that organization. Still, there are differences of nuance in the reports. In some years, the reports are based primarily on a reading of the press and external sources, while in other years, firsthand information was obtained by members of the American Jewish Committee staff in Syria. The writers of these reports include distinguished scholars of the Middle East such as Walter Z. Lacqeuer, Don Peretz, and George Gruen. Don Peretz, for instance, has developed a view quite critical of both the Arabs and Israel in their policies and can hardly be characterized as simply "pro-Israel." The reports of all three show that Syrian Jews are subject to some special restrictions because of their Jewishness. Since the observers use firsthand material and since the authors are sophisticated observers, many of the AJYB reports try to achieve a balance between reporting and advocacy that is not found in most other articles and books.

Since 1986, new works on Syria have appeared. An increasing number of scholars have written on conditions in Baathist Syria.[8] While these scholars usually ignore the tiny Jewish minority, their work helps us place data on the Jews into the larger context. While Saul Friedman's book on the "the plight of Syrian Jewry" is lachrymose and highly partisan, it documents incidents of harassment and torture systematically. While many recent emigrés from Syria were reluctant to speak with journalists, both Friedman and Joseph Sutton have used these accounts in their works. Sutton includes several detailed and textured testimonies on life in postindependence Aleppo in his book.[9] In the future, when emigrés are able to speak more freely, we can expect to improve our understanding of this period in Syrian Jewish history.

The parallel development of Zionism and Arab nationalism and the consequent struggle for Palestine, viewed by many Syrian Muslims and Christians as an integral part of Syria, isolated Syrian Jewry. Many Syrian Jews, like their compatriots of other religions, participated in the great emigration to Egypt and then to the Americas in the search for economic opportunity. During the 1930s, as economic need and the anti-Zionist fervor of their neighbors increased and as the doors to the United States were shut, many Syrian Jews slipped over the border to Palestine. This was especially true during the period of the Second World War and its aftermath, when the French Vichy regime implemented anti-Semitic policies and the heat of the Arab-Jewish struggle for Palestine became more intense.[10] Tensions culminated in the Aleppo Riot of 1947, when the United Nations General Assembly passed a resolution enabling the partitioning of Palestine and the establishment of a Jewish state. The riot was aimed at Jews and synagogues, many of the latter being destroyed. As in similar events elsewhere, the authorities either encouraged this violence or were unable to control a large segment of the populace. Most synagogues in Aleppo, including the Great Synagogue, were damaged. As a result of this pogrom, large numbers of Syrian Jews fled from Syria to Lebanon. Many remained in Lebanon, while others found their way to Israel and to the various countries of the Diaspora.

The Arab defeat in the Arab-Israeli War of 1948 resulted in the overthrow of the parliamentary regime that had ruled since independence. Syria now was subject to a series of military dictators, which were sometimes in coalition with civilian parties, a situation that has continued up to the present. The first of these dictators, Husni el-Zaim, permitted the emigration of large numbers of Syrian Jews. Approximately five thousand went to Israel. The governments that succeeded Zaim maintained a policy of severe restriction on Jewish emigration and on Jewish activities in general until 1992. The restraints on the small, impotent, and diminishing Jewish communities, located primarily in Aleppo, Damascus, and the town of Qamishly on the Turkish border, were often severe, even in comparison with other Syrian nationals.[11]

Syrian Regimes

In the period from 1948 until 1970, Syrian history was punctuated by coup d'etats and countercoups. This includes the brief period in which Syria was the "northern region" of a United Arab Republic, headed by Gamal Abd-el-Nasser of Egypt (1958–61). Conflicts along rural-urban, class, and ethnic lines underlay this instability, while coalitions were formed that included civilian politicians and military officers. Army officers affiliated with the Baʿath party came to power in 1963. Hafez el-Assad, one of these officers, took the reins of power in 1970, and has held them ever since. Assad's control is based on balancing a number of competing factions and interests within the Syrian elite. He has also put down certain opposition groups, including the very bloody suppression of the Hamah rebellion in 1982, which had been led by the Muslim Brotherhood.[12]

While some diversity of opinion has been allowed, the regime has kept tight surveillance on the people in general and has suppressed opposition. Travel and currency restrictions have applied to everyone.

Despite conflict, there has been consensus in Syria on certain issues, including the continuing confrontation with Israel, which is not considered a legitimate state. The small and declining Jewish minority, while symbolic of the "Israeli enemy," has been powerless and has became another object for displaying either one's power to one's fellows or one's toleration to outsiders. The Jews have been subject to extortion by government officials, especially those in the security forces, and by civilians who have perceived them as being fair and easy game.

The Syrian Jews, as has been indicated, were restricted in their ability to leave Syria. In addition to travel restrictions common to all Syrian nationals, the government tried to prevent emigration to Israel and thus made any travel abroad for Jews particularly difficult. This essentially meant that they were trapped in Syria.

Pattern of Recent History

While the 1950s and 1960s were marked by political instability and the period from 1970 to the present has been a period of relative stability under Assad, the pattern of Jewish life in Syria changed little between 1950 and 1992. The Aleppo Riot of 1947, the Arab-Israeli War of 1948–49, and the brief Zaim dictatorship, which resulted in the 1949 Armistice agreement between Israel and Syria and permitted emigration, were dramatic events. From that time forward until 1992, the pattern was one of alternation between periods of intense restriction and of letup. Just after the fall of Husni ez-Zaim, for instance, two hundred Jews were arrested and two motorboats seized for illegal emigration.[13] During the dictatorship of Shishakly (1953–54), it was reported that Syrian Jews "lived under a regime of terror mitigated only by inefficiency and corruption." After Adib Shishakly's overthrow, their status improved.

Various laws passed under the early military regimes included laws to insure that property of emigrés remained in Syria, including a ban on selling property (1948), the freezing of all Jewish bank accounts, and distribution of the property of Jewish emigrés to Arab refugees. Certain community buildings, such as schools, were seized.[14] It was also reported that Syrian citizenship was restricted to Arabs (and therefore denied to Syrian Jews), although the authenticity of this fact is unclear. In addition, the movement of Syrian Jews was restricted. While the *American Jewish Yearbook* reports that Jews were not legally barred from leaving Damascus in this period, they could not move freely in practice. In addition, there was unofficial harassment. Jews were attacked in public places, such as markets and streets; synagogues were stoned; and Jews were arrested periodically. A few escaped to Lebanon, which faced pressure to extradite them. The *Yearbook* report indicates that the communal leadership had been taken over by "people without a public record." The middle class in Damascus had fled and only the very rich and the very poor remained.

The situation changed somewhat in 1954, although the changes were seen as minor. Administration of Jewish affairs was still in the hands of the police. The Jewish chief of the afforestation department in the Ministry of Agriculture (who presumably had been employed previously) was dismissed for actions "on behalf of Jewish commercial establishments." There also were reports of the murder of a Jewish merchant in Aleppo, with possible political motives, and of the arrest of alleged spies or border-crossers. Still, after November 1954, Jews were again permitted to leave Syria, and there was one report of emigrés who left via Turkey. Jews also demonstrated against their own leaders, accusing them of corruption.[15]

This alternation of restriction and easing of restriction continued throughout the 1960s. Coup followed coup, finally culminating in 1970 with the accession of Hafez el-Assad's Alawi-dominated faction to power. Travel restrictions, whether generally applicable or specific to Syrian Jews, continued to mark this period. For instance, it was reported that in March 1964, Jews were forbidden to travel more than three miles from home without permits. Those who were permitted to leave the country could take only one hundred dollars with them and had to abandon all other belongings.[16] In addition, the government took control of Jewish schools, admitting non-Jewish students and hiring Muslim principals. As always, those favorable to the regime justified the restrictions on the basis of the state of belligerency between Israel and the Arabs.[17] Others saw them in a different light.

Sutton illustrates the effect of travel restrictions through the story of a merchant who secured a travel permit to a distant town. When he arrived at this destination and before he left, he had to register with the police. At his return, the police accompanied him to the bus and ordered the bus driver "not to permit the Jew to descend from the vehicle until the arrival in Aleppo." When the Jew indicated that he had to go to the toilet at a rest stop, the driver refused to let him get off. Later, when the bus was under way, however, the driver did show mercy by letting the Jew get off for a minute at the side of the road.[18]

During the 1970s, Syrian Jews were occasionally in the news. A number of incidents highlighted the restricted situation of Syrian Jewry. In 1971, twelve Jews, including children, were arrested for trying to flee. In 1974, after the Yom Kippur War, four Jewish girls who tried to emigrate from Syria were raped and murdered. The brother-in-law of one of the girls, along with another Jew and two Muslims, was accused of the murder. In that year, a thousand Jews, joined by some Arabs, protested in Damascus. A Committee of Concern, chaired by General Lucius Clay, was organized in the United States. This committee charged that Jews in Syria were living under a reign of terror. Charges were presented that Jews who had attempted to emigrate had been imprisoned and were subjected to torture. A Lebanese Jewish leader who had been kidnapped in Beirut was reported to be imprisoned in Syria.

The situation of the Jews in Qamishly, a town near the Turkish border, was of particular concern. Qamishly is a fairly new community, built mainly under the French Mandate, when there was development of the Jazira region in the Euphrates River valley. The area is highly sensitive, since it is close to the borders of both Iraq and Turkey. The Jews there were only permitted to travel within the town, and they had to report to the Jewish quarter at night.

They eked out a living only with the help of Jewish charity from abroad. There were charges that some Muslim individuals loitered about the Jewish quarter in a threatening manner, annoying Jewish girls in particular. Military intelligence personnel were said to enter Jewish stores in Qamishly and help themselves to merchandise. The Syrian government forcefully denied all of these charges and attributed them to Zionist propaganda.[19]

In the wake of these reports and the sensitivity of the Assad government to American public opinion, Mike Wallace of *60 Minutes* was allowed to review the situation of Syrian Jews in Damascus. His first broadcast was considered to be an apologetic for the Syrian government's position, explaining away any discrimination as understandable because of the belligerency between Syria and Israel. After criticism of his broadcast, Wallace returned to do a second report. Both of these programs have been seen by the Syrian government and its supporters as vindication of their position that Syrian Jews are treated on par with other citizens of that country, except for minor restrictions.[20]

After 1974, the Syrian government apparently lifted certain restrictions, but not on emigration. Religious life, education, and commercial activity proceeded in a normal fashion. The government also allowed several Jewish girls to be married by proxy to Syrian Jews in the United States and to emigrate. Some Syrian Jews were allowed to travel abroad for business reasons, provided that they made a deposit of money and the remaining family members remained in the country.[21]

With the end of the Cold War, Syria lost its major ally, the Soviet Union. It now needed to be conciliatory toward the United States. Thus it joined the U.S.-led alliance in a limited fashion against Iraq in 1990, and it agreed to negotiate with Israel in the framework of the Madrid talks, initiated in 1991. Relaxation of restrictions against the Jews was part of this conciliatory stance.

The Restricted Remnant

The review of recent history, however fragmentary, focuses on government policies, which vary. While some laws were aimed at Jews, most were not. Yet there was differing enforcement vis-à-vis Jews, depending on the part of the forty-year period and the place. Some regimes were more restrictive than others. Foreign intervention might call forth a defensive reaction that restricted the Jews more, or it might bring alleviation of their lot. Extortion exists in Syria, but a targeted minority is more subject to its effects than are others, whether perpetrated by majority-group members or by corrupt officials.

Despite such restrictions and extortion, many mature (but not elderly) Jews were able to earn a living and even prosper. Some youths were allowed to study in a university and enter the professions, while others went into business. Even Jewish women attended Aleppo University and graduated as physicians. Others lived on charity from abroad. Jewish schools were supported from abroad as well.

Relations with non-Jews were obviously colored by government policies and practices, but elements of traditional relationships remained. Aslan Bewabeh, a Jew born in Aleppo in 1946, describes relations with Muslims as generally good. His father told him that during the disturbances in 1947, a Muslim neighbor stood at the door and told the rioters to go away because the Bewabeh home was Islamic. He said that most Aleppo Jews continue to observe the Sabbath, and that in many cases Muslims go to their homes to turn lights on and off.[22]

The traditional view that Muslims were friendlier to Jews than Christians were is still held by recent emigrés, but they note the effects of anti-Israeli government policies and official anti-Semitism. For instance, Morris Antebi said: "my personal observation is that Muslims might be even friendlier to Jews one day if the anti-Jewish propaganda is relaxed. They can be friendly. The Aleppo Muslims are business people who are not interested in 'boloney' topics like 'Judaism' and 'Zionism.' The minority of Christians there really have a more deep-seated dislike for Jews."

He went on to say that despite the Qur'ān's anti-Jewish expressions, Muslims reciprocated Jewish civility. Still, propaganda has had an effect. Muslims will say that Jews are not true "Beni Yisrael" (Israelites) and that the Torah is not true either. However, Sunnis are now so antagonistic to President Assad's Alawi sect that they say they would prefer that their daughter marry a Yezidi (a Kurdish sect) or a Jew than an Alawi. They deny that the Alawis are true Muslims.[23]

The fact that much of the community had emigrated and that the government and non-Jewish populations shared a general enmity toward Jews, seeing them as symbols of the Israel enemy, made emigration attractive to the young. Such Jewish emigration has been a fact throughout the Arab world, not only in Syria.

Since emigration was restricted and generally illegal, it was dangerous. It was even more perilous for women than for men. In a society where "free" women may be fair game and where the honor of the family is bound up with the chastity of the women, it is not surprising that men may escape more easily than women. Thus women of marriageable age were caught in a trap that led either to marriage with Gentiles or to celibacy, both undesirable states in a traditional society.[24]

As noted, Jews were often victims of extortion, but this must be seen in the wider context of the police state, which Syria is. Fear of the secret police is widespread in Syria, especially in cities like Aleppo, where there are many pockets of resistance to the "new classes," which support the Baathist regime. The old urban bourgeoisie and middle classes have felt that they have been deprived of power by the new elites, particularly formerly rural members of the Alawi sects. For this reason, many old urbanites now support the Muslim Brothers and other opposition groups. That support makes the members of these classes subject to special surveillance by the secret police.

G. Darrow Zenlund, an anthropologist who was a participant-observer in Aleppo during the 1980s, describes interaction with the police on a number of occasions. For instance, he shows how shopkeepers in the Gold Sūq, where items for wealthy tourists and others are sold, make periodic payments to municipal policemen. In other incidents, merchants told Zenlund of their fear of the secret police, who make life in this market full of fear through arrests, physical threats, and demands for bribes. Through such terror, the Baathists have profited and become wealthy in their own right. Zenlund's description complements Samir al-Khalil's description of Iraq under Saddam Hussein, and his analysis of the totalitarian roots of Baathist ideology in his book, aptly named *The Republic of Fear* (1989).[25]

Many of the Jewish merchants in Aleppo worked side by side with Muslim and Armenian merchants. For instance, the husband of Lillian Antebi Abadi, the victim of a brutal murder in Aleppo, was in the gold trade.[26]

Aslan Bewabeh, a native of Aleppo who left in 1983 and who was in the gold trade, indicates that many Jews who remained in Aleppo were goldsmiths and dealers in gold jewelry. His own shop was located at the heart of the jewelry center (presumably the Gold Sūq). His customers included Syrians, as well as Kuwaitis and Saudis. Bewabeh described an incident that involved dealing with the police.

One day a Saudi came into his store. The Saudi was looking for an Armenian merchant, but found that Bewabeh's goods were more to his liking than those of the Armenian, and he bought from him. When the Armenian discovered this, he threatened Bewabeh because he had "stolen" his customer. The threats were, however, reported to the police. The police vouched for the Jewish dealer and told the Armenian to lay off. Here the Jew received police protection in a case involving an Armenian Christian, a more traditional rival than the Muslims. Still, the background is one of threats of violence of one against the other.[27]

There have also been situations in which Jews were favored by government officials. Morris Antebi was an intern at an Aleppo hospital when an official of the *mukhabarāt* (secret police) who had been wounded in an attack was brought into the hospital. While he was a Sunni Muslim, he was a Baathist. Because Antebi became friendly with him, this official made it possible for Antebi to obtain an official passport and leave Syria.[28]

While some wealthy members of the community prosper, members of a remnant community are likely to have low morale—at least with regard to their continued existence in a particular society. Generally where emigration is free, the young simply go abroad to study and never return. Where restricted, such emigration is frustrated and must be secretive. The small and declining size of a minority remnant community makes the community even more politically impotent than it may have been previously. The Jews' lack of importance may also make the Jewish community in such a situation less conspicuous and less of a target. A stable government may, under such conditions, use the community's fate as a bargaining chip, as indeed the Assad government did in the late 1970s, and again when they permitted emigration in 1992. Still, the community's improvement and the relative prosperity of some of its members can also be a stick with which the opposition can beat the government.

In many cases the effects of foreign intervention on behalf of a minority can be both a blessing and a curse. On the one hand, competing foreign and domestic interests can bring improvements in the minority's lot, as regimes seek to curry international favor. On the other hand, a change in political conditions can also bring to power a regime that finds it benefits politically from thumbing its nose at outsiders.

In the case under discussion here, the former would seem to be the case. Some of the improvements in the condition of Syrian Jews and their ability to emigrate were clearly the result of overseas interest. The announcement in April 1992 that the government of Syria was lifting "a travel ban on its 4,500 Jewish citizens" coincided with Syria's need for closer ties with the United States and with its participation in negotiations with Israel, obviously indications of a linkage. A substantial number of Jews emigrated after the ban was lifted. By the time of the lifting of the ban, most Aleppo Jews had already left via Turkey. The Qamishly Jews who had moved to Aleppo and many Damascus Jews soon emigrated as well, but at the end of 1992, emigration again was restricted. By 1995, there were almost no Jews left in Aleppo.[29]

In any case, except for a small number of individuals, the history of the Jewish communities in Syria has ended. As indicated here and in chapter 2, Ottoman pluralism resulted in quite distinct identities and communities, which shared many common cultural features. Trade networks and early emigrants provided social networks for those leaving Syria later. In the final analysis, the Syrian Jewish communities, like those in other Arab lands, were pushed out as a result of the conflict between Arab nationalism and Zionism, which made the position of the Jews in these countries untenable. Syrian policies preventing emigration by force succeeded only in making the position of the Jews more uncomfortable, and the agitation of Jews abroad to free Syrian Jewry were finally successful.

Courtyard, Ancient Synagogue of Aleppo, c. 1940.
(A. Dothan, "On the History of the Ancient Synagogue of Aleppo."
By permission of Ben Zvi Institute, Jerusalem.)

Interior, Ancient Synagogue of Aleppo, c. 1940.
(From A. Dothan, "On the History of the Ancient Synagogue of Aleppo." By permission of Ben Zvi Institute, Jerusalem.)

A family in a ḥōsh (traditional courtyard) in Aleppo, early twentieth century. (Courtesy of Sadie Safdie. From The Spirit of Aleppo. *By permission of the Sephardic Archives of the Sephardic Community Center, Brooklyn.)*

Western clothing was adopted by many middle-class people in Aleppo in the late nineteenth and early twentieth centuries. (From Hamui, Los judios de alepo. *By permission of Maguen David, Mexico.)*

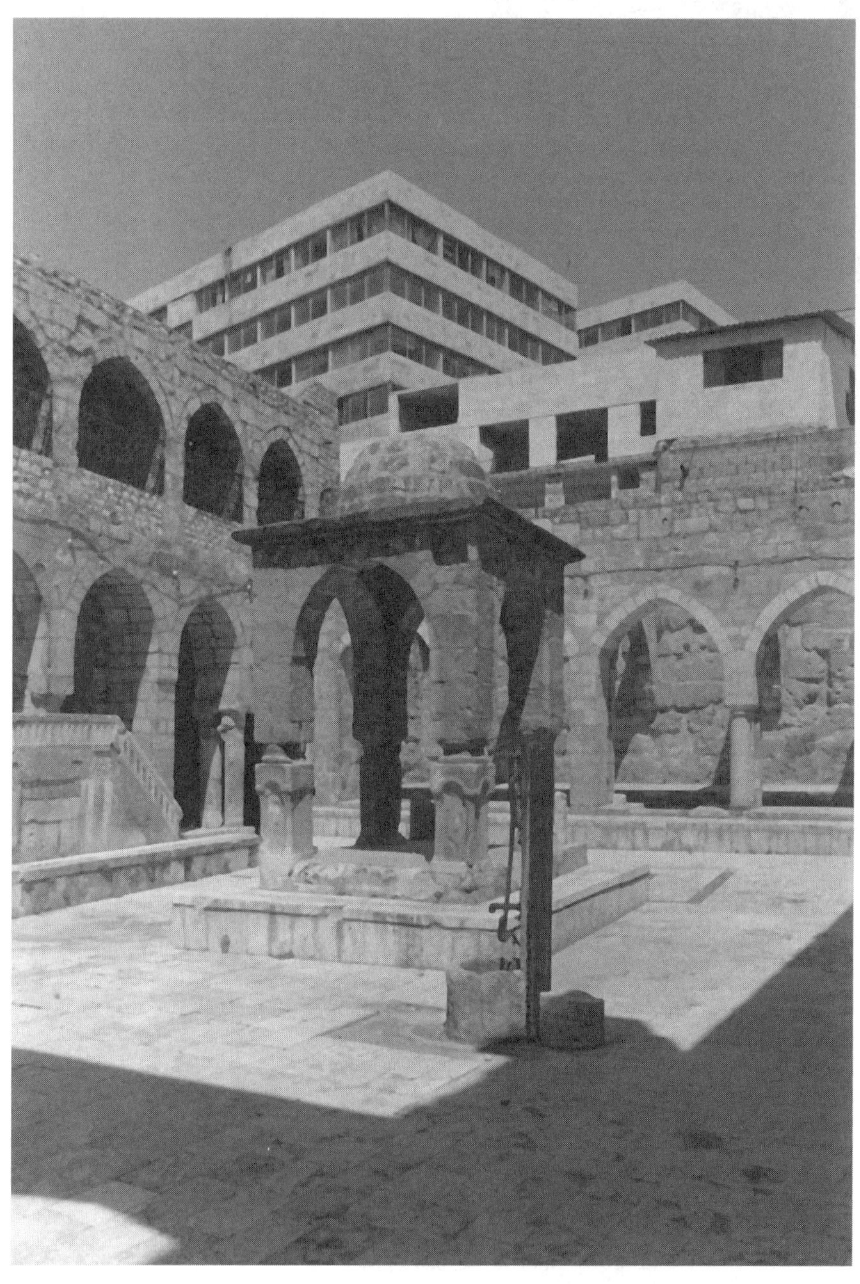

The courtyard, Ancient Synagogue of Aleppo, 1995.
Note the state of disrepair and the high-rise buildings.
(By permission of Robert Lyons and the World Monument Fund.)

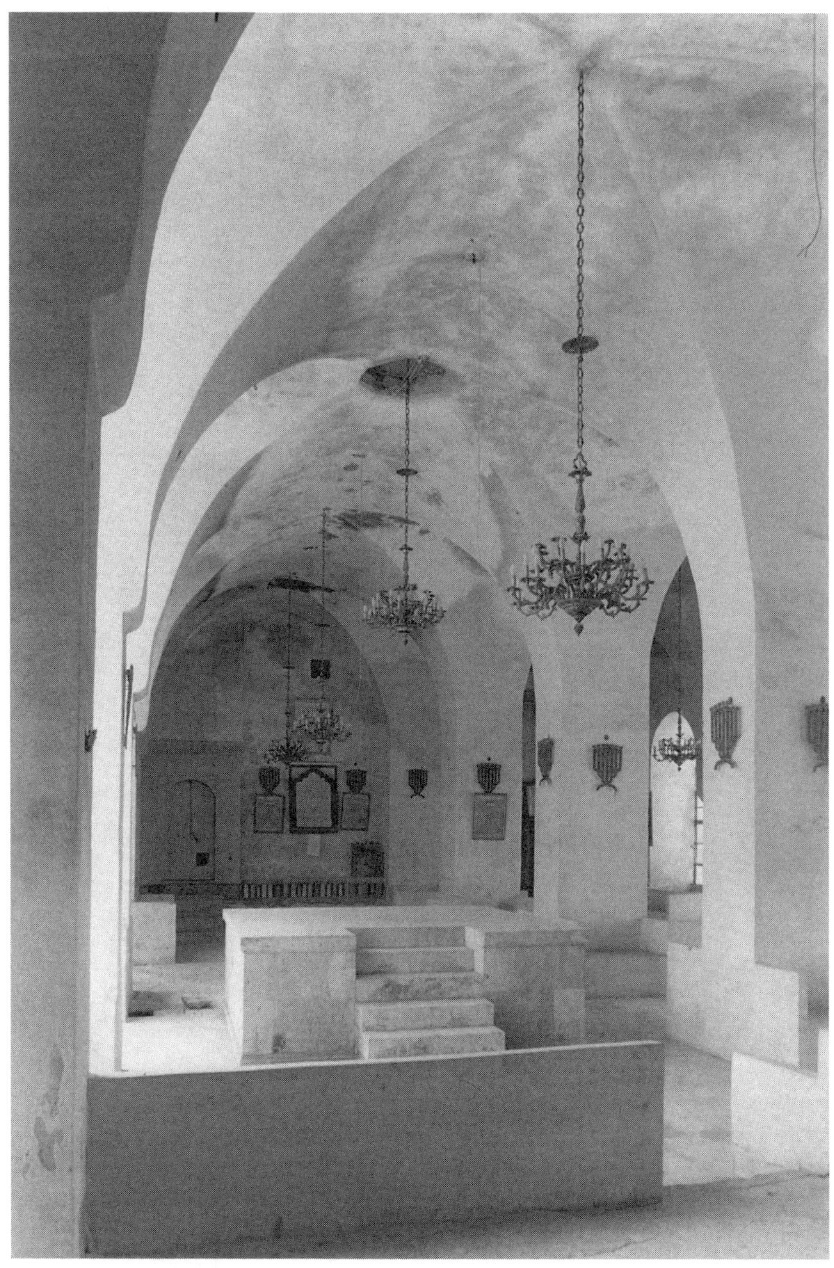

Interior of the Ancient Synagogue of Aleppo, 1995.
(By permission of Robert Lyons and the World Monument Fund.)

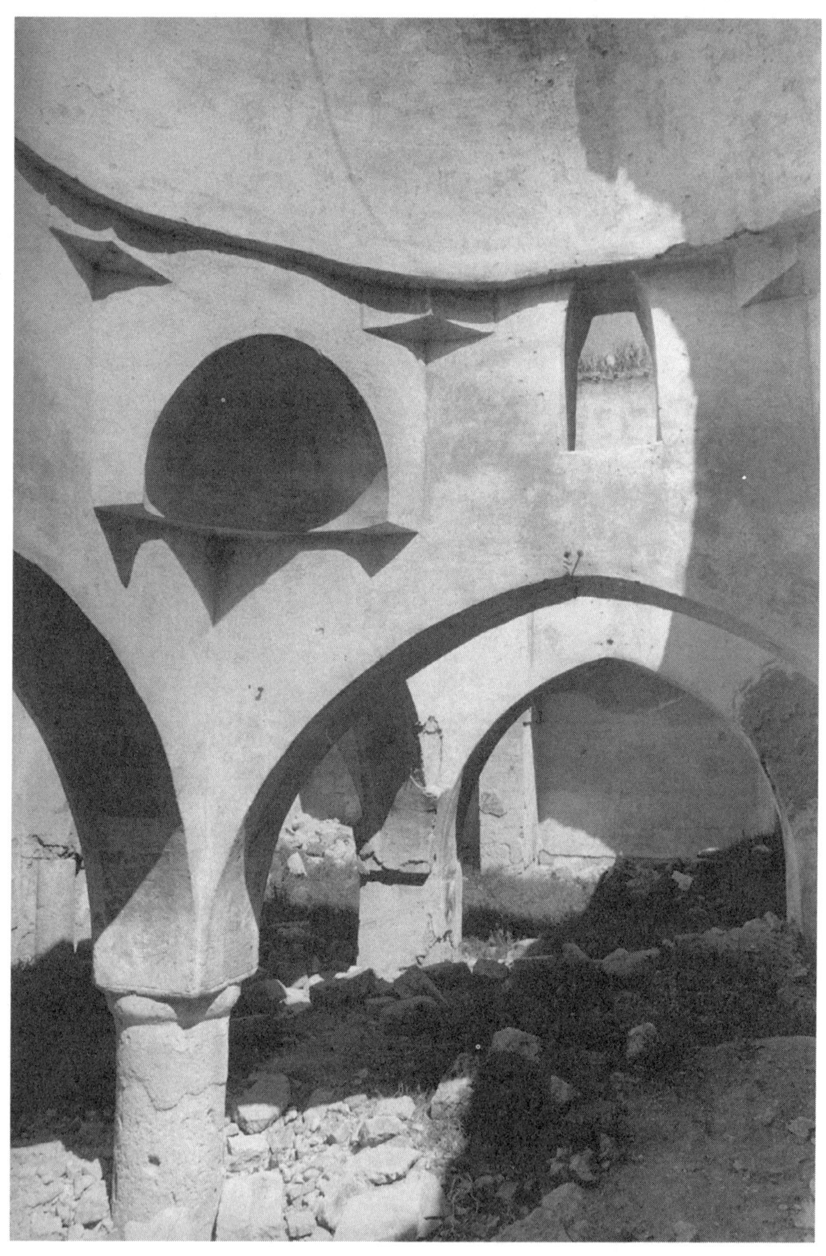

The synagogue at the cave of Ezra the Scribe, Tedef al-Yahud, Syria, 1995. (By permission of Robert Lyons and the World Monument Fund.)

View of the bimah *from the women's gallery, Sha'are Sedek Synagogue, Manchester, England, 1987.*
(Photo by author.)

CHAPTER 4

Bourgeois Immigrants: Syrian Sephardim in Manchester

Introduction

Changes in the trade relations of Southwest Asia changed the economic position of Aleppo for the worse in the nineteenth century. The Industrial Revolution, the decline of the overland caravan trade, and the opening of the Suez Canal had a particularly negative impact on the North Syrian metropolis. Some places in the Middle East prospered as a result of these changes, including Beirut, which grew during the nineteenth century. Jews, as well as others, migrated there from inland cities. Later, in the period between 1947 and 1975, when Lebanon was briefly insulated from other Middle Eastern conflicts, it became a refuge for Syrian and other Middle Eastern Jews; its Jewish population increased to about five thousand in 1958, after which it began to decline, culminating in wholesale emigration as a result of the civil war that began in 1975.[1]

The modern European-oriented sectors of the Egyptian economy also flourished during the late nineteenth and early twentieth centuries. Egypt's Jewish population multiplied to over eighty thousand at its apex as a result of migration from Europe, Southwest Asia, and North Africa. Among these were Jews from Damascus and Aleppo, including prominent individuals such as Joseph Bey de Picciotto. Most, however, came from humble backgrounds. They had started their lives in Egypt as village peddlers or ran small enterprises such as the bicycle shop owned by Andre Aciman's Aleppan grandfather in Alexandria.

In these new settings, Aleppan Jews interacted more freely with non-Jews than they had in Aleppo. Many went to European-run schools together with non-Jews. It is not surprising to find people with Aleppan-connected surnames in Cairo and Alexandria who represent a wide gamut of viewpoints, including Zionists, converts to Catholicism, and communists, as well as rabbis striving to stem the tide and uphold Orthodox Judaism. In Egypt, most Jews from Syria mingled freely and intermarried with other Jews. For most, their observance of traditional Judaism diminished, but many, especially those who immigrated to Brooklyn after the "Second Exodus" (the emigration between 1941 and 1967) renewed their ties with their cousins of Aleppan descent.[2]

Some Jews from Aleppo migrated eastward. Baghdad was another city where the Jewish population grew during the nineteenth century, and Aleppan Jews were among the newcomers. While sharing some characteristics with the new entrepôts in Egypt, Baghdad was less cosmopolitan. While most of the Middle Eastern Jews in South and East Asia in the eighteenth and nineteenth centuries were Baghdadi, occasionally an Aleppan crops up among Jews in India and China. The Sephardic community in Kobe (Japan) began when that city became a port for foreign traders in 1867. In the twentieth century, Aleppans lived in both Kobe and Manila, trading in such goods as pearls and infantwear. Aleppans, often coming from New York City, have also been involved in the export of electronic goods from Hong Kong, as well as from newer industrial centers such as Thailand.

The immigrants to the European continent were more likely to be from well-to-do families than were the immigrants to Egypt and the Americas. For centuries, Jews in the Levant had had commercial ties to Europe, and individual merchants moved in both directions. As noted in chapters 1 and 2, the *signores francos* in the eighteenth and nineteenth centuries had particularly close ties with both Aleppo and Livorno. Therefore, it is not surprising that Jews from Aleppo and other Ottoman cities would send family members to reside in Europe and to conduct business as agents of their firms. In the first decades of the nineteenth century, a number of Aleppan families moved to Marseilles. Later, Ottoman Jews were living in many of the major cities of Europe, including London, Paris, Vienna, Milan, and Manchester.

European passports and education made it possible for many from wealthy families to go to Europe and "hit the ground running." Most came as agents of their family firms and viewed their stays in these European cities as sojourns. With time and changes in the course of trade, some moved on to other locales, such as Latin America. Some, however, stayed and loosened their ties to the old trade diaspora.

Milan, one of Italy's major industrial centers, had a substantial Sephardic community, both before and after the Second World War. Some Syrian Sephardim living there were killed during the war by the Nazis, or they fled. For a time after the Second World War, the Syrian Sephardim had a separate *minyān* (prayer group) in the Milan synagogue and dominated a Jewish social club there.[3]

One of the most significant places where Sephardic immigrants, including Aleppan Jews, made their mark was in Manchester, England. This is the only British city outside of the London area where there have been Sephardic congregations since 1850.

Manchester: the name is a byword evoking images of the early Industrial Revolution, with crowded factories; overworked men, women, and children; hardheaded, grim factory owners; liberal capitalism at its height; labor unions; strikes; and Friedrich Engels, the Communist capitalist. By the 1970s and 1980s, however, Manchester had acquired a very different image. It was now seen as part of Britain's "rust belt," full of radicals, Asian immigrants, and empty parcels of unused land. Like other such areas of the world, it has also had its pockets of high-tech rejuvenation.

In the summer of 1987, I spent a month in that city, seeking to amplify my knowledge of what has been called the "Manchester connection" in the history of the Jews of the Mediterranean and Southwest Asia. As in the rest of my work on Syrian Sephardim, my working hypothesis has been that maintenance of the Aleppan identity was tied to involvement in commerce with other Syrian Jews. Important in this has been the maintenance of international kin ties. Most of the descendants of Syrian Jews whom I interviewed in Manchester were in their seventies and eighties. These were people who had come of age in the 1920s and 1930s, when the Sephardic community was at its apex.

Over the years, several of the Syrian Jews whom I knew had mentioned having spent some time in Manchester or having relatives in Manchester. I also was aware of the presence of Sephardic Jews in Manchester through the writings of various Jewish authors.[4]

Manchester was the center of the textile trade during the Industrial Revolution. It was the capital of the "Cotton Kingdom," which stretched from the U.S. South to the Middle East and India. The Sephardim from Gibraltar, Morocco, Tripoli, Corfu, Baghdad, and Aleppo were all involved in a centuries-old trade diaspora, carrying on trade between Christendom and Islam. By the mid-nineteenth century, the need for such mediation had diminished but had not disappeared. The families involved in the textile trade decided that to meet the new direction in trade, they must send family members as agents to the industrial core.

The Mediterranean Jews were not alone in this desire. From its start as a manufacturing center in the late eighteenth century, Manchester was a base for many foreign traders. After all, German families like those of Friedrich Engels and Solomon Levi Behrens, a prominent Jewish leader in Manchester, were represented in this city. Among those from the Mediterranean and

Southwest Asia, one finds Greek Christians, Armenians, Moroccan Muslims, and Syrian Muslims and Christians, as well as the Sephardim.[5] All of these merchants and entrepreneurs realized that in order to profit from the trade in cotton goods they must be at its source. Thus we find a paradox in modern imperialist capitalism. Many of those who engaged in trade between the metropole and the colonies (whether direct or indirect) were natives of the colonies.[6]

The foreign merchants in Manchester from nonindustrial countries were not simply "comprador capitalists" or "pariah capitalists," whose commerce was solely of benefit to the bourgeoisie in Britain, as Marxists might describe them; they participated in modern capitalistic activity at its center.

The Foundation of the Sephardic Community

The first Sephardic Jew of record was Samuel Hadida, a Gibraltarian commission agent, who arrived in Manchester in 1843. The first Syrian Jew, Abraham Btesh, an Aleppan merchant born in Killiz, visited Manchester in that year.[7] The census of 1851 records a number of Sephardic Jews, several of whom were Gibraltarian or from Constantinople. Some families from Corfu also were represented during the 1850s. They included a Hebrew teacher and a confectioner, as well as cotton traders. By the census of 1861, two Aleppan families were represented. In this period, Christian and Muslims, including some of the latter from Fez and Damascus, had settled in Manchester.[8]

The period of migration began in the 1850s and lasted into the 1920s. After that time, only small numbers moved to Manchester, which had passed its peak as a center of trade. It is hard to gauge the total number of Sephardic Jews in Manchester in the 1920s. H. M. Nahmad suggests that the number of those who were Syrians of all denominations was around five hundred at its height, using Fadlo Hourani's estimate of between two to three hundred Syrian-born and their descendants in Manchester around 1940.[9] He also suggests that a higher estimate of two thousand is exaggerated. A difficulty in any estimate is that there were always individuals and families who sojourned in Manchester for a number of years before moving on to other points, such as Syria itself and Latin America. While the Aleppans and other Syrians were a large part of the Sephardic community, they were probably less than half of that community. The Syrian proportion of the total Sephardic community may have been greatest around 1930. This would make the Sephardic community as a whole around four hundred at its height.

Most of these Mediterranean Jews still belonged to the Great Synagogue of Manchester, but moves to form a separate congregation began in North Manchester during the 1850s.[10] A congregation was founded on Cheetham Hill Road in 1871. It included most of the Sephardim in Manchester. The

Aleppans resisted merging with the other Sephardim for a time, but eventually they did join with the others in forming the new congregation. The Cheetham Hill Synagogue was helped by the Bevis Marks Spanish and Portuguese Synagogue in London and it adopted the prayer book and usages of that synagogue. It also acknowledged the authority of the London Haham (Sephardic chief rabbi).

By the beginning of the twentieth century, most Sephardic cotton traders had moved to the South Manchester suburbs of Withington and West Didsbury. Many of the other Middle Easterners, such as the Armenians and the Syrians of all denominations, also resided in Withington. This was not a segregated area, and it was affluent, with private homes, some of which were sumptuous. There were even a few businesses, such as Mansour's Grocery, which catered to Middle Eastern tastes.

There two congregations formed at that time which continued in that neighborhood until they merged to form the Sephardic Congregation of South Manchester in 1997. Both synagogues maintained the decorous services that marked the Cheetham Hill Synagogue. The buildings of both congregations were completed in the 1920s. The Withington Congregation of Spanish and Portuguese Jews was founded in 1904 and it was led by a Ladino-speaking Jew. The Shaʿare Sedek Congregation split off from the Withington Congregation before World War I. It was identified as an "oriental" congregation, predominantly Aleppan and Baghdadi. However, in the Withington congregation there were also Aleppan and Baghdadi families.[11]

The ritual differences between the two congregations were minor. In both an air of formality was maintained, symbolized by the wearing of top hats by the Parnas (president) of the congregation during the service. In both, the Spanish and Portuguese Prayerbook prepared by David da Sola Pool of New York was used. The most significant difference between the two lay in the recitation of the Musāf (an additional prayer that is recited only on Sabbaths, festivals, and new moons). This prayer follows the reading of the Torah. In the Withington congregation, the beginning of the Musāf is chanted by the cantor and the congregation together, while the congregation recites the rest of this prayer silently. When this is done, the Kohanic or priestly blessing is not recited by Kohanim (those who trace their descent to Aaron the high priest). At Shaʿare Sedek, members of the congregation recite the Musāf silently, followed by the cantor's repetition of the Musāf, including the Kohanic blessing. The latter is the custom of Syrian Sephardim.

The extended family was the important social unit within the Sephardic community. It should be understood that family networks were crucial in understanding this community. Some of the families represented in Manchester belonged to the mercantile-consular and rabbinic elites of Aleppo. Manchester had members of the de Picciotto, Hamwi, Ades-Tabboush, Abadi, and Anzerout families, among others. Whether this helps to explain the upper-middle-class ambience of the community from the mid-nineteenth century to the present is not clear, but it stands in contrast to the history of the New York Aleppans, whose stories fit the Horatio Alger "rags-to-riches" pattern.

The Business of the "Shipping, etc.,. Merchant"

In the city directories of Manchester, which were published until 1969, the kind of business in which the Sephardim engaged was described as "Shipping, etc.,. Merchant."[12] The entries for this line of trade took up about thirty pages in the pre–World War I directories, but declined thereafter, until they occupied only five pages in 1965, the last year I examined. The entries include name, address, markets, goods, payday, telegraph address, and telephone number. An example follows:

> HAMWEE, A.& SONS 2 & 4 Beaver St. Syria & Egypt Manchester Goods: Tues. 11 to 1;TA:"HAMWEE',Manchester.TN 5,724 Central.[13]

A superficial perusal indicates that trade with the Levant, including Syria and Egypt, was concentrated in the hands of those with Arabic, Jewish (both Spanish and Hebrew), and Armenian surnames. Other trade, including markets in "all parts" of the world, was spread among those with English and other surnames. After World War I, the Middle Easterners increased their trade with Latin America and West Africa. The "payday" indicates the day of the week when the trader was present at the Cotton Exchange in Manchester, standing by a particular pillar, waiting for clients.

The goods sold by most of the Middle Easterners were Manchester cotton goods, sometimes including specialties. For instance, Keyhayglou's sold only greys (grey cloth); Joseph Levy sold both Manchester goods and machinery. Non–Middle Easterners, on the other hand, included merchants who sold safes or vulcanized rubber goods.

Most of the firms into the 1950s bore personal names, presumably those of the proprietors. This was even true in 1965, though by then we also find corporate names in the directories, like Anglo-Swiss Textiles or Nahum's Union Mills (Yarns), Ltd. Such corporate designations make identification of the presumed proprietors somewhat more difficult than the former variety. Most of these firms were either personal proprietorships or family firms. Often a brother, cousin, or son was brought into the firm. Clerks, secretaries, and workers might come from outside the family. The firm required an office, usually in the central part of Manchester, off Oxford Street or near Deansgate, Princess Street, or a similar area. Warehouse facilities were required, as was access to the cotton exchange, where each merchant had his corner. The overseas customers in the Levant and later in Latin America who received the Manchester or Bradford piece goods were often, though not always, kin. It was in the post–World War I period that the purchasers of goods in the target countries began to be non-kin. Many Syrian Jews in Manchester sold goods to West Africa, where there were many Lebanese merchants but few Jews.

H. M. Nahmad writes about them as follows:

> The Syrian Jews, like the Syrian Christians, the Armenians, and the few Moslems from the Near East, and the Maghrebi colony (who lived in the Moss Side area of Manchester) were, in the main, engaged in the textile trade. They carried on their businesses in offices in the center of Manchester (four or five miles from where they lived). Some of them had large establishments and were well-to-do; others were in a more modest way of business. Their main occupation was the export of cotton-piece goods to the Near East, South America, and other markets. Some added woollen piece goods to their trading activities, and at one time the Syrian merchants would travel to Bradford, Yorkshire, usually every Wednesday to buy wool. . . . (The writer, on a visit to Manchester . . . , met one member of the community, a native of Beirut and in his eighties who told him that he still went to Bradford regularly.)
>
> Trading was carried on a lot between members of the same family—close or extended. Thus a merchant in Manchester might have a brother in New York, another in Mexico City or Buenos Aires, and a cousin or brother-in-law in Aleppo or Beirut to whom he shipped Lancashire manufacture.[14]

When the Sephardim arrived, they came from different places. Educationally, some had a fair amount of schooling and a good command of English and other languages, while others did not. Nahmad, who dealt mainly with Syrian Jews, notes that some knew just enough English to get along in their business. "Those from the Levant had to correspond with clients in the Middle East. One told me [H. M. Nahmad] that they would write letters in Arabic." They used a special ink, and then they pressed the letter on a machine to produce a copy. Young men in the second generation who were expected to carry on correspondence with Syria did learn Arabic.

Prior to World War I, participation in the textile trade was lucrative, but it was far from risk-free. One elderly gentleman said that he had heard that fathers in Syria would slap their baby sons on their rear and say, "Go to Manchester and become rich." Yet, many became bankrupt, even in the prewar period. Traders sometimes helped each other with loans, and interlocked networks occasionally collapsed when one individual had overextended himself. Cash flow problems of this kind were not uncommon.

Relations with Gentiles

The subject of financial transactions with Gentile competitors is a sensitive one, where we find some negative stereotyping of Syrian Jews in particular. When questioned about this, most of my informants said that the Sephardic Jews had generally good relations with their fellows. This may reflect my lack of sufficient rapport or the acculturation of more recent generations to the English scene (most of those with whom I spoke were English-born).

Two allegations of improper behavior did, however, come to my attention. One was told to me by a young member of the Sephardic community, who had been in Britain for about ten years and had heard this from older men. He said that some Syrian businessmen had established exclusive relations with a local shipping merchant and then dropped him, thus forcing him into bankruptcy or into selling his business to one of their relatives at low cost.

The other instance was alleged to have occurred in the 1890s and was reported in the quasi-satirical paper, *The Spy*. This paper, which was published in the 1890s, was generally anti-alien and anti-Semitic. The articles appeared in *The Spy* in 1892 and were titled "Levanters and Their Doings," with sequels. The author, who used the pseudonym Kinder, claimed that some fifteen Syrians had borrowed money from Manchester bankers and merchants and had then declared themselves bankrupt. He wrote that "it was clear to me that sweating calico printers and grey cloth agents was too slow a process of getting rich for them, and that they were using their remittances for the purpose of gambling in stocks and shares instead of paying their debts."

"Kinder" also alleged that Abram Besso, a Sephardic of Corfiot origin, was in business with this "ring" of Syrian Jews, later calling the "ring" one of Syrian, Egyptian, and Corfu Jews and including other Middle Eastern Gentiles in the schemes. Essentially, *The Spy* alleged that these "Levanters" fraudulently borrowed money and obtained goods on credit with no intention of paying for them. The paper claimed that these Jews were in business to obtain money, not to engage in ongoing trade. The manner in which the author constantly referred to their origins, their kin and business ties, and their "race" and "religion" is what demonstrates his underlying xenophobia. The December 17, 1892, issue of *The Spy* noted that Abram Besso had made an application to bring criminal charges against *The Spy*, but the application had been denied. In my perusal of *The Spy*, I found no more articles on the Sephardim, although the paper continued to campaign against the Russian Jewish immigration until it ceased to publish a few years later.

It is difficult to evaluate these allegations. The first was transmitted by someone too young to verify them. If the second were true on a wide scale, the Syrian Jewish shipping merchants could never have established themselves.

On the other side of the ledger, there were also family traditions about firms that made a point of repaying their creditors fully after having been forced into bankruptcy due to a cash-flow problem. Such businessmen stand in sharp contrast to the stereotypic Levantine portrayed by "Kinder."[15]

Socially, the first generations created their own connections and clubs.

Middle Easterners of various religions maintained correct ties, but outside of the business areas they generally were somewhat distant from each other, as they had been in the Middle East. Among Jews, Aleppans preferred each other's company to that of other Sephardim, even those from Baghdad. The various Middle Easterners did exchange visits on each other's holidays, such as Christmas, Sukkot, and ʿĪd al-Aḍḥa (the major Muslim holiday), as they would have in Syria. Relations between Jews, Christians, and Muslims were affected by external politics. During World War I, Syrian Christians were not affected by restrictions on enemy aliens, but Jews and Muslims were. After 1918, Christians and Muslims tended to support the creation of a Greater Syria, while Jews were torn between support for a "Jewish homeland" in Palestine and their concern for their relatives in Aleppo.

Relationships between Middle Eastern traders and their British counterparts were often cool. The British middle classes were not eager to engage in social relations with these exotic non-Christians.

"You Need a Passport to Go from North to South"

The small stream of Sephardic immigration coincided with the mass immigration of East European Jews to Manchester. The East Europeans generally gravitated to north Manchester, such as the Strangeways neighborhood, which Louis Golding described in his novel *Magnolia Street.*[16] Gradually the movement of veteran Jews, especially the Sephardim, to the southern "inner" suburban areas got underway.

By the early 1900s, most of the Sephardic families had moved to Withington and West Didsbury. They were part of the elite that controlled communal philanthropies. By the 1920s, even the leading Ashkenazi Jew of Manchester, Nathan Laski, sometimes called the "king of the Jews," belonged to the Withington Congregation of Spanish and Portuguese Jews. Since a Sephardic tie was required for admittance, he obtained membership through his wife, Sissie Gaster, a daughter of Moses Gaster, the Haham of the British Sephardim.

Even though the vast majority of Sephardim in Manchester were recent immigrants from the Mediterranean and Southwest Asia, their congregations projected the aura of the entrenched Anglo-Jewish-Portuguese Jews who were the pioneers of Jewish resettlement in England. The top hat, the ritual found in Bevis Marks in London, and the term *Portuguese* all symbolized their connection to this tradition. It marked their superiority over the new immigrants from Eastern Europe.

The Eastern Ashkenazim resented this snobbery. One quoted for me a saying that "You need a passport to go from the north [of Manchester, where most Jews lived] to the south [where the Sephardim held sway and excluded Ashkenazim, especially those who were poor]."

The Sephardic Jews did not hide their Jewishness, but they maintained their separation. For instance, in the Urmston cemetery, the Sephardic section is separate from that of the Ashkenazim, and the gravestones are quite distinct. The Sephardic ones have a shape reminiscent of Muslim gravestones, where the marker is in the shape of a coffin. The Ashkenazic gravestones resemble those of other Europeans who had vertical or horizontal headstones.

The upper-middle-class Sephardim associated primarily with other Sephardim and Ashkenazim of a comparable class. They encouraged their young to marry other Jews of comparable class. As late as 1930, I was told of a woman who acted as a matchmaker. There also were various social, literary, and Zionist clubs that engaged the attention of the young. Most of the families observed the dietary laws in their homes. While many attended the synagogue, some did carry on business on the Sabbath and ride to their social clubs in automobiles.

By the 1960s and 1970s, non-Jewish Mancunians saw both Sephardim and Ashkenazim as Jews. Ironically, West Didsbury was sometimes referred to as "Yidsbury" and Palatine Road as "Palestine Road." Also by this period, membership in the Sephardic congregations became more and more open to Ashkenazim.

Later Generations

It is now more than 140 years since the first Mediterranean Sephardim settled in Manchester. The congregations and even some of the firms that they established survive into the late twentieth century. However, since the trade in cotton piece goods has moved from England to other parts of the world, fewer and fewer of those who have stayed in Britain continue in the trade.

Some families only had brief sojourns in Manchester, followed by migration to other places, where they continued to engage in export-import business of one kind or another. An Urfali-Ḥalebi family with connections in Panama, Colombia, and Palestine spent a few years in Manchester before returning to South America. One Aleppo-born merchant went to Jamaica, where he married and then began to do business in Central America. During the 1930s, he joined a brother living in Manchester in his business but decided that Central America was a more lucrative site for his enterprises. Of nine Manchester-born children of an Aleppan merchant, six remained in Manchester. A daughter married a Syrian Jew from Colombia. Later she and her husband moved to the United States. The other children stayed in Manchester; most married Ashkenazic Jews there. In fact, several Aleppan immigrants married non-Aleppan Sephardi women, while many of their children married Jews of other origins in Manchester. There were some cases of intermarriage with Gentiles.

The younger generations early on began to move into the professions or other lines of business. We find this pattern as early as the turn of the century. *The Jewish Yearbook*'s Who's Who for 1901/2 includes Elizabeth Abadi, whose entry follows:

> Abadi, Miss Elizabeth, B.A., Headmistress, Jews Free School. b. Manchester. Educated at Askia High School for Girls and University College, Aberystwyth [Wales]. Graduate of London University with Honours. Appointed Vice-Mistress of Jews Free School in 1897. Head mistress, June 1900. Member of several communal committees. Synagogue: Hammersmith. Address—18 Rockley Road, West Kensington.[17]

I asked "Cecil Altaras," a second-generation gentleman, about his choice of occupation and that of his siblings. He was one of seven sons and two daughters, and he was born around 1910. Cecil's father sent two of his brothers to open a branch in Buenos Aires, when Japanese textiles threatened those of Lancashire. They were followed by one of their sisters. Two brothers died in their twenties. Two brothers emigrated to Canada, one having become a physician while the other was not very successful in business. One became a solicitor, while another became a barrister. None went into the cotton trade in Manchester itself.

"Frieda Sitt," a woman whose family had lived in Manchester prior to returning to Colombia after her father's death, described her father's house (probably around 1930):

> He set up a beautiful establishment (in Manchester on Palatine Road). He set up the first Sephardic synagogue in Lansbury Road. We grew up half English, half Syrian. My parents ate with flat Syrian bread. We grew up with English nurses, knife and fork. We were sent to (school in) a Roman Catholic convent. My younger brother was sick and mother went with him to Paris. (At home) it was polite to scream and shout. At the same time, we were sedate and wild, English and Syrian.

"Ralph Ades" also lived on Palatine Road. He went to a Church of England boarding school, after his parents had returned to Panama. He learned Jewish subjects in Mendoza's United Sephardic School. They learned little Hebrew, it was so noisy. Mr. Mendoza was able to quiet the children. Ralph liked Jewish history. At public school, when Ralph and other Jews were challenged by Gentiles, they fought back. Ralph also sat at the back of religion classes in this Anglican school. He learned the New Testament quite well. For people like "Ralph Ades," who moved between New York City, Latin America, and Great Britain as children, the number of discontinuities was great.

The Great Depression and the two world wars had a profound impact on both men and women raised in Manchester. The standard of living for the previously prosperous cotton-trading families went into a decline. One woman whose husband died during this period was forced to give up her maids and make her home in West Didsbury into a boarding house. Another widow and her children were forced to move to a smaller home in this period, before her sons became established in business.[18]

Even young women were forced to go to work, a fact that made the traditional familial control over their lives more difficult. Women were conscripted into auxiliary forces or worked in war industry during World War II. Whereas the schoolmistress Elizabeth Abadi (see above) was probably singular in her generation, Yvonne Tabboush, who became an international civil servant, was less unusual in hers. Joseph Sutton, who interviewed her, met her at a reception given in New York by other prominent Aleppan Jews from Jerusalem and Dublin, with whom Yvonne Tabboush was related. She is part of an international Ḥalebi kinship network, even if much of her life is lived outside of the community.

Yvonne Tabboush was the product of a marriage between an Aleppan Jew and a woman of Livornese origin. They had married in Egypt prior to moving to Manchester. Yvonne was the fourth daughter, and she became a journalist rather than getting married. She took a job with a British paper while staying with relatives in Cairo. Later she worked for the United Nations as a public relations officer and translator. At the time of her interview, she was living on the Upper East Side of Manhattan, not in Brooklyn, and she also had a condominium in Mexico. Her life is that of an independent woman.[19]

Today one finds few firms of Sephardic origin in the piece-goods trade, and even some of these are on the verge of closing down. Scions of the Manchester Sephardic community work in many different capacities, including as solicitors, barristers, diplomats, metallurgists, and university professors. The community has also been augmented by the acceptance of some Ashkenazim into the congregations and by small numbers of immigrants. Some of these are of Syrian or Iraqi origin, as well as Iranians. One noted Iranian immigrant, David Alliance, has been involved in various corporate takeovers and was involved in the establishment of Coats Viyella, described as "the creation of the world's leading textile business" in 1987.[20]

In 1987, before their merger, the two synagogues—the Withington congregation on Queens Road, and Shaʿare Sedek, a block or so away—remained. Each was smaller than in its heyday. Since 1987, however, they have shared services. In the summer of 1987, the two congregations held one Friday evening service on Queenston Road, while each had its own Sabbath morning service. The Withington congregation's Queenston Road building is now used by the amalgamated congregation. Many congregants have left the old neighborhood of West Didsbury and moved to suburbs in North Cheshire, and they must drive to services. The original Manchester Sephardic congregation, which is now in Kersal, in the northern part of the metropolitan area, has many Ashkenazim as members, as well as some new immigrants from Gibraltar and Morocco. Another group of more religiously observant immigrants from Morocco have founded the small Nefusot Yehudah synagogue and the Pinto Yeshivah and synagogue in North Manchester, where ultra-orthodox Ashkenazim live.[21] These congregations continue to represent the Sephardic tradition outside of the London area, though the era when cotton was king is long gone.

Conclusion

What is the significance of the Manchester Sephardim for our understanding of Aleppan Jewish ethnicity? This study is obviously only a preliminary glimpse at this group. Still, a number of considerations emerge.

We have a tendency to associate the perpetuation of ethnic identity with deprived groups. Elite groups, of course, can utilize the same kinds of social ties which perpetuate their identity, whether openly or invisibly.[22] The Sephardim of Manchester maintained their ties over a long period of time. Some of this was associated with the cotton trade, which made international networks pay off. These Sephardim, however, were also Jews, members of a group with its own religion and a history of persecution. Even if the Sephardim were prosperous, they were conscious of being identified with the poor Russians in Manchester itself and with persecuted Jews elsewhere. Indeed, one Syrian Sephardi in Manchester was a refugee from Belgium in 1941.

As the descendants of the Sephardic immigrants to Manchester have drifted away from the cotton trade and into other professions, the community has become less central to the global network of Syrian Sephardim.[23] This does not mean that they have lost memory of their ancestry, but one could not label the community surrounding Sha'are Sedek "Aleppo-in-Didsbury," the way Joseph Sutton has spoken about "Aleppo-in Flatbush." The community is much smaller and the pressure to conform to British society has been greater. Yet the persistence of the small Sephardic community in Manchester for nearly a century and a half testifies to its resilience.

CHAPTER 5

THE MIGRATION OF SYRIAN JEWS TO ERETZ YISRAEL, 1880–1950

This chapter will describe how various streams of Syrian Jews immigrated to Israel and laid the foundation for their integration and assimilation into Israeli Jewish society. Unlike the Syrian migrations to other countries, religious and ideological considerations were uppermost in Jewish migrations to Palestine\Eretz Yisrael. This ultimately contributed to the dispersal of Syrian Jews in various sectors of Israeli-Jewish society and to their assimilation.

THE BOUNDARY BETWEEN SYRIA AND ERETZ YISRAEL

There are several ways to demarcate the boundary between the lands labeled "Palestine," "Eretz Yisrael," and "Syria." There are different ways in which the selfsame territory is conceived by Jews, Muslims, Christians, and the different political powers who have ruled these lands. In many periods, all of these territories were seen as part of a single region. It might be called Syria, but its boundaries crossed many contemporary state borders (Roman, Ottoman, Mandatory, post-Mandatory). Sometimes provincial lines also cut the lands now identified as Israel and/or Palestine into different provinces of an empire.

Certainly in Talmudic times and possibly earlier, Jews made a distinction between Syria and Eretz Yisrael (roughly translated Palestine, but not identical to the Mandatory territory of Palestine). Geographically, there is no natural separation of Palestine from the rest of the "Syrian lands." For Arabs and others, Palestine could be considered part of a larger entity. Jews, however, considered Eretz Yisrael to be a holy territory, while "Syria" was partially sanctified. Sacred memories were attached to it, since parts of this territory had been under the hegemony of King David, and such biblical figures as Elisha and Ezra had visited it.

In Jewish law, tithing of agricultural produce was a practice generally limited to Eretz Yisrael, but payments of certain tithes were mandatory in Syria. Syrian Jews, like other coreligionists, considered migration to Eretz Yisrael to be a sacred duty. They also discussed which cities in Syria were, for one purpose or another, to be considered part of Eretz Yisrael.[1]

There were other differences between Syria and the "Holy Land of Israel." For instance, Syrian Jewish communities were dominated by Arabic speakers, while Palestinian Jewish communities, especially the four holy cities (Jerusalem, Safed, Tiberias, and Hebron) were more heterogeneous and contained several speech communities in the nineteenth and probably earlier centuries. While Jews in Syria were expected to be self-supporting, Palestinian Jews regularly sought assistance from Diaspora communities through special emissaries. This set these communities apart from communities in the Diaspora, that is communities outside of the Holy Land. While Jews from different speech communities were somewhat separated from each other, they also consciously shared a common religious motivation.

Jewish Divisions in Eretz Yisrael

Since Eretz Yisrael has always attracted pilgrims from different parts of the world, its Jewish, as well as Christian and Muslim, populations have always been heterogeneous. For the past three centuries, there have always been groups who could be labeled as "Sephardim and ʿEdot ha-Mizraḥ"—that is, Sephardic (Ladino-speakers)—and the "congregations of the East" (i.e. Middle East). In the early eighteenth century, the number of Ashkenazim was negligible. In the nineteenth century this changed, even before the beginning of Zionist settlement in the 1880s, which involved primarily East European Jews.

By the end of the Mandatory period, during which the Jewish population of Palestine had grown to about 600,000, the Sephardic and Middle Eastern proportion of that number had declined to about one-fifth of the total. This proportional division changed again with the mass migrations from North Africa and Southwest Asia (i.e., the Middle East) in the 1950s and 1960s. By the 1970s, the two groups were nearly even, with the Middle Eastern proportion growing at the expense of the European, due to both immigration and higher birth rate. In the 1990s, the large-scale migration of Jews from the former Soviet Union has changed this proportion again.

Prior to the 1880s, the Jews of Eretz Yisrael were all Orthodox Jews, of one variety or another. The Zionist movement, however, introduced secular Jewish nationalism, or the adherence to secular expressions of Jewishness. This secular nationalism became dominant during the Mandatory period and remained dominant until c. 1980, when it faced the challenge of a reinvigorated orthodoxy.

These divisions have important political and economic ramifications. During the Mandatory period, a Sephardic mercantile elite in the urban centers lost power and influence. By the time the State of Israel was established, being Sephardi (or Oriental) was increasingly associated with poverty, low status, and cultural backwardness. This was true for both secular and Orthodox Jews. During the mass immigration of the 1950s and 1960s, Jews from Middle Eastern countries were subjected to harsher efforts at acculturation than were European Jews, including encouragement to settle in agricultural and other communities in remote parts of the country. Since most of the Syrian Jews, especially in Jerusalem, had arrived prior to this period, they were less affected by such programs. They were, however, affected by the general atmosphere in the country, which stigmatized the Middle Eastern segment of the population.[2]

Migrations of Syrian Jews to Eretz Yisrael, 1870–1920

The immigration of Syrian Jews must be seen against the background of the changes going on in Palestine in the late nineteenth and early twentieth centuries. The nineteenth century witnessed the domination of Ottoman Palestine by the Christian powers of Europe, especially France, Britain, and Russia. This was a period when Christian tourism and pilgrimage increased and when churches and other Christian institutions began to dominate the landscape, especially in Jerusalem. Jews as well as Christians benefitted from the protection of the Europeans. From the 1840s onward, large numbers of European Jews came to live and die in the holy places. Jerusalem, in particular, acquired a Jewish majority.

The early migrants were mainly religious Jews from Europe and the Middle East. The Europeans in particular lived under what has been called the *ḥaluqah* regime. This arrangement meant that most of those living in Jerusalem and other Holy Cities subsisted off the contributions of the pious abroad. Few were engaged in productive occupations. Most of the Ottoman Jews did engage in trade and the crafts, but some probably were subsidized.

From the late 1870s, a break with this regime occurred that may be said to mark the beginning of Zionist settlement. In the 1880s, some European Jews began to establish agricultural settlements. Although initially many of these settlers were Orthodox Jews, the agricultural settlements were influenced by secular Zionism, which began to organize in that period.

No figures for Syrian immigration are available for the period prior to

1919, since no international boundary existed between Syria and Palestine. As noted above, there were differences between Syrian and Palestinian Jewish communities in the nineteenth century. The former were expected to be self-supporting, though both Aleppo and Damascus had fallen on hard times during the late nineteenth century. Also, in Jerusalem and the other Holy Cities, Syrian Jews found themselves surrounded by Jewish speakers of Yiddish, Ladino, Persian, and strange dialects of Arabic.

Still, unlike Europe or Yemen, Syria was sufficiently close geographically for some Jews to undertake the pilgrimage to Jerusalem or Safed several times in their lifetime. For instance, poor young peddlers from Damascus and even Aleppo would go up to Jerusalem and Safed in the period between Passover and Pentecost. Migrations in either direction between Syria and Palestine were not uncommon. As a consequence, family names such as Safadi were common for both Jews and non-Jews in Syria.

In Jerusalem, "committees" of various *ʿedot* (singular *ʿedah,* national origin groups) registered with the Ottoman authorities in the late nineteenth century. Such registration marked the breakup of the previously unified Jewish *millet* (officially recognized religious community). This breakup began in the early nineteenth century, when the Ashkenazim seceded from the Sephardic-controlled community. They were followed, at least for certain purposes, by the Maghrebis (Moroccans and Algerians) in 1844, the Georgians in 1863, the Bukharians in 1868, and the Persians in 1877. A synagogue, called Aram Ṣōbā, was established in the Old City of Jerusalem in 1876. The Ḥalebi *ʿedah* registered itself in 1880.[3] The degree of autonomy these groups enjoyed is uncertain. In the late Ottoman period, for instance, the Ḥalebim had no burial society, while the head of the Bukharian rabbinic court was a Ḥalebi rabbi, who served in the same capacity for the Ḥalebis.

Before 1870, the number of Syrian Jewish scholars in Eretz Yisrael was very small. Until the mid-nineteenth century, most such scholars who immigrated to Eretz Yisrael went to Tiberias. After 1870, many of the leading rabbinic scholars moved from Aleppo to Jerusalem. Many of the immigrants were mystics. Some had worked in other occupations in Aleppo, but in Jerusalem they devoted themselves to sacred study. Included among these immigrants were some of the most original scholars of the period.[4] Those who were engaged in sacred study spent time in *midrāshim* (or yeshivot). While we often think of such institutions as places for young students or scholars, these *midrāshim* were for adults as well. There they studied Talmud and Zohar in particular. The *midrāshim* were small rooms that had books set aside for this purpose. They could also be used as synagogues for prayer. The scholars were not only Ḥalebim, but also included Talmudists and Kabbalists from other parts of the Middle East and even a few Europeans. Such close interaction between peoples of different origin resulted in some intermarriage between the children of Ḥalebi rabbis and non-Ḥalebim. Most such unions were with offspring of Sephardic families from the Balkans, Southwest Asia, or North Africa.

The interaction with European Jews in Jerusalem led to a recognition of the gulf between Jewish secularists and the Orthodox. The Aleppan rabbinic circles felt the threat of secularization. From 1900, and especially after the British occupation in 1918, Ḥalebi rabbis allied themselves with the *ḥaredi* (ultra-Orthodox) Ashkenazim. These groups opposed the influence of secular Zionism.[5]

Those Ḥalebim who were unable to study because of financial circumstances or lack of previous education became tradesmen or workers, such as tailors. Old-timers said that while such a thing was uncommon among religious Ashkenazim, a Ḥalebi rabbi felt no shame in opening a shop if he could not support his family while engaged in full-time study.

The First World War had a disastrous impact on all the countries of the Levant. Military conscription was imposed on all Ottoman subjects. The military draft coupled with the Balkan wars and then the First World War caused young men to flee the country. Many were separated from their families for years. People also suffered from wartime shortages, natural disasters, and an influenza epidemic. Some families returned from Palestine to Aleppo, though that city was undergoing the same traumas.

The Mandatory Period, 1920–48

With the establishment of the Palestine Mandate under British rule and the Syrian Mandate under the French, an international boundary separated Syrian Jewry from the Yishuv (the Jews of Palestine). Now people had to obtain passports, visas, and other certificates in order to go from one country to the other. While many people continued to cross this new international border without documents, they could now be arrested for illegal entry. Some were deported from Palestine several times, but some did obtain immigrant certificates. Joseph Schechtman, using Jewish Agency figures, estimates that 9,118 immigrants entered Palestine from Syria and Lebanon from 1919 to 1948. From 1948 to 1958, 5,660 arrived in Israel. Thus the vast majority of Syrian Jews immigrated to Israel either before or just after the establishment of the State. Unlike other Middle Eastern groups, nearly twice as many Syrians and Lebanese had arrived before 1948 as after that date.[6]

In Jerusalem, the majority of Syrian Jews were Ḥalebim (Aleppans), from Aleppo and from other communities in the former north Syrian/south Turkish province of Halep.

The rate at which Syrians entered Palestine and in which years is difficult to gauge. In 1939, there were a total of 1,763 Syrian and former Syrian citizens among the Jews of Jerusalem. Of the 1,312 former Syrians, 35.59 percent had been Palestinian residents for more than five years. Another

16.46 percent had been Palestinian residents for ten to fourteen years. As for the 451 Syrian nationals, 221 had been residents of Palestine for between five and ten years. During the interwar period, the period of heaviest Syrian immigration was between 1929 and 1935. The Arab Revolt in Palestine between 1936 and 1939 discouraged potential immigrants.[7]

During the 1930s, the demand for immigration certificates to Palestine increased with the large-scale exodus from Germany. Fewer certificates were available to Middle Eastern Jews. At one point, the Urfali Committee in Jerusalem, representing Jews from southeastern Turkey, put in a request for certificates for their region. This request was opposed by the people in charge in Aleppo, who wanted certificates for Syrians. An orphanage in Aleppo requested certificates for its charges.[8]

The situation in Syria deteriorated in the late 1930s as pro-Palestinian nationalism sharpened and hostility toward the Zionists took on an increasingly anti-Jewish tone. This was heightened by German Nazi and Italian Fascist efforts to woo Arab nationalists. With the fall of France in 1940, Syria came under the rule of the anti-Semitic Vichy regime. Although the pro-Vichy government was ousted by the British in 1941, Syrian Jews did not feel secure.

During this period, a mass flight of Jews to Palestine occurred. Schechtman estimates that 4,811 Jews from Syria and Lebanon arrived in Palestine between 1942 and 1947. The Aleppo Riots in 1947 resulted in many Aleppan Jews seeking refuge in Lebanon, but access to Palestine was barred by the British until May 15, 1948. Only 585 Jews arrived in Palestine in 1947 and early 1948. A further 3,690 immigrants arrived through 1951. After that, immigration from Syria tapered off.[9]

Stories of immigration show what a casual process immigration was in the 1930s. One man who immigrated during the 1920s said he crossed the border in a car with some Arabs. Another, who was twenty at the time, had performed a rare feat of calligraphy by painting an entire book of the Bible on an eggshell. He exhibited this eggshell at a book fair in Tel Aviv and then simply stayed in Palestine.

A shopkeeper in Jerusalem told me about how he and his two brothers reached their decision to emigrate during World War II, when the "great hatred which both Arab and Christian had in their hearts" reached its apex. Two brothers had an antiquities shop in Damascus, and one had a shop in Beirut. All three were married. One Passover, when the Germans threatened the Middle East (c. 1942), the three signed a pact to leave immediately for the land of Israel. They did this without consulting their wives or their elderly parents—it was their decision to make. They applied for and got certificates from the British Mandatory authorities and arrived in Palestine with their entire families. Two settled in Jerusalem, while the other lived in Tel Aviv.

One man came to Palestine but returned to Syria. A few years later, his family decided to immigrate. When they crossed the border illegally, they were captured and interned. Around 1940, the two oldest daughters in another family were smuggled across the border on donkeys. They found work as domestics until their parents immigrated.

One man who immigrated to Jerusalem at the beginning of World War II left behind a pregnant wife, a nine-year-old daughter, and three smaller sons. His wife miscarried and died. The children were taken in by their mother's brother, but they wanted to join their father. The nine-year-old girl and her three younger brothers set off with a group of illegal immigrants. They reached Damascus by truck and spent the night in the city's cemetery.

In the confusion, one of the brothers was lost. Since the leader of their group did not want to wait for them to find the lost boy, she and the other two brothers got off to look for their brother. The truck left without them. They found their brother and all four had to wander through the streets of Damascus.

There they met a Jewish shopkeeper who wanted the girl to mop his floor for a few piasters. She did not know how and the shopkeeper wanted to throw her out, but she cried. When he heard her story, he sent them back to Aleppo. Later her uncle sent them to Jerusalem via Beirut.

Some illegal immigrants were betrayed to the authorities. One man related how a kinsman had cheated his father in Syria. Later, when the narrator and his father arrived in Palestine, this relative informed on them to the British authorities and they were deported. Still later, when they returned to Jerusalem, another cousin, who was well established in Jerusalem, let them stay in his house and helped them financially.

There were some organized efforts at illegal immigration. In 1944, when Yehoshua Levy, a native from Damascus, was nine, he was part of a group of forty children who were taken to an old Muslim cemetery near the center of the city. There they hid behind the tombstones until two members of *Palmaḥ* (a pre-State Jewish underground army) took them by truck to the Syrian-Palestine border in the Golan region. From there they walked on foot some twenty miles to a kibbutz in Galilee. They were apprehended by the British army while walking to a second kibbutz. Although the British threatened to return these children to Damascus, they were given legal status, and Yehoshua Levy went to a kibbutz where he has lived ever since.[10]

It was no accident that Yehoshua Levy ended up on a kibbutz. In Damascus, there was an active Zionist youth movement affiliated with HeḤalutz, a kibbutz-oriented socialist branch of Zionism. Some members of this group immigrated to kibbutzim in Israel, as indicated in the above story. Later they aided several illegal immigration efforts in Syria. Other Syrians also immigrated as part of the Zionist movement. The novelist Amnon Shamosh's family immigrated in the footsteps of a brother who had become a lecturer at the Hebrew University.[11]

Ḥalebim in the Mandatory Yishuv

An immediate problem facing new immigrants was how to make a living. Some aid was available from the Jewish Agency, from the Ḥalebi Committee, and above all, from kin. Most of this aid was of short duration. Most men had been peddlers or shopkeepers and were otherwise unskilled. They were not interested in agricultural labor, which the Zionists were promoting. The market for gold ornaments and other items that craftsmen in Syria had made was not great. Most men became unskilled laborers. Such labor was in demand during World War II, when Palestine served as a major base for the British army in the eastern Mediterranean.

In this period, the pioneering sector of the Zionist movement became dominant in the Yishuv. This segment stressed the growth of Jewish agricultural settlement, generally in the form of communal and collective settlements. In addition, the new cities grew, especially the all-Jewish city of Tel Aviv and the port city of Haifa, which was the country's major port and naval base. There was also some growth in Jerusalem, which was the administrative capital and the site of the Hebrew University, although the secularist Labor Zionists tended to de-emphasize Jerusalem.

The Jewish population of Jerusalem was much more Sephardic and much more religious than that of the other regions of Palestine. Syrian Jews, for the most part, were not in the pioneering sector, but were concentrated in the large cities. Some immigrants from Damascus, in particular, had joined HeḤalutz there and had joined kibbutzim on their arrival in Israel. Some Ḥalebi youth were attracted to the organizations for working youth set up by the Histadrut and other socialist organizations. This also led some to the kibbutzim.

Many Syrians lived either in predominantly Middle Eastern Jewish neighborhoods (e.g., Naḥalaot in Jerusalem) or on the borders between Arab and Jewish areas, such as the Kerem Ha-Teimanim area between Arab Jaffa and Jewish Tel Aviv or the areas between the predominantly Jewish Hadar Ha-Karmel and lower Haifa, which was where most Arabs lived.

Some women who had worked as seamstresses or domestic servants in Jewish homes in Aleppo continued this work in Palestine. Some immigrant girls married before the arrival of their parents in Palestine. For a few this was a means of gaining support. Several of these marriages were outside of their origin group (*ʿedah*). One girl became the second wife of a well-established Yemenite in a polygamous marriage. Another married a Persian, an *ʿedah* then considered inferior by the Ḥalebim.

The unevenness of migration upset the social life of Syrian Jews in other ways. In many families, fathers and husbands were separated from their children and wives because of migration. In a period of illegal immigration this was exacerbated, as the above examples indicate.

Many suffered disillusionment after arrival. One woman reported that many Ḥalebim wanted to return to Syria. Many years later, immigrants often idealized the circumstances of their lives in Syria or Turkey. For instance, in the 1960s, they would describe the large size of the houses, the low cost of living, and the variety and quality of foods. When questioning one woman about her family's poverty, she replied that they were poor because of successive efforts to go to Palestine.

After arrival, there was often internal migration. In some cities, Syrian Jews first settled in neighborhoods on the border between Arabs and Jews, such as in the Kerem Ha-Teimanim area between Tel Aviv and Jaffa or near Damascus Gate or in the Old City in Jerusalem. Jews living in these areas sometimes moved to areas of greater Jewish concentration after the Arab-Jewish conflicts such as those in 1929, 1936–39, and 1948.

The economic marginality of most Syrian and other Middle Eastern Jews also had political manifestations. Whereas most European Jews supported the main Zionist parties such as the various Labor parties, many Middle Eastern Jews were particularly attracted to the more extreme nationalist Revisionists. During the 1930s and 1940s, they were disproportionately represented in the ranks of the Irgun Zvai Leumi (known by the acronym Etzel) and the Loḥamei Ḥerūt Yisrael (known as the Stern Gang or Leḥi, its Hebrew acronym). During the period of the underground war (1946–47), the various Jewish factions often fought among themselves. A veteran of that period, who had been in Etzel and who had brothers in Leḥi and the Haganah, described the war of the walls, when members of one group would put up a poster and members of another group would deface it or remove it. Sometimes members of one group would beat up members of the other factions.[12]

The rabbinic elite also was affected by the changes of the Mandatory period. The Porat Yosef yeshiva, a leading Sephardi rabbinic institution, was established in the Old City in 1923. It had been funded by Joseph ben Shalom, a Baghdad Jew living in Calcutta in 1909, but completion of the building was delayed by World War I. Ḥalebi rabbis served at this yeshiva in a leading position from the opening of Porat Yosef. Rabbi Ezra ʿAtiyeh, another Aleppan, was the head of the yeshiva for many years. In this period, several of the Ḥalebi rabbis strengthened their ties with the Ashkenazi *ḥaredi* (ultra-Orthodox community) and its political wing, Agudat Yisrael, which rejected Zionism.[13] While the core of the rabbinic elite and its offspring were strengthened by these connections, some of the children of rabbis were attracted to Zionist youth movements of both the Left and the Right, like others in the Yishuv.

So far, the emphasis of this chapter has been on the religious and working-class sectors of the community. There were, however, Syrian Jews, including Ḥalebim, who entered middle-class and elite sectors of the emerging Yishuv during the Mandatory period and later. There was a Ḥalebi presence in the small west Jerusalem suburban area of Bayit ve-Gan. The Commercial Center, built in the 1930s near the King David Hotel in Jerusalem, was founded by Eliyahu Shamah, an Aleppan who had lived in Manchester and in Jamaica and who was an active civic leader in Jerusalem. Amnon Shamosh's brother was appointed to a position at the Hebrew University; Amnon and his mother immigrated from the middle-class Jamaliya to a middle-class section of Tel Aviv. Like many other urban middle-class youth of the 1930s and 1940s, he went to a gymnasium (academic high school) and was attracted to a secular Labor Zionist youth movement. In his work, he describes some of the cultural conflict that he faced, but it is within a middle-class context.[14]

Conclusion

Early on, the Aleppan Jews in Eretz Yisrael became dispersed throughout the Jewish communities, dividing along a number of different lines. The rabbinic families formed one group, especially in Jerusalem, aligned with similar elites of other origins. Working-class Aleppans similarly had already mingled with Jews from southern Turkey in Aleppo and when they found themselves living side by side with Jews from Turkish and Iraqi Kurdistan, they found they also had much in common. The Zionist ideology prevalent in pre-State Palestine encouraged assimilation, and this continued into the early State period. Since the Aleppan group was relatively small, they could easily mingle and merge with other compatible ethnic and ideological groups, a pattern that has continued up to the present.

A Sephardic synagogue in Bayit ve-Gan, western Jerusalem, 1962. Bayit ve-Gan was a place where middle-class Ḥalebim lived. (Photo by author.)

Dabbah Synagogue, a Ḥalebi synagogue in Jerusalem, 1962. (Photo by author.)

Ḥalebi father and son, Nahalat Zion neighborhood, Jerusalem, 1962. (Photo by author.)

Ḥalebi mother and daughter, Jerusalem, 1962. (Photo by author.)

Ḥalebi boy at his bar mitzvah, Jerusalem, 1962 (note phylacteries and prayer shawl). (Photo by author.)

Rabbi David Laniado and his wife, Mazal Laniado, Jerusalem, 1965. Rabbi Laniado was the author of La-Qedoshim Asher Ba-Are"ṣ. *He continued to wear the traditional cloak and tarbush of Aleppan rabbis. (Photo by author.)*

A couple in Jerusalem, 1993. The husband is of Aleppan descent, while the wife is from a Kurdistani family. (Photo by author.)

East Talpiot, Jerusalem, 1992. This is one of the new neighborhoods of high-rise buildings built in Jerusalem since 1967. Many people who formerly lived in the older neighborhoods in West Jerusalem now live in these new developments. (Photo by author.)

The ʿAdes Synagogue in the Naḥalat Zion neighborhood, Jerusalem, 1993. This is the main Ḥalebi synagogue in Jerusalem, though most who worship there are not Aleppan. (Photo by author.)

The Monte Sinai Synagogue was the first in Mexico City. This photo was taken in 1959, after most Jews had moved to other neighborhoods. (Photo by author.)

Aleppan Jewish peddler with his Mexican porter, c. 1920–1930. (From Hamui, Los judios de alepo. *By permission of Maguen David, Mexico.)*

Sedaka u-Marpe Synagogue (also known as Templo Rodfe Sedek), Colonia Roma, Mexico City, 1959. (Photo by author.)

An Aleppan Jewish wedding in Mexico City. (From Hamui, Los judios de alepo. *By permission of Maguen David, Mexico.)*

Gravestones of Sephardic Jews in the Jewish cemetery in Guatemala City, 1989. (Photo taken by Rachel Zenner for the author.)

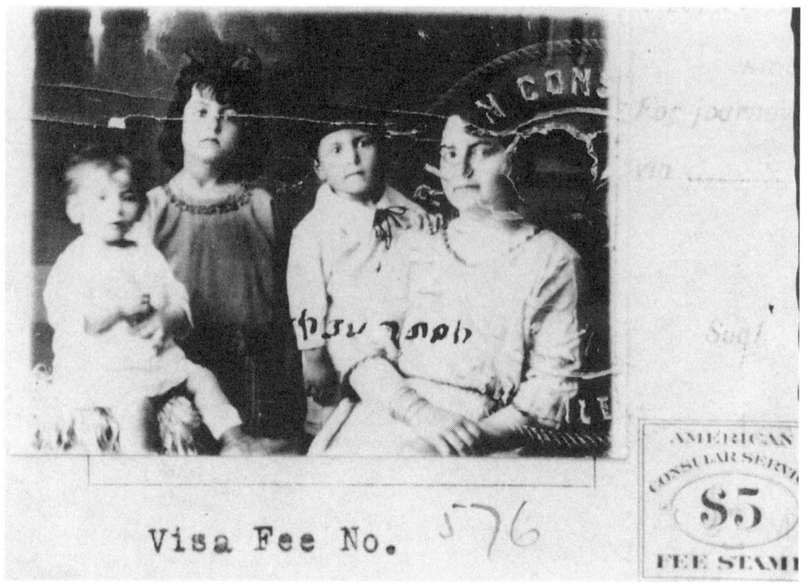

An immigrant visa to the United States, 1924. (Courtesy of Esther Abadi. From The Spirit of Aleppo. *By permission of the Sephardic Archives of the Sephardic Community Center, Brooklyn.)*

Isaac Shamie in Brooklyn, 1986. He is shown holding the cash register from his father's grocery store on the Lower East Side. The shop was the oldest Syrian grocery store in that area. (From Spirit of Aleppo. *By permission of the Sephardic Archives of the Sephardic Community Center, Brooklyn.)*

Oriental pastry shop, Bensonhurst, Brooklyn, 1958. (Photo by author.)

A home in Deal, New Jersey, 1995. (Photo by author.)

Torah dedication, Kol Israel Congregation, Bedford Avenue/Avenue K. (By permission of the Sephardic Archives of the Sephardic Community Center, Brooklyn.)

Gifts are collected on the occasion of a brīt mīlah *(circumcision ceremony). Mickey Kairey carrying Seniyel; Alice (Harari) Labaton lighting candle. (By permission of the Sephardic Archives of the Sephardic Community Center, Brooklyn.)*

CHAPTER 6

THE DESCENDANTS OF ALEPPO JEWS IN JERUSALEM AND ISRAEL, 1962 AND 1993

INTRODUCTION

The previous chapter told the story of the manner in which various streams of Jews from Syria arrived in the land of Israel and of the places that they found for themselves in what became Israeli society. The account in this chapter carries their story forward to the 1990s. It shows how the descendants of Aleppan (Ḥalebi) Jews in Israel have become integrated into Israeli society, but also how many remain tied to the transnational network of Aleppan communities. It shows how Aleppan Jews have changed, both since their migration and since the early State period (c. 1961–62). Here the situation of Aleppan families studied in the 1960s will be compared with that of the 1990s.

In 1961–62, I did a study of Syrian Jews in Jerusalem, concentrating on about ten extended families, as well as on a number of communal organizations.[1] Most of these families lived in the neighborhoods surrounding the Maḥaneh Yehudah market in West Jerusalem, including the Naḥala'ot, Romema, and Geula. The families were of Aleppan (Ḥalebi) origin and several were rabbinic families, related to a number of old rabbinic dynasties. Several of these families had been in Jerusalem since the 1890s. Others had originated in the south-central Turkish hinterland of Aleppo, were of proletarian origin, and had immigrated in the Mandatory period, as described in the preceding chapter.

In 1992 and 1993, I interviewed members of some of these families. I also investigated the condition of a number of Syrian Jewish institutions that I had studied previously or that had been established in more recent years. Certain trends I noted in 1962, such as the dispersal of origin group members into the larger Israeli-Jewish society, have continued, while other trends, such as movement to certain new neighborhoods and strengthening of the Orthodox institutions, are the result of larger changes in Israel.

Syrian Jews as a Small Ethnic Group

The Syrian Jews represent one of the smaller origin groups in Israel. These groups generally entered Israeli society without causing massive social problems. In fact, some were part of the Sephardic community that was part of the "Old Yishuv," as noted in the previous chapter. Their community was generally too small to make great waves in the society. They were thus unlike the German Jews, the Moroccans, Kurds, Iraqis, and Yemenites of the 1950s and 1960s, or the Russians of the 1980s and 1990s. Unlike these groups, they were not seen as the source of major social problems. In addition, there were no collections of jokes or sayings in which Syrians were stereotyped. They are useful in studying how the various divisions within Israeli society, such as the social divisions between affluent Ashkenazim and impoverished Mizraḥim (Middle Easterners), between religious and secular Jews, or between nationalists and socialists, may deepen or may be bridged. Walter Weiker, for instance, has called another small group, Jews from Turkey, "the unseen Israelis."[2] By this, he points to their lack of visibility as a distinct group.

Weiker tests the suggestion that small immigrant groups will assimilate fairly rapidly. In his 1988 book, Weiker concluded that the children of Turkish immigrants would be indifferent to their parents' culture. But in a 1994 article, he acknowledged that, in reality, they had considerable interest in their heritage. Still, the process of assimilation was proceeding. For instance, Weiker's findings include almost universal intermarriage with Jews of other origins. Thus the grandchildren will be interested in the parents' heritages (plural). His work suggests that small origin groups like the Turks, the Bulgarians, and the Syrians assimilate into other groups of Israelis in the second generation, even if they retain a positive attitude toward their origins.[3]

Integration and Assimilation

As has been frequently noted, Israeli policies of immigrant absorption have generally supported rapid and intensive integration of Jewish immigrants into the society and economy. These policies, which preceded the establishment of the State of Israel, encouraged repudiation of attributes brought by immigrants from the Diaspora, including personal and family names, language, and the like. While these policies have not been totally effective, they have helped in the creation of a Hebrew-speaking national Israeli identity. Certain new immigrants have also been encouraged and possibly coerced into agricultural settlements. This was especially the case in the 1950s. In the 1970s and 1980s there was a lifting of assimilatory demands, and greater voice was given to Middle Eastern cultural expression.[4]

In 1961–62, I was concerned with the degree to which the Syrian immigrants and their descendants had maintained or lost their particular local identities and merged with the Sephardic and Middle Eastern segment of the Jewish population. I noted at that time that there were few specifically Syrian institutions or organizations. It seemed that Aleppan Jews were dispersing as a group, though many had both ambivalence toward and pride in their ancestry.[5]

In the 1960s, I concluded that Syrian Jews were not concentrated residentially, nor did they have many institutions that were marked "ethnic arenas" for Syrians. The synagogues and even the charities supported by Syrian Jews abroad and mediated through Syrian Jews in Israel served a larger clientele. Like most national white ethnic groups in the United States, Syrian Jewry in Israel had been reduced to a recognition of ancestry and the performance of a few customs, particularly culinary and musical, which also were not their exclusive heritage.

In 1993, I sought to interview members of families I had met previously and to return to sites where I had spent much time. I also interviewed leaders of the World Center for the Traditional Heritage of Aleppo Jewry. My goals were the same. I wanted to set this study in the context of studying other Syrian Jewish communities in other countries. As noted, some of the Diaspora Syrian Jews have vigorously maintained their communal structure, while others have not.

Jerusalem 1962 and 1993

The changes between Jerusalem in the early 1960s and in the early 1990s, needless to say, have been great. In 1962, Israeli Jerusalem was part of a truncated metropolitan area, somewhat isolated from the population and economic center of the country on the coastal plain. It was a city of a little over 150,000 people, mostly Jews. Connections with the Jordanian Jerusalem metropolitan area were few, mediated primarily by the United Nations at the once-famous Mandelbaum Gate checkpoint. While Jerusalem was the capital, most governmental buildings in the city were modest. Most building, such as the Hadassah Hospital complex in ʿAin Karem and the Hebrew University's Givʿat Ram campus, was in the west. Building along the then-international border was not very often done. The *ḥaredi* presence was still small, though much more visible in the Holy City than in the rest of the country.

Jerusalem in the 1990s is far different. The city as a whole has a population of over 400,000, although it is larger when combined with that of surrounding suburban communities and villages. The united Jerusalem is still a divided city, as Michael Romann and Alex Weingrod amply illustrate in their volume, *Living Together Separately*.[6] The divisions include those between Arabs and Jews, as well as between *ḥaredim* and other Jews.

Large government, residential, and commercial buildings now cover many of the hills from north to south and east to west. In 1960, Bethlehem was far from Jerusalem, while now the high-rise apartments of the Jewish development of Gillo tower over the Arab towns of Ephrata.[7] The *ḥaredim* are now a much more important segment of the population throughout the city than they were in the 1960s and they include substantial numbers of Sephardim as well as Ashkenazic Jews. For instance, the Reḥavia area, which in the 1960s was a predominantly secular middle-class neighborhood with a large number of Hebrew University professors, now has large numbers of people wearing *ḥaredi* dress. As we will discuss later, the yeshiva population among Middle Eastern Jews has grown.

Gentrification has been another force in Jerusalem. Several old and poor neighborhoods have been targeted as places where middle-class families can find good and attractive housing with the patina of age. Among these is Naḥala'ot, with its small houses with courtyards and winding lanes. A consequence of such gentrification is that the cost of housing in such neighborhoods rises. Naḥala'ot itself now also has been renamed *Lev Haʿir* (The city's heart), following the old Talmudic proverb: Change of name is change of destiny.[8]

Changes in Residence and Neighborhood

The Levi family had lived in Naḥala'ot and Givʿat Shaul, a western neighborhood in the 1960s. Naḥala'ot in particular is in walking distance of the market of Maḥaneh Yehudah, while Givʿat Shaul is farther out. Naḥala'ot is an old Middle Eastern–style quarter with closely packed one- or two-story houses, often with courtyards. Jacques Levi lived in a two-room house with kitchen and bathroom and a small courtyard on one floor. He did not have a telephone at that time.[9]

Jacques Levi and his wife, Jamila, were both born in Aleppo and had immigrated to Jerusalem in the 1940s. They had married early. Jacques was a truck driver selling vegetables to market shops. Later he became a grocer. He is now dead. He has seven surviving children. Only one continues to live in Naḥala'ot. Another has a shop in Maḥaneh Yehudah. Most of the rest have moved to the southeastern neighborhoods and live in high-rise apartment buildings there. I did not see one of the daughters in 1993. According to her brothers, she has become "religious" (Orthodox), which the Levis were not.

When I asked one brother if he was "religious," he indicated that he was not irreligious.

Ezra Levi, who also had lived in the central and western neighborhoods, now lives in East Talpiot. Nearby live a daughter and her Ashkenazic husband. One son lives in Gillo, while another lives in Bakʿa in an older apartment building. Both Gillo and East Talpiot are neighborhoods that have been built in the last twenty years as high-rise apartment areas in the former Jordanian zone.

Those Ḥalebim who are professionals often live in other areas, such as in southwestern areas of the city, where there are many nonreligious Ashkenazim. This is not a change from preceding decades, as these people already lived outside the areas surrounding Maḥaneh Yehudah in the 1960s and they generally lived together with nonreligious and moderately religious Ashkenazim.

In 1962, I followed one teenager, Raful, as he left school and got a job as an apprentice.[10] At the same time, Sima, his sister, had succeeded in gaining admission into an academic high school. I inquired about them in 1993.

Raful, who is now known as Rafi, is a taxicab driver living in the southeastern suburbs. He lived in the Negev for a few years before returning to Jerusalem. He owns his own cab, but he is employed by a company. His wife, a woman of Kurdish origin, is a civil servant and one of his daughters is a university student. His sister never finished high school. She, too, married a man of Kurdish origin and they run a business in one of the villages near Jerusalem. If we look at their outward appearances, Raful and Sima have risen in terms of status, despite the disadvantages of being school dropouts.

What is true of Raful and his sister also can be applied to the other families I visited. Both the families of people who worked in the market and those of rabbis have a higher standard of living in the 1990s than they did in the 1960s. Many are engaged in middle-class occupations. Foreign travel is not uncommon, and most households have televisions and telephones. Whereas in 1961 a visitor would just drop in, now visitors are expected to call ahead. Some of those who have prospered the most have done so abroad. A member of one of the rabbinic families went to work in the United States for a company founded by other Sephardic Israelis, and he has become an important executive in this company. There are, of course, some exceptions to the general improvement in standard of living, such as one young man who was paralyzed as a result of driving over a land mine in Gaza. Still, the general trend has been favorable.

Family Life

In 1961–62, much of my fieldwork was devoted to observation of family life in the Ḥalebi households I visited. In my much shorter update, I was unable to make equivalent observations. There are some hints, however, that trends noted in the 1960s have continued. It is likely that what is often seen as the traditional ideal, in which wives obey husbands and children heed their parents' words, was never a perfect reality. In addition, the discontinuities that have marked Syrian Jewry since the beginning of the nineteenth century have added to contradictions and conflicts in these relationships. The *moredet* (rebellious wife) has been known for centuries. Such women often ran away from their husbands' homes to return to their parents, complaining of abuse on the part of husbands and husbands' parents. Such an action might occasion negotiations, in order that the wife might return to her husband, or it might precipitate a divorce. Disobedient children appear in both the responsa literature and accounts of foreigners resident in Aleppo. For instance, a woman who was an Alliance teacher in Aleppo reported that once a father brought his adolescent son to her so that she could punish him. She indicated that parents expected teachers to punish their pupils for disobedience to parents.[11]

The disruptions of and changes in traditional family relationships I found in my 1962–63 study included: (1) Marriage against parental wishes, (2) Wives disobeying husbands, (3) Disobedient children and inconsistent parental behavior, and (4) Grandmothers acting as baby-sitters and living near children, while the mothers worked outside the home. Most of these changes indicate that the family had become less patriarchal and authoritarian. A woman might go to Tel Aviv to visit relatives without her husband knowing she was going, or might consider voting against his political party.

I did not have the opportunity to observe households in 1993, but from conversations with the Ḥalebis, now in their forty, I found that relationships between spouses seemed fairly relaxed. In most cases, wives worked outside the house, sometimes at jobs of higher status than those of their husbands. Grandmothers continued to baby-sit for their daughters and daughters-in-law.

Another trend that has appeared is "traditionalizing" among those who are Orthodox. This includes continued arranged marriages and greater "modesty" in women's dress. This is especially marked in rabbinic families, where the model of the Ashkenazi *ḥaredim* is especially strong. Several older male members of rabbinic families, who were not themselves rabbis, complained about the ways of their younger relatives. One said that his nieces would not shake his hand.

At the other extreme, one finds members of Ḥalebi families who are unattached and lead an almost bohemian lifestyle. One individual, about forty years of age, has traveled extensively and lived abroad. While he has returned to Jerusalem, he is unmarried, although he has had a succession of girlfriends.

Intermarriage

In the 1960s, Syrian Jews in Israel already had a high level of outgroup marriage. I was able to trace this through people I interviewed, but this was also verified by data that I requested from the Central Bureau of Statistics (CBS). The categories used by the CBS were different from my own. They did not differentiate between Aleppan Jews and Damascus Jews and certainly would not consider a second-generation, Israel-born descendant of such Jews as a Ḥalebi (Aleppan) or a Shāmī (Damascene). Approximately one-third of Syrian and Lebanese brides and grooms who married in 1956 married other Syrian and Lebanese. If people of Syrian and Lebanese origins, such as "Israeli-Oriental," Egyptian, and Turkish individuals are included, the percentage rises to about two-thirds of the total. In 1961, between 25 and 30 percent married Syrian- and Lebanese-born spouses. If the other categories are included, this figure rose to about 62 percent. The percentage of those marrying spouses of European origin was over 15 percent. In the early 1960s, most younger Jerusalem Ḥalebim were Israeli-born.[12] Most of the Aleppan-born individuals I interviewed in the 1990s varied in age between forty and seventy and were married to non-Syrians. One man, whom I had known in Jerusalem when he was about twenty and who now lives in the Syrian community in New York, was married to a non-Syrian Sephardi. One man was not married, although he had a woman friend. The daughter of one nonreligious, working-class Aleppan couple was married to a non-Jewish Englishman and lived in England, but she kept in touch with her parents. In another family, a daughter had moved to France. In general, maintaining a "pure Aleppan family" did not seem to be an important value in seeking a partner. For the religiously conservative, religiosity was a much more important value.

It is also noteworthy that most of the younger couples in these families had two to four children, rather than the six or more children characteristic of the families in which they grew up. The small family size of nonreligious Israelis is prevalent among those Ḥalebim who are moderately traditional to nonreligious.

Political and Religious Orientations

The families I visited in 1993 all had ties with the "nationalist" (right wing) camp within Israel. While I did know some Ḥalebis who were affiliated with the "workers' parties" (MAPAI, Aḥdut Ha-ʿAvodah, MAPAM) in the 1960s, these were not the ones with whom I had contact in 1993. I should also indicate that political topics did not always come up in conversation in my encounters. I judged religious orientation as much by behavior as by the actual statements people made. I visited some of my friends on the Sabbath, and I could see how they behaved in their homes, or I saw them in synagogues.

People who were thirty-something or around forty when I was in Israel in the 1960s are now in their late sixties and seventies. They were the generation that experienced World War II and the struggle for independence. One had been a prisoner of war in Germany, after having joined the British army at the behest of the Jewish Agency. Others had been in various underground organizations. Many of these people felt profoundly disillusioned at what had happened to the State of Israel. One felt inadequately compensated for the sacrifices he had made and scorned the belated honors that veterans received. Another, a veteran of the revisionist underground army (Irgun Zvai Leumi) and an activist in the political parties that succeeded it (Ḥerut, Likud), recalled the heroism of men accused of terrorism by the British who went to the gallows with Zionist songs on their lips, thus showing the purity of their motives. Now he feels that the Likud Party no longer stands for the ideal of a Jewish state with boundaries on both sides of the Jordan.

In 1992, my wife and I watched the opening of the Knesset on television with a couple in their East Talpiot apartment. This was when the late Yitzhak Rabin was sworn in as prime minister. They knew all the political leaders. As veteran Likud voters and residents of a new East Jerusalem neighborhood, they were not happy with the new Labor government. In the summer of 1993 (before the Oslo Agreement) these same people predicted that Rabin was going to give the Arabs what they wanted: the return of the Golan to Syria and recognition of a Palestinian state.

The Jewish attitude toward Arabs in 1993 was not completely different from what it had been in 1962, except that Arabs are present in the Jerusalem of the 1990s. Between 1948 and 1967, few Arabs appeared on the streets of the Israeli sector of a still-divided Jerusalem. Today, especially in areas like East Talpiot, not only can one see Arab villages and neighborhoods, but Jews and Arabs interact with each other on a daily basis. For instance, the park area near Government House (the old British high commissioner's residence) is in walking distance of Ezra Levi's apartment. Arabs and Jews both stroll there, and Arab children play in the park. As we took a walk together through this park, Ezra Levi commented on then-mayor Teddy Kollek, who was seen as appeasing the Arabs. Levi saw Kollek as clever, but he expressed fear that Kollek was giving the Arabs too much. Several times during our walk he called attention to the Palestinian boys who were playing soccer. He also pointed to the memorial for those who had died fighting on this spot in 1967, including a cousin, thus underscoring the sacrifices Israel had made.

He also said that while he used to go to the Old City frequently, since the *intifāḍa* (the Palestinian revolt against Israeli rule, 1987–93), he went only to go to the Western Wall.

The attitudes of these older Arabic-speaking Jews toward Arabs are not totally negative, however. A Syrian-born woman expressed a desire to visit Syria if there is peace. While generally viewing Arabs as "dirty," when pressed they will admit that many Arabs are "clean." The stereotypes have a situational character and are related to anxiety about the future. There were also individuals who dissented from the attitudes expressed. One man in his forties who had traveled considerably had a much more positive attitude toward the Palestinians.

These elderly Ḥalebim also expressed dissatisfaction with their Jewish neighbors. An older woman in East Talpiot expressed her displeasure with the way apartments had been allocated in her housing development. She complained that older couples had been given upper apartments in buildings without elevators, that people had obtained apartments through political favors, and that welfare was given to women whom she considered "whores." My friends here were engaged in "griping," which the Israeli scholar Tamar Katriel sees as a communal ritual. It is a way of releasing pent-up emotions.[13] Still, their frustration over their position in Israel—living in a contested sector of Jerusalem—makes them feel vulnerable to forces beyond their control.

An important sector of the Ḥalebi community is Orthodox. Its political orientation will be considered in the next section, when Ḥalebi yeshivot are discussed.

The Middle Eastern Heritage

In 1963, the attitude that Jerusalem Sephardim, including Ḥalebim, had toward their Middle Eastern heritage could at best be characterized as "ambivalence" intermingled with a good deal of disdain for the old ways.[14] Some of this ambivalence continues today, but there is currently a much larger dose of pride mixed in than there was then. This is not just toward the Aleppan heritage, but toward other heritages as well.

While in the home of one Ḥalebi married to a Kurdistani-born woman from the Jerusalem neighborhood of Katamon, we watched a Kurdish Jewish music program. They watched this show without any self-conscious comments. There were no ethnic jokes about Kurds, as there might have been in the 1960s. (In the 1960s Kurdish Jews were stereotyped as "numbskulls.")

For Eli, one of Jacques Levi's sons, a popular television series based on Amnon Shamosh's *Michel Ezra Safra and Sons* brought back many of his feelings about his parents' difficult past. The novel and the television series portray the fictional history of a wealthy Ḥalebi family from the late 1930s to the late 1970s. This mercantile family, which must be considered separately from the real banking dynasty of the same name, was quite affluent. The fictional Safra family had branches throughout the world and led a privileged life.[15] *Michel Ezra Safra* won critical praise and acclaim from many Middle Eastern Jews because it broke with the stereotypical view of Middle

Eastern Jews as impoverished and ignorant. This work showed a proud and powerful Middle Eastern family, the equal of those of Germany or Poland.

This book and other works by Shamosh that deal with Aleppo generally portray a bourgeois milieu, most often set in the middle-class Aleppo suburb of Jamaliye. The stories reflect Shamosh's own background.[16] Eli, however, felt that Shamosh had misrepresented Aleppan Jewry. Shamosh had told only one side of the story, and it was not the story of Eli's forebears. Eli said that he had written to Shamosh about this, but he was not satisfied with Shamosh's reply. He strongly felt that his mother's story of impoverishment and discrimination against her by wealthy Jews in Aleppo must be told. He said that the rich (like the Safras) would only employ the poor as maids, and played favorites when giving out charity.

This ambivalence toward their Aleppan past is present among the Orthodox as well as the secular Ḥalebim. Paradoxically, religious institutions also stand at the crossroads of pride and disdain. In the early 1960s, Orthodox religious institutions were in a much more defensive position than they are in the 1990s. A number of Sephardic yeshivot existed at that time, alongside Ashkenazi ones. For instance, the Porat Yosef Yeshiva, which had been established in the Old City, had rebuilt its buildings in the Geula section of West Jerusalem. But yeshivot in general were considered marginal to Israeli society at the time.

Even though kibbutzim were not as strong as they had been in the 1930s and 1940s, they still were connected to the dominant forces in Israeli society, while yeshivot were not. In the 1960s a troubled child was more likely to be sent to a kibbutz than to a yeshiva. If all yeshivot were marginal, Sephardic yeshivot were doubly stigmatized. The cultural ambivalence that marks them today existed at that time as well. While some of the older Ḥalebi rabbis continued to wear the cloak and tarbush of Middle Eastern *ḥakhāmim*, younger rabbis wore black suits with ties and black hats in the style of the Ashkenazi rabbinate. Many of these younger rabbis had studied in Ashkenazic yeshivot. Since that time, Sephardic yeshiva students have begun to wear the black-and white garb, which is an Ashkenazic style. Even though the Sephardic Orthodox have broken politically with Ashkenazim by founding the Shomrei Oraita Sephardim (SHAS) Party, they stylistically and in other ways imitate the styles of the Ashkenazic yeshiva world. Even though the spiritual leader of this political movement, Rabbi Ovadiah Yosef, wears distinctive garb, no attempt has been made to revive a more distinctive Middle Eastern style for rabbis and yeshiva students.

In the rabbinic families the split between those who favor a fairly open attitude to the nonreligious world, which is seen by some as the traditional Sephardi way, and those who favor rejection of cultural modernity, is most apparent. Several sons of rabbis, who had secular occupations, expressed some hurt and dismay at the conduct of their more religious siblings who were rabbis or married to rabbis. Shaio pointed out that his father, who was extremely pious, always was pious for himself, not for others. He tolerated others. Shaio himself was fairly traditional. He had worked for the Israeli government abroad in various capacities and always tried to attend synagogue services. As noted above, Shaio was put off by the fact that several of his nieces, children of a sister, would not shake hands with him. He felt that this new breed of rabbis did not represent the true Ḥalebi and Sephardic traditions.

Ties between the Aleppan community in Jerusalem and those abroad have been quite important. Many of the rabbinic families and yeshivot have supplied rabbis for communities overseas, while the Diaspora communities have sent money to help Jerusalem institutions. Several Aleppan rabbis who have served overseas communities, such as Mordecai ʿAtiyeh, who was rabbi in Mexico City for many years, have retired to Jerusalem.[17] Today, several of the Jerusalem-born rabbis who serve congregations in the Americas spend each summer in the Holy City.

In the early 1960s, organized activity along origin group lines for old-timers was sporadic and not particularly visible. The Committee of Aleppo Jews was not very active, although it had previously transferred funds, received from Ḥalebis abroad, to impoverished Ḥalebis in Israel. More active was a Ladies Committee, which occasionally met and raised money for the poor by special sales of linens, which they received from abroad.[18]

A *bet din* (rabbinic court) of Aleppan rabbis also was convened from time to time to supervise the ʿAdes Synagogue in Naḥalat Zion. Several Ḥalebi rabbis and leaders, as representatives of the Aleppan community, disputed the efforts of President Ben-Zvi to claim ownership of this sacred relic for the State of Israel. This dispute continued from the bringing of the Codex to Israel in 1958 until an endowment agreement was issued in 1962 between Ben-Zvi and the Ḥalebi community.[19] In any case, as far as the majority of Ḥalebi Jews in Israel were concerned, the communal organizations were atrophying during this period and were less and less relevant to the daily lives of the people.

The revival of interest in the Aleppo heritage is centered in Tel Aviv. The World Center for the Heritage of Aram Ṣōbā is located in a synagogue in a Tel Aviv neighborhood, near Kerem Teimanim, where Syrian Jews also have lived. The center is indicative of a broad change, whereby Jews in Israel, especially those of Middle Eastern origin, are searching for their Diaspora roots and are not afraid to assert this interest. For instance, there is now a Museum of Iraqi Jewry in Or Yehudah near Ramat Gan. Public celebrations of the Moroccan Mimuna and the Kurdistani Sirḥana are also part of the Israeli scene.

The World Center has a fairly broad view of the Syrian Jewish heritage, valuing both religious and secular aspects. It has published occasional bulletins highlighting aspects of Syrian Jewish life in Syria, Israel, and the Diaspora. It organizes meetings on Syrian Jewish culture in Tel Aviv, Haifa, and Jerusalem. The most active leader involved with the center is Menaḥem Yedid. Yedid is the son of a well-known rabbi, Yomtov Yedid, but his father died when he was young. After immigration, Menaḥem became a member of the Irgun Zvai Leumi during the 1940s and was active in the Ḥerut Party, founded by Menaḥem Begin. In the early 1960s he was leader of that party in Shekhunat Ha-Tiqva, an impoverished neighborhood in southeast Tel Aviv. He was a Likud member of the Knesset before his retirement.

In the early 1960s, Yedid's work included the establishment of a high school near Rishon LeTziyon, with the help of a Syrian Jewish philanthropist from Los Angeles. In 1973, he was active in the campaign on behalf of Jews in Syria. The establishment of a cultural center is a product of his more recent work. In addition to the World Center, he has also established a small yeshiva in memory of his father.

Other activists include Moshe Kohen, Shlomo Toussia-Kohen, and Ya'akov Choeka. Moshe Kohen, a younger man, was born in Aleppo and in 1993 resided in Bat Yam. Shlomo Toussia-Kohen is a well-known lawyer, living in Jerusalem, who has also been active in Likud. Choeka, a Jerusalem resident, is a professor of computer science at Bar Ilan University in Ramat Gan. His father, Rabbi Aharon Choeka, was born in Aleppo but served as rabbi for many years in Egypt. Ya'akov Choeka has been involved in projects at Bar Ilan involving the application of computers to the study of response and other genres of Jewish legal literature.

The participants in programs of the World Center, according to the activists, are primarily the older generation of Syrian natives, rather than their children. Except for Professor Choeka himself, few Egyptian Ḥalebis participate in these programs. As noted above, many of the younger generation are either the children of mixed marriages or have intermarried with Jews of other origins.

The activists do not see themselves as promoting the separation of Syrian Jews from others, but rather as keeping alive the consciousness of the Syrian heritage. Most of the activists said that today most Ḥalebis marry people who are not Ḥalebi, and they do not view this negatively. They see their job as helping others to value the Syrian heritage as part of the broader fabric of Judaism. Although Yedid and Choeka are privately religious, the center has promoted and included the work of Amnon Shamosh, the novelist and poet who is a Labor Party member and a kibbutznik. This contrasts with the position of *ḥaredim,* who view people like Shamosh as antireligious. When Shamosh was in New York in the 1980s, for example, several rabbis, including some with Israeli *ḥaredi* connections, forced the Sephardic Community Center in Brooklyn to cancel events honoring him and his work. In any case, for the World Center, the remembrance of Aleppo in Shamosh's writings is compatible with the assimilation and integration of the descendants of Aleppo Jewry into the larger Israeli nation. The publications of the World Center show an interest in the secular side of Aleppo Jewry also, and include old advertisements and wedding invitations from Aleppo.[20]

The same combination of integration and symbolic ethnicity surrounds the ʿAdes Synagogue in Naḥalat Zion (Jerusalem). The building is noted for its inlaid mosaic woodwork on the Aron HaKodesh (ark). It also at one time had painted decorations made by artists from the Bezalel school, though much of this has been destroyed. The synagogue was founded by Ḥalebis, with financial support from the ʿAdes family, which had settled in Egypt. Its affairs were under the control of a court of rabbis from Aleppo (discussed previously). By the 1960s, however, fewer and fewer of the residents in the neighborhood were Ḥalebis and most worshipers were Kurds. The synagogue had no marker denoting its origin. Now, however, there is a sign outside the building, noting that it is an Aleppan synagogue. The building has been restored, with funding by Syrian Jews abroad, some of whom come to celebrate their children's bar mitzvah there. In the 1960s, the furnishings in the synagogue were traditional but were becoming run-down. By 1993, there were new furnishings and lighting in the synagogue.

The synagogue remained Ḥalebi in form. The cantor at that time was a Ḥalebi rabbi, Ezra Shaio. It was a place where *baqashot,* the Hebrew hymns sung to Arab melodies, were sung from 2 A.M. to sunrise during the winter, as noted earlier. Singing of *baqashot* is a Ḥalebi custom, although it has since been adopted by non-Ḥalebi synagogues in Naḥala'ot. Even in 1961, the ʿAdes Synagogue was only one of several sites for such activity in the neighborhood. In 1993 *baqashot* were sung at the ʿAdes Synagogue on Shabbat between *minḥah* (afternoon service) and *ʿarvit* (evening service) during the summer, as well as during the winter. Some Ḥalebis and others came to the synagogue specifically for that purpose on Shabbat, though there were other synagogues where one could sing *baqashot* on Shabbat.[21]

The ʿAdes Synagogue is also the site of a yeshiva, in its courtyard. This yeshiva is named for Rabbi Ezra Shaio and is run by one of his sons. While this institution receives some funding from Ḥalebis in the United States, the students come from a variety of mostly Middle Eastern backgrounds. With the proliferation of yeshivot, in part spurred by the subsidies given to them as a result of coalition politics, individual yeshivot have tried to develop specialities.

Rabbi Yosef Shaio wanted to start a yeshiva for young people, and he wanted to maintain the traditional (Sephardic) separation between *talmud torah* (the study of the Torah) and *parnassah* (making a living). At his yeshiva, students study in the morning and teach in the afternoon. He encourages them to become skilled in other occupations. He does not necessarily mean secular occupations, but rather skills such as those he and his father have practiced: cantor and scribe. Another yeshiva in the area has a slightly different specialty, training its students to become community rabbis and rabbinic court judges.

The men who go to the yeshiva wear white shirts and black suits, as well as black hats. Since it was warm at the yeshiva when I visited it in July 1993, most did not wear coats, but simply rolled up the sleeves of their white shirts. The traditional feeling that one must be occupied in Torah study at all times was emphasized. While I was waiting for Rabbi Shaio to arrive for our appointment, a young man asked me if I wanted to study something while I waited, such as the weekly Torah portion. The yeshiva occupies a fairly small space, taking up just two rooms.

Politically, there is a connection between the ʿAdes Synagogue and the Sephardic Torah Guardians (SHAS) Party. This political party emerged in the 1980s in Jerusalem. Its first representatives in the Knesset (parliament) were elected in 1984. In 1996, the party succeeded in electing ten members to the Knesset, and it is currently (on the eve of the 1999 election) the largest religious party in that body. It is both a religious and an ethnic party. In fact, it is the most successful "ethnic" party since 1948. Like other religiously Orthodox parties, it supports public observance of Jewish law, including prohibiting activities such as the opening of cinemas on the Sabbath, and supports subsidies for Sephardic yeshivot. It also protests discrimination against Sephardic-Middle Eastern Jews, within both the Orthodox and the secular sectors of Israeli life.

Rabbi Shaio told me one story about the founding of this party. According to him, it began one Tish'a b'-Av (the fast day for the destruction of Jerusalem) when a worshiper at ʿAdes announced his candidacy for a seat on the city council. Rabbi Shaio was also familiar with some Sephardic *ḥaredi* activity which long preceded the founding of SHAS. For instance, we discussed *Qol Sinai*, a Sephardic *ḥaredi* publication, usually marked by a picture of a rabbi on the cover, that had a run of several years, beginning in 1961. Its editor was Menashe Halevi, who has an electric appliance store in the Geula neighborhood and who has been close to Ovadia Yosef, the spiritual leader of SHAS.[22] While Shaio still has many dealings with Ovadia Yosef and his successors, he is no longer active in SHAS.

The synagogue also serves as a community welfare station. When I arrived there one morning, several old women were there to receive food. Together with the yeshiva, Rabbi Shaio also is in charge of a charitable institution, called *arukha u-marpe*. This succeeds an earlier fund, *ṣedaqa u-marpe*, that had served the Ḥalebi community. The *ṣedaqa u-marpe* was an activity of the Ḥalebi committee in the 1960s, in which Rabbi Shaio's father participated. Rabbi Shaio was asked by various rabbis to take over the fund's operations on his father's death. For legal reasons, he could not combine the operations with those of the yeshiva, so he started the *arukha u-marpe* fund.

He said that he does not like to do fund-raising. He tries to get goods in kind, such as strictly kosher food from hotels, and uses the voluntary labor of the competent younger elderly. Rabbi Shaio's activity as a *sofer* (scribe) was apparent when our interview was interrupted by a woman who wanted him to check a *mezuzah* (the parchment containing Biblical verses which is placed in a container fixed on the door of each Jewish home).

The dependence on remittances from abroad has its price. When businesses abroad were in trouble, as during the recession of the early 1990s, so were institutions in Israel, such as the yeshivot in Naḥalat Zion. The bankruptcy of several prominent supporters of Orthodox institutions in general and Ḥalebi philanthropists in particular obviously affected these institutions.

In the 1960s, some Ḥalebi rabbis who were unconcerned about maintaining the particular Aleppan heritage did use their "Ḥalebi card" when dealing with potential contributors from abroad. In dealing with potential contributors, they would emphasize their common Ḥalebi ancestry. In general, these institutions show the same pattern: while appeals abroad target Aleppan Jews, thus highlighting the Aleppan heritage of the institutions, the participants in these institutions come from many different backgrounds. The Israeli leaders disclaim any interest in discriminating among those whom they admit to the yeshiva, seeing this as a form of "racism" (*giz'anut*). They thus emphasize a Jewish "universalism."

Representations of Aram Ṣōbā in Israel

Even though the Ḥalebi origin group in Israel is dispersing, Israelis have been important in reformulating the images of the Jewish community in Aleppo, which have been spread throughout the world. Several images stand out. One is the religious image of Aleppo as having been a city of scholars and saints where men rose early to pray and where the common folk submitted to rabbinic authority. Another image is that of a community of shrewd traders, whose families enjoy a privileged, worldly existence. Neither image is new, but both have been burnished by writers in the twentieth century.

A good example of the former representation is David Laniado's *La-Qedoshim Asher Ba-Are"ṣ*. The heart of Ḥakhām David's book, especially in its most recent edition is a biographical dictionary, along with legal decisions and legends of the rabbis. The biographical dictionary contains 527 entries, mostly rabbis, but also a few communal leaders. Many of these figures lived in Eretz Yisrael, while others have served the Diaspora in Egypt and the Americas. Since the dictionary is arranged alphabetically by family name, it is easy to see the large number of families whose scions were rabbis. Laniado also includes photographs of many of these rabbis. These pictures reinforce the image of piety and learning. This representation has particular appeal to religious Ḥalebim and other traditional Jews.[23] For the more secular, it provides a valuable counterpoint to the stereotype of the commercial cleverness and opulence of Ḥalebim.

Ḥakhām David Laniado, the author of this book, himself exemplified the piety that is represented in the book. He was Aleppo-born, but fled with his family from Hebron during the pogrom of 1929. He then settled in Jerusalem and lived modestly in the area north of the Maḥaneh Yehudah market. He received all visitors graciously and invited them to eat with his family.

The second image—that of the clever and opulent businessman—can be found in the work of Amnon Shamosh, which has been referred to previously. While in his various works—fiction, autobiographical sketches, journalistic essays, scholarly writing, and poetry—Shamosh has written about many facets of Aleppan Jewry, both in Aleppo and throughout the world, he does not live in an urban neighborhood with many other Aleppan Jews. He is in many ways the Israeli equivalent of an "out-of-towner" (see chapter 9). As an adult, he has made his home on Kibbutz Maʿayan Barukh, on the Lebanese border, far from the urban centers where most Syrian Jews reside. Maʿayan Barukh is a secular kibbutz, which has generally been affiliated with the Labor Party. In fact, during the 1984 election, Amnon Shamosh was a candidate for Parliament on the Labor Party slate.

In his work, Shamosh has given particular attention to the contrast between the hard-driving, individualistic, and familistic Ḥalebi and the socialist kibbutzniks. He shows both their similarities and their differences. While the kibbutz in the past had elements in its goals that were antifamilistic, such as communal children's homes, these have been replaced by a very nuclear-family-friendly approach.

Shamosh is also concerned with the integration of Middle Eastern Jews into Israeli society. His stress on middle-class and well-to-do Ḥalebis is partly a product of his own experience. He also, however, is fighting the stereotype of Sephardic and Middle Eastern Jews as eternally impoverished and backward. The title character in his novel *Michel Ezra Safra and Sons* exemplifies this. Michel Ezra is certainly a shrewd, even unscrupulous businessman, conventionally pious and observant, but not deeply religious. While Michel Ezra Safra and his counterparts in other stories by Shamosh are not role models for Israelis, Shamosh suggests in his work that the Ḥalebi culture has been successful for a long time and that it offers some values for emulation that serve to moderate certain tendencies in Israel. These include political extremism, unrealistic attitudes toward coexistence with the Jews' Arab neighbors, and total rejection of traditional Judaism. In short, Israeli Ashkenazim have much to learn from their Sephardic fellow citizens. Immigrant absorption, Shamosh is saying, is not a one-way street.[24] In their various writings, both Shamosh and Laniado show that Ḥalebis in Israel have strong connections with their own Diaspora, which offer important models for Israeli society.

Conclusion

The example of the Aleppan Jews shows the dispersal of descendants of immigrants from a small origin group into larger segments of Israeli-Jewish society (that is, structural and identificational assimilation, as well as acculturation). This example shows that assimilation does not necessitate complete amnesia about the past of the individuals integrating into the new society. There are both psychological and structural reasons for this remembrance. Many, though not all, human beings have a need for some kind of origin narrative. Such writings as those by Shamosh and Laniado help relate this one specific heritage to the greater Jewish and Israeli whole.

The existence of strong and wealthy Diaspora communities of Aleppan Jews makes connections with them a valuable resource for the descendants of Aleppo Jews in Israel. In Israel, the Ḥalebis and their descendants may be seen as members of a particular origin group, as part of the larger Sephardi-Oriental segment, or simply as Israeli Jews. More than Aleppans elsewhere, they have a strong identification with the Jewish state. This identification with Israel continues among those who emigrate. Thus both the assimilation model and the diasporic discourse are of value in understanding the Ḥalebis of Israel.

CHAPTER 7

"You're from America— Do You Know My Cousin in Buenos Aires?"

Early in my fieldwork on Syrian Jews in Brooklyn, I encountered visitors from Latin America and men who had "imported" a bride from that part of the world. In Israel, when I said I was from America, people would ask me if I knew relatives of theirs in Mexico City and Buenos Aires. While I have not done fieldwork in Latin America, I have met many people with Latin American connections and I have interviewed a number of these people. Several of the characteristics that mark the modern Syrian Jewish dispersion have been crystallized in Latin America.

The purpose of this chapter is to provide a survey of Syrian Jewish communities in the Western Hemisphere between the Rio Grande and Patagonia as derived from published works and from my own interviews. Except for two brief visits to Mexico City, I have not worked in Latin America, but as noted above, I have encountered many Jews of Syrian origin who have spent considerable time in that region. Since Latin American Jewry is not as familiar to North American readers as are the backgrounds of Jews in the United States and Israel, I provided more background on this region than I have for other areas. In this chapter, I utilize statistical studies of the Jews of Latin America, along with individual biographies. Many characteristics of Syrian Jews noted for Aleppans in England, the United States, and Israel are found in Latin America as well.

In my consideration of Syrian Jews in Latin America in particular, I have been struck by a number of features:

1. Aleppan and other Syrian Jews have continued to be concentrated in a small number of commercial occupations. This is unlike the situation in Israel, but similar to situations elsewhere in the world.
2. Syrian Jewish identities have been transferred and reinterpreted in a Latin American context. In this region, Syrian and other Mediterranean Jews are as likely to be seen as *turcos* (Turks) or *arabes* (Arabs) as they are to be identified as Jews. Both *turcos* and Jews have been seen at times as undesirable or unassimilatable immigrants.
3. The maintenance of Syrian Jewish identity is related to participation in transnational family, kin, and commercial networks.
4. Until fairly recently, Syrian Jews have generally maintained a relatively tenuous connection to their present places of residence. This is even more characteristic of those in Latin America than of those in England or the United States, especially for first- and second-generation Syrian Jews in that region.

The short biographies I have studied are marked by what Paul Siu called "sojourning."[1] Sojourning is a condition where people live in one place but see their residence in that place as temporary. The behavior of sojourners manifests this attitude, in contrast to that of "permanent settlers." Manifestations of this sojourning include a reluctance to take citizenship, indifference to politics in the land of residence (except with regard to one's own economic interests), liquidity of resources, sending remittances home, and lack of investment in permanent facilities. Sojourning is the result not only of a personal attitude but also of the milieu and policies of the receiving society. In general, sojourners are less committed to the country or locale in which they live than are those who settle there permanently. The differences between sojourning and settling are not absolute and range over a continuum. Consideration of the usefulness of the concept of sojourning will be made at the end of this chapter.

The Americas south of the Rio Grande loom larger in the history and psyche of Sephardim than they do for Ashkenazic Jews, even though there are many more Ashkenazim than Sephardim in Latin America as a whole. According to one estimate, 20 percent of Latin American Jews are Sephardic. Despite this, the proportion of Sephardim to Ashkenazim is greater in Latin America than in the United States and Canada. The Sephardic Jews include both those who were originally Spanish-speakers from Morocco and the Balkans and those who were originally Arabic-speakers, particularly Syrians.

Most of the Syrian Jews who were interviewed by Joseph Sutton and me had lived in one or more of six countries: Argentina, Brazil, Mexico, Panama, Colombia, and Guatemala. Demographic data on Jews in Latin America is largely conjectural; it is even more so with regard to estimating the relative proportions of Ashkenazic and Sephardic Jews. Table 1 gives only the general data on these six countries.

Table 1
Estimated Jewish Population of Six Latin American Countries (end of 1982)

Country	Total Population	Jewish Population
Argentina	28,085,000	233,000
Brazil	121,547,000	100,000
Mexico	71,193,000	35,000
Panama	1,940,000	3,500
Colombia	28,776,000	7,000
Guatemala	7,481,000	900

Source: Sergio DellaPergola, "Demographic Trends of Latin American Jewry," in *The Jewish Presence in Latin America,* Judith L. Elkin and Gilbert W. Merkx, eds. (Boston: Allen and Unwin, 1987).

Together with Venezuela and Cuba, these countries were the recipients of much of the Sephardic Jewish immigration to Latin America. Syrian Jews were an important component of this immigration. For example, in Guatemala City in 1970, one of three congregations was Sephardic (predominantly Syrian). In Mexico City, out of approximately 5,500 Jewish families affiliated with synagogues, nearly 2,700 were Sephardic. Of these, 700 were affiliated with the Damascene Alianza Monte Sinai and 1,150 with the Aleppan Maguen David (formerly Sedaka u-Marpe).[2]

Latin American Jewry Before 1880

Much has been written about the participation of *conversos,* or New Christians of Jewish origin, in the Conquest and colonization of the New World by the Spanish and Portuguese. The records of the Inquisition are particularly useful in noting those who were accused of judaizing in the New World. Here, as on the Iberian Peninsula, there is speculation about which people were victims of false accusations, made out of malice, and which were true heretics/martyrs, such as Luis de Carvajal the Younger.[3] While undoubtedly people like Carvajal did participate in the colonization of the New World, it is difficult to assess their importance. Except for a few obscure retentions, like that of family traditions that candles be lit on Friday evening, most traces of Jewishness among the Creoles (New World–born Spaniards) may well have vanished by the Wars for Independence, though reports of hidden Jews among the Hispanics in New Mexico and other parts of Latin

America continue, and some Hispanic families have reclaimed their Jewishness publicly.

The formation of Jewish communities in the New World began with the Dutch occupation of Recife, in Brazil, from 1630 to 1654. For the first time an openly Jewish community appeared, including both former *conversos* and Jews from the Netherlands. When the Portuguese reconquered Recife, Jewish refugees from Brazil helped initiate congregations in Surinam, the Antilles, and New Amsterdam. The communities around the Caribbean, especially in the colonies of Britain and the Netherlands, as well as in North America have survived to the present day.

In many places, the next wave of immigrants came from the Germanic lands, from Alsace to Silesia and Posen. Immigrants from this region were among the first modern Jewish settlers in Guatemala, as well as founding the modern community in Mexico.[4] There was also a Sephardic immigration during the nineteenth century, especially from Morocco.

After 1880: European Jewish Immigration from 1880 to 1930

Latin America's Jewish population, like those of North America and Western Europe, increased after 1880 with the widespread immigration of East European Jewry. In particular, Jewish settlement in Argentina was greatly augmented by a deliberate effort to resolve the Jewish problem in the Russian empire through agricultural settlement on the pampas. These efforts began in the 1880s, when the Russian government moved in a rightward direction and instituted a new policy to restrict Jews and encourage their emigration. The Russian Jewish immigration to Argentina was motivated by the desire to make Jews into agriculturalists. Efforts to that end were financed by Baron de Hirsch, who funded similar movements in the United States and elsewhere. The agricultural immigration was, however, only a part of the general Jewish immigration, even to Argentina. Most Jewish immigrants outside of rural Argentina went to urban areas. During this period, Jewish and non-Jewish emigration from the Ottoman Empire also increased.[5]

Middle Eastern Immigration to Latin America

Immigrants from many countries were attracted to Latin America. Argentina became the home of Italians and Spanish, Germans and British. There was even a sizable Welsh population in parts of Patagonia. People from Mediterranean countries predominated. Spanish and Portuguese, especially from the northern areas of the peninsula, were part of a large modern immigration to various parts of Latin America. Entrepreneurs and adventurers from Europe and North America tried their hand at coffee plantations, mines, railroads, oil prospecting, and the like. The building of the Panama

Canal and the rubber boom in Brazil attracted many, including Jews from Morocco.

The Ottoman Empire, especially the Arab provinces, was an important source of immigrants. Many were Christians, but Muslims, Druzes, and Jews were also represented. All were referred to by Latin Americans as *turcos* or *arabes*, including Ladino-speakers and Armenians. The former term was most commonly used, even though most of the immigrants were not Turks in an ethnic sense. Armenian immigrants resented being labeled with the name of their persecutors. In addition, the term *turcos* had pejorative connotations. Most of the Arabic-speaking immigrants came from Lebanon, Syria, and Palestine.

The immigration of Arabic-speakers began in the 1880s. In Argentina, as in other countries, peddling became their niche. Many sold trinkets and objects of religious significance.[6] In Argentina, Maronites apparently were the first, but they were followed by Syrians of other religions. By 1908, there were more than twenty-three thousand Syrians in Argentina, more than nine thousand arriving in that year alone. They were concentrated in peddling and small commerce. The concentration of these people in trade was viewed negatively.

People of Syro-Lebanese origin are sprinkled throughout Latin America. Col. Omar Torrijos, who was dictator of Panama in the 1970s, is an example of a leader of Lebanese origin. Col. Mohammed Sineiddin, leader of a military revolt in Argentina against the Alfonsin administration in 1987, and Carlos Saul Menem, who became the Peronist standard-bearer and president of Argentina in 1989, are both of Syrian Muslim origin and have become Catholic. In 1989, there were presidential candidates of Arab origin in Honduras and Brazil as well. In Guatemala, a presidential candidate of Sephardic origin was disqualified in 1989, while a Sephardic Jew ran for vice president. Shafik Handel, head of the Salvadorean Communist Party, is of Palestinian origin. Honduras has a substantial community of Palestinian immigrants, primarily from the Bethlehem area.

When various countries have sought to restrict immigration, both Jews and Arabs have been considered undesirable immigrants. The negative images of both groups have continued into the present. In the late 1980s, when an Arab-Argentinian, Carlos Menem, was elected president, many anti-Arab images came to the fore. The Latin American images of Middle Easterners will be considered further in the following.

Traces of Latin America returned with some of those who went back to the Middle East. One section of the Galilean city of Nazareth was called the Spanish Quarter, because it had been built by money sent from Cuba.[7] In the 1960s, there were Druzes in Lebanon and in the Upper Galilee who drank maté, a drink they had discovered while sojourning in Argentina.

In addition to Arabic speakers, Armenians and other nationals migrated to Latin America. The first major wave of Armenian immigrants to Argentina came during the Balkan and World War I period (1909–21), when there were large-scale massacres of Armenians. The Armenians came mainly from Cilicia (southern Anatolia). Personal networks and formal institutions played an important role in starting the community in Buenos Aires, the main metropolitan area in which they settled. Because the real estate market favored buyers, Armenians were able to own land on which to build their homes, schools, and churches.

Many East European Jews (at least those who were not agriculturalists) and the various Middle Eastern immigrants, including Sephardim, occupied similar economic niches. Most began as rural and urban peddlers and later became shopkeepers, manufacturers, and professionals. They faced the usual anti-Semitic prejudice directed against exotic, "unproductive" middlemen. While they came with their own prejudices against other groups from their homelands and elsewhere, members of the different Middle Eastern groups also collaborated with each other. For instance, many Armenians immigrating to Buenos Aires chose a café owned by a Sephardic Jew in a Syro-Lebanese neighborhood as their meeting place in the early 1900s. Jews and Maronite Catholics could be invited to a dinner in which the Armenian community honored one of its notables. Occasionally they might contribute to Near Eastern war relief or invest in each other's enterprises. After the outbreak of the Arab-Israeli conflict in 1948, such cooperation diminished.[8]

Stereotypes of Jews and *Turcos*

Both Jews and *turcos*, or Middle Easterners, in Latin America are seen as basically unscrupulous. These stereotypical *turcos* (as all Middle Easterners were called) have appeared in Latin American literature.

In Gabriel Garcia Marquez's short novel, published in English as *A Chronicle of a Death Foretold*, the murder that was predicted was that of the scion of an Arab family. The Arabs were portrayed as clannish and as sellers of cloth and trinkets. They had different culinary ways from the majority Latins and they had spoken a strange tongue for two generations.

In the novel, when the daughter of a prominent local family is married to a rich American, the bridegroom discovers that she is not a virgin. When she is asked who has deflowered her, she says it was Santiago Nasser, and her brothers murder him. Garcia Marquez implies that he was a convenient scapegoat, even though after the assassination the townspeople fear vengeance from the Arab community. The Lebanese as described in the novel are seen as strangers, still alienated from their Latin neighbors.[9]

The prejudices against Middle Easterners in general are related to and mingled with anti-Semitism. Both streams of stereotypes view the targets of their prejudice as sharp traders, cheats, members of foreign groups, and often non-Christians. While Latin Americans might, at times, romanticize both groups as part of the admixture that gave Spain its unique culture, both groups were usually despised. Both were seen as unassimilable. The fact that many early immigrants from the two groups were poor peddlers helped to reinforce this stereotype. In Mexico around 1910, people of various political persuasions debated the desirability of non-Catholic immigration from Europe, but there was a consensus about the undesirability of the Middle Easterners. One newspaper called them "beggars" and dirty, while another saw their immigration as "not propitious" for Mexico.

A liberal Buenos Aires daily wrote in 1898 that "ethnographers would do well to watch the immigration returns. Are we becoming a Semitic republic? The immigration of Russian Jews is now the third largest on the list, whilst Syrian Arabs (Turcos) and Arabians are now flocking to these shores. The last two races are, however, Christians."[10]

There were some who encouraged the immigration of the Eastern Sephardim, possibly viewing these people as being of Spanish speech and stock. Francisco Rivas, a Mexican Jew, advertised the fine qualities of Mexico in Ladino publications in the Ottoman Empire. In addition, American Jews, already hard pressed by the large East European immigration, encouraged Levantine Jews to go to Cuba, Mexico, and elsewhere.[11]

The fact that Jews, Muslims, and even Christian Arabs and Armenians were not fully accepted into Latin American society made their settlement in the area more tentative than it might otherwise have been. The perception that these "Semitic traders" were not desirable immigrants added to the Middle Easterners' insecurity and encouraged them to see their settlement as a sojourn.

The Sephardic Immigration

The first Sephardim from Muslim lands who immigrated to Latin America in the nineteenth century were from northern Morocco, particularly the areas near Tangier and Tetuan. Their favored destinations were Venezuela and Brazil, particularly the Amazon basin, during the rubber boom around 1900. At the time, there was a string of Moroccan communities from Belem to Manaus.[12]

Jews from the Ottoman Empire, like their Christian and Muslim counterparts, began to immigrate to Latin America in the 1890s. Some were Ladino-speakers from the Balkans and Anatolia, while others, in some places the majority, were Arabic-speakers. The numbers of such Sephardic immigrants could be counted in the hundreds and thousands, as noted previously. Krause describes the ones who went to Mexico as peddlers who went into the interior with backpacks filled with soaps, notions, and images of saints.[13]

Sophie Ashkenazi's father first went to Mexico from Aleppo in 1908. A schoolmate named Isaac already lived there, and Sophie believes he was the first Syrian Jew there. Her father had a "modern" education, but he was also very religious. Because he was not sure of the kashrut of food in Mexico, he learned how to slaughter chickens in a ritually appropriate manner. She reports that the stream of immigrants from Syria grew slowly. At first, only men immigrated to Mexico. For several years, her mother was the only Syrian Jewish woman there.

At fifteen, Sophie married Ezra Ashkenazi and moved with him to New Orleans, returning during the Depression to Mexico, where they lived until 1936. In Mexico, her husband, like most Syrians in that period, worked as a peddler.[14]

Sephardim were peddlers in other countries as well as Mexico. Several Jews from Jerusalem worked in Panama and Colombia. They lived for years as single men peddling their wares in the countryside. Sometimes they set up households with native women. Some remained in Panama, while others returned to Palestine. Some became shopkeepers in the Holy City. For instance, I met two Jerusalem proprietors of a haberdashery, one a Ḥalebi and the other, his partner and brother-in-law, an Urfali (of southeast Turkish origin). Both had been peddlers in Colombia between the wars.

A Brooklyn-born rabbi gave this description of his mother's family in Panama: "My grandfather on my mother's side . . . came to America (from Cairo). It was too cold for him, so he went to Panama and married. That was where my mother was born. My father went to Panama and married. I went to Mexico and married."

This is "Frieda Sitt's" story of her father:

> He came from the poverty of the Near East. He was a tinsmith. I remember something about polishing stuff with his feet. He knocked around Aleppo and Alexandretta. He made some brass steeples for churches and paid his passage to Panama. He made a fortune in Panama. My father was broad, open, and expansive—strange for a Syrian. He had records of *Romeo and Juliet* in Arabic. He was Arab in one sense, his openness to the world.
>
> Mother went from Aleppo to Argentina. . . . She came from a "high" Sephardic family. Her father was a tax collector for the Turks [unclear how her parents met]. Her father had three houses in Syria and Lebanon, Aleppo and Damascus.

"Flora Cohen," a woman who was born in Guatemala, told the story of her father's immigration:

> My father came from Syria, I think Aleppo. His father died when he was a little boy in Syria. I don't know at what age they emigrated, I guess when he was 15 or 16. He went first to Panama. When I don't know, but on one of his trips, his boat stopped in Jamaica. It was one of the Jewish holidays and he went to the synagogue. There he was invited to a Jewish home, and in that home he

> met my mother. . . . Then they went to live in Panama. My sister was born in Panama. . . .
>
> He had some relatives in Guatemala. . . . He must have had an uncle or a cousin in Guatemala. The situation there was good. . . . He moved to Guatemala in 1919. . . . So my father had a store in Guatemala, a retail store. He also sold wholesale. He imported and then he sold. . . . He wanted a better life. Guatemala was not wonderful. He left the store in charge of other relatives and took the ship to Manchester.

Later he and his family returned to Guatemala.

Some families prospered even prior to World War I. Such was the Mizrahi family, an Urfali family that built the Edison Theater, the first cinema in Jerusalem. This family gained a fortune, and after World War I family members moved to Palestine, where they invested money in various enterprises, including a banana plantation in the Jordan valley. This family later supplied honorary consuls for Panama in Israel.

Some individuals went to Latin America via Manchester in order to import cotton manufactures from Britain. The "shipping merchants" from the Levant started by exporting mainly to their former homes. After World War I they increasingly sought markets in Latin America, which had previously been in the hands of exporters of British origin. Flora Cohen's uncle shipped to her father in Guatemala. When her father later moved to Manchester, he could ship to his own partners in Guatemala.

The first synagogue in Mexico City was organized by these "Arabian" Jews early in the century. They first met in a private home in 1900 or 1901. Around the outbreak of the Revolution of 1910, Ashkenazic, Syrian, and Ladino-speakers formed the Alianza Monte Sinai, which by 1918 had its own synagogue and cemetery. By that date, however, the congregation was primarily Sephardic. Gradually it became the synagogue of the Damascene Jews, with its first building located near the Zocalo (central Mexico City). Later it moved to the middle-class Colonia Roma area. Aleppan Jews arriving in Mexico first joined this congregation, but later they built their own synagogue.[15]

Fewer Syrian Jews immigrated to Cuba than to Mexico or the United States. Syrian Jews preferred the latter two countries, where large Syrian-Jewish communities crystallized.[16] For many, as for their coreligionists of other origins, Cuba was a way station, although this was not the case for many Ladino-speakers. In general, however, the Syrians in Cuba accommodated themselves to the ways of the larger number of Ladino-speaking Sephardim.

The pattern of immigration to Colombia and Panama was similar to that of the preceding countries. In Barranquilla (Colombia), the first traces of Jews go back to the nineteenth century. In 1879, a formal deed setting aside part of the cemetery for Jews was registered. The first Jewish inhabitants were either Germans or Curacao Sephardim. Most of the descendants of the latter had become Catholics by the beginning of the twentieth century. Three Syrian Jewish families settled in Barranquilla in 1908. From the start, they conducted religious services, although they did not receive official permission to perform ritual slaughter of meat until 1926. Their synagogue was formally established in 1928, but was not incorporated until 1945. Meanwhile East European Jewish immigrants had arrived. They were joined by German refugees in the 1930s. Most Syrian Jews had been in petty trade in the Middle East. They became peddlers in Colombia, as did many of the East Europeans. Their economic mobility was rapid.[17]

The Syrian Jewish immigration to Argentina, more than any other, was overshadowed by the much larger immigration of Jews from Russia and Rumania. Many of these immigrants started in agricultural colonies during the 1880s, but eventually most moved to urban centers, especially Buenos Aires. Argentina had the largest Jewish community in Latin America.

The first wave of Sephardic immigrants to Argentina were Moroccans, as was also true for Brazil and Venezuela. By 1900, in fact, the Moroccan community had a second, Argentine-born generation, unlike those from Eastern Europe and the Ottoman Empire. Most of the Moroccans came from Tetuan, where Spanish influence was greatest. While Christians and Muslims had preceded Jews, by the 1890s Jews from the Ottoman Empire were immigrating to Argentina in substantial numbers. The Jews from different areas were separated in their residential patterns. The Ladino-speakers from Istanbul and elsewhere settled near the port. By 1904, Aleppan Jews veered toward the Once precinct of Buenos Aires, where they have continued to concentrate. Damascenes settled in the Boca and Barracas area, where many Italian immigrants had also settled.

Most Syrian Sephardim started as single men working as peddlers. Many came to work for a few years and then return to Syria. After the Young Turk revolt of 1909, when conscription was imposed on Jews and Christians in the Ottoman Empire, many brought their families over and became permanent residents.

In the first decades of the twentieth century, the West Europeans in Argentina were the most prosperous. Many were involved in export and import. The East Europeans were the most diversified. Many of them had opened factories. Large numbers of Jews from all groups, however, were peddlers.[18]

In Argentina, the Syrian Jews, especially those from Aleppo, were noteworthy because of their fairly fervent practice of Judaism and submission to rabbinic authority, at least compared with their coreligionists from other areas, both Sephardic and Ashkenazic. The Aleppan rabbi, Shaul Setton Dabbah, held firm control over the community. He was extremely conservative, and was one of the rabbis who set a precedent in banning intermarriage and conversion in Argentina (and for Syrian Jews in the Western Hemisphere). He was anti-Zionist and close to those Aleppan circles that favored the anti-Zionist Orthodox organization, Agudath Yisrael. Syrian Jews also were almost alone in trying to keep their children home from school and keeping their shops closed on the Sabbath.[19]

While most of the immigrants to the Amazon were North Africans, there were also some Syrians. Eduard Farhi told Joseph Sutton that his uncle and other Syrians imported linen from England and silk from France to Manaus. Later, however, they left Manaus because the small size of the Jewish population posed a threat to their children's Jewishness. Manaus was the center of the rubber export trade early in the century. By the 1920s it had declined, however, and was well past its prime when Farhi moved there. Later Rio de Janeiro and Sao Paulo became the centers of the Jewish population.[20]

Circulation between Communities

Syrian Jews, like other immigrants, circulated among different communities, moving from declining communities like Manaus to flourishing cities like Rio. Some immigrants circulated between Brazil and Argentina. The circulation between Panama and Colombia was substantial, perhaps due to the fact that Panama had been part of Colombia until 1903. Syrian Jews who wished to enter the United States often sojourned for a time in Mexico or Cuba. During the interwar period, British Aleppans went to Latin America to make their fortunes, while several families from Latin America settled in Manchester. There were also Syrian Jews who returned to the Middle East, especially to Jerusalem.

Accounts of Life from World War I to 1946

In the period after the initial immigration and well into the latter half of the twentieth century, most Syrian Jews in Latin America remained "sojourners" there. While a degree of sojourning may describe immigrant groups in all countries, the phenomenon appears to have been most characteristics of colonial and neocolonial settings in which immigrants never completely identified with the native society.

There are a number of reasons why sojourning was so particularly characteristic of Syrian Jews in Latin America:

1. Premodern Jewish communities were seen as separate from their host societies. The Enlightenment in Europe brought strenuous efforts to incorporate and assimilate the Jews, but such efforts did not spread to the Ottoman Empire until the period just prior to World War I, and they were unsuccessful in Syria.
2. Latin Catholic nations may have had particular difficulty in accom-

modating those who were neither Catholic nor Latin, because of the heritage of conformity inherited from Spain.

3. The economic gap between rich and poor, foreigner and native, in many Latin American countries made even poor foreign immigrants disdain the natives.
4. The frequent movements of many Syrians made it difficult for them to put down roots in or identify fully with any one country.

These characteristics, of course, vary in different countries and regions. The strength of the "imagined national community" has probably been more marked in Mexico and Argentina than in Panama, whose "independence" was a consequence of North American manipulation. Much of this lack of identification comes out in the various life histories.

In New York, when I was first doing research on the Syrian Sephardim, I met "Ralph Ades," a native of Brooklyn, whose family was based in Panama and Colombia. Shortly after he was born, his family moved to Manchester. He went to school in England and then in New York, before the family decided to move to Panama when he was about fourteen. At first he continued school in the Canal Zone. He had a late Bar Mitzvah, learning the *brakhot* (Hebrew blessings) from his uncle. His uncle was a poor *ḥakhām*, living in the red-light district. The women of the area came to this *ḥakhām* for charms. He sent his children out to peddle. During World War II, they prospered. At the time of my interview (in 1959), his uncle was living with his children in a big house, but he thought that he had been happier in the old days.

When Ralph was about sixteen or seventeen, he went to work in a rayon factory in Bogota. He told me that during this period, he and his brothers went "whoring" and drinking in brothels with other Syrians. But Ralph liked to read, and he found that Bogota was full of bookstores. It was there that he found a history of the Jews, which later led him to Zionism.

His experiences in the U.S. Army were crucial. He describes his decision to volunteer, something atypical for Syrian Jews in the Canal Zone:

> When the Japanese bombed Pearl Harbor, I went home to Panama. I volunteered for the U.S. Army. It took me a year to be inducted, because of a problem with my American citizenship. I was inducted in October 1942. . . . My parents were perturbed. One boy who had been in England with me said, "Why should you fight? It's not our fight. Sure we want Hitler beaten, but let them fight." My mother, the *ḥakhām,* all tried to persuade me, but I went.

Ralph served in the U.S. Army, then subsequently participated in helping illegal Jewish immigrants into Palestine. He and his family moved to New York City for several years. He returned to Latin America to help his brother in his business in 1960.

Frieda Sitt (mentioned previously) had a family history similar to that of Ralph Ades. Her mother had moved from Aleppo to Argentina, and then to Brooklyn. Colombia and Manchester were also way stations in her life's journey. Frieda lived in Manchester during her childhood. Her mother was her father's second wife. After Frieda's father's death (around 1936), the family moved to Cali, Colombia. Family members belonged to the wealthy San Fernando Club. When Germans tried to expel Jews from the club in the 1930s, one of her half-brothers led a Jewish resistance.

She found that her family's way of life took on the ways of their neighbors. In England, they had been near-English, while in South America, they were very Latin. At the same time, the family remained within the Syrian group. They lived in an upper-class manner wherever they were.

The two or so years that she lived in Cali were not a pleasant experience. The family fortunes had declined (a typical pattern during the Depression years for all parts of the Syrian dispersion). Her brother's businesses failed and her deceased father's investments were tied up in various places, including money in Panamanian banks and real estate in Brooklyn. In 1939, her family moved to Brooklyn. Frieda was an intellectual, and for a time she became a leftist. When I interviewed her in 1959, she was living in Greenwich Village.

Flora Cohen's father returned to Guatemala from Manchester during the Depression. Business was bad. The store in Guatemala had not fared well under his cousins' management. He thought he could set things aright, so his family stayed in Guatemala.

During World War II, some Syrian Jews who had lived in Europe settled in Latin America. "Joseph Politi," an Italian national, left Milan after the anti-Semitic decrees of 1938. A native of Egypt, he had lived in Milan since the age of thirteen. He had sold piece goods there. He went to Guatemala because he had a brother there. He moved back to Milan for a few years after World War II, but eventually he returned to Guatemala, where his family had started a textile mill.

In this period, there were Jewish communities in both Panama City, on the Pacific Coast, and Colon/Cristobal, on the Caribbean. An American who had been an army chaplain in 1946 reported that Cristobal had three Jewish congregations: the old Spanish-Portuguese congregation, founded by Caribbean Sephardim; a "Polish" Ashkenazic synagogue built around the time of World War II; and the Syrians. The chaplain became the rabbi for the Ashkenazim, while the older congregation had no one to act as spiritual leader. They required help in circumcising their young and in writing Hebrew inscriptions on gravestones. Meanwhile, the Syrians had their own *ḥakhām*. He served as ritual slaughterer, scribe, and teacher. He also helped the Sephardim from time to time.

The Syrians were looked down upon by the others. They were reputed to be uneducated and it was said that they did not send their children to school. They were indistinguishable from the Panamanians. Still, the chaplain did meet several who were among the Panamanian citizens who had volunteered for the U.S. Army and who were stationed in Panama.

When this former chaplain returned to Panama in the late 1970s, he was able to find only very few traces of the Jewish community in Cristobal. Cristobal had declined in importance, though Panama City still had a substantial Jewish community.

The significance of religious institutions in the lives of Latin American Ḥalebim varied. Still, they appear to have played a greater role for them than for other Jewish groups. The rabbis who arrived, even early in the century, were from the same families who led Aleppan communities elsewhere. Sophie Ashkenazi, for instance, describes Selim Labaton a *shoḥet* (ritual slaughterer) and *ḥakhām* who arrived in Mexico early in the century and served the community for twenty years (into the 1930s): "He was a truly wonderful man. For (the) twenty or more years that he lived in Mexico, he never took a peso from anyone for any religious services whatsoever, for marriages, divorces and circumcisions, everything. He did everything. There was no one in the world who did not love that man. His livelihood he earned by working, just like everyone else."[21]

Later, the Aleppan community was led by *Ḥakhām* Mordecai Atiyeh. He immigrated to Mexico in 1922. He is credited by some with reviving and perpetuating traditional Judaism there. Two rabbis who served the Syrian Jewish community in Argentina were more controversial, but also had a great influence on their communities. They were Shaul Setton Dabbah and Yitzhaq Shehebar.[22]

From 1946 to the Present

In 1959, I visited Mexico City. At that time I was still a student at the Jewish Theological Seminary, as well as preparing for my doctoral comprehensives at Columbia University. A friend who was serving as rabbi in Mexico City met me on my arrival. He and some members of his congregation immediately took me to a Middle Eastern restaurant in Colonia Roma, a middle-class neighborhood. Thus my first meal in Mexico consisted of humus and tahini. The restaurant, Cafe Miguel Oriental, was owned by a Damascus Jew. It was decorated with large paintings emphasizing the sybarite life of an Oriental potentate, with food, drink, and harem women.

The Syrian synagogues at that time were located in Colonia Roma. One was the Damascus synagogue of Monte Sinai, which was in a large, modern building, probably the largest synagogue in Mexico City. The congregation still maintained the older building in downtown Mexico. The Ḥalebi congregation Sedakau-Marpe (the congregation has since been renamed *Maguen David*), was then located nearby and was smaller. The services at Sedaka u-Marpe were well attended. Young people were present in substantial numbers. On the streets of Colonia Roma, there were school buses for the various Jewish private schools in Mexico, including one for the Aleppan community and another for the Damascus group.

The East European and Sephardic-Levantine Jews were well aware of each other, but they were concentrated in different neighborhoods. In addition, the Jewish component of Mexican society had been augmented by German refugees in the 1940s and by North American leftist refugees and "mainstream" businessmen and retirees in the 1950s. The lower-middle-class Ashkenazim, still partly Yiddish-speaking, were concentrated in the Hippodromo neighborhood, while the Syrians were in Colonia Roma. The movement toward the outlying areas, such as Polanco, Tecomachalco, Lomas de Chapultepec, and Truiet, was underway. As in Colonia Roma, both Aleppans and Damascenes live in these neighborhoods and have built synagogues and established private clubs there.

For Eduard Farhi, a native of Aleppo, Mexico City turned out to be a way station between Rio and New York. He arrived in Mexico in 1966 and met and married his wife there. He became the proprietor of a button factory, but he failed in this business. He served the Aleppan community as cantor briefly, and then he became cantor, Hebrew teacher, and ritual slaughterer for the Damascus congregation. He supervised the kosher meat used by both Aleppans and Damascenes. Farhi described the Mexican community as strong, with vigorous Jewish education and limited intermarriage.[23]

This perspective on the Mexican community is confirmed in Sergio DellaPergola's study of Mexico City's Jews. In 1991, Syrian Jews (both Aleppans and Damascenes) constituted 40 percent of the total Jewish population. Ninety percent of these Syrian Jews were Mexican-born. Most lived in areas where the majority of their neighbors were Jews. Occupationally, most were self-employed or in family businesses. Many were involved in garment manufacturing. While about 30 percent of the Jews were professionals, the proportion of Syrian Jews in the professions was below 20 percent. In Mexico, most Jews continued to marry Jewish co-ethnics. This was particularly true of the two Syrian communities. While interethnic marriages among Jews are increasing, DellaPergola reports little intermarriage between Syrian Jews and non-Jews, a point disputed by some of Sutton's interviewees. Seventy-five percent of all Jewish children studied in Jewish day schools; 47 percent of these studied in the day schools of the two Syrian communities. Members of the two Syrian congregations were above average in their observance. In any case, the Syrian Jews of Mexico City have had an active community life, comparable to that found in New York.[24]

A number of Latin American countries received Jewish immigrants from the Middle East during the 1950s. Like Eduard Farhi, some came from Syria and Lebanon, while others left Egypt in the wake of the Arab-Israeli wars and the harassment of Jews under Abdel-Nasser. Among these was Edmond Safra.

Safra, the scion of an important Aleppan banking family, arrived in Brazil in 1952, when the country was still booming. Until Edmond and his father could obtain a Brazilian license to start a bank, they had to trade in a wide variety of goods, including machinery and agricultural commodities, as well as monetary exchange.[25]

The Safras became Brazilian citizens, and Edmond moved to Geneva in 1956 to start an international bank. He was aided in part by seed money obtained from some Brazilian businessmen. In his new Geneva bank, Safra attracted deposits from Sephardic businessmen in Brazil and Argentina, among others.[26]

Eduard Farhi had left Syria at the time of the 1947 riots in Aleppo, which were sparked by the United Nations resolution that partitioned Palestine. He immigrated to Brazil, where his uncle lived. While Syrian Jews were concentrated in São Paulo in this period, Farhi moved to Rio.

In Rio, Farhi set up a business employing commission agents who worked as peddlers, selling various goods that they carried or that they ordered by catalogue. Since most customers paid on an installment plan, however, and because Brazil's currency was constantly being devalued by inflation, Farhi was unable to make a living. He then moved to Mexico City and finally to New York.

Farhi knew the Arabic-Ḥalebi musical tradition and became a cantor in various communities, both in Rio and in Mexico City. As he describes it, Syrian Jews in Brazil were either Ḥalebi or Jews from Saida (in Lebanon), with only a few Damascenes. In the 1950s, most Syrian Jews lived in Rio, but more and more migrated to São Paulo, the commercial center. After the new capital, Brasilia, was completed in the 1960s, some Syrian Jews went there. Many Jews who emigrated via or from Beirut went first to Milan and from there to São Paulo (following a path similar to that of Edmond Safra). Farhi's view of the situation in Brazil in the 1960s, when he left for Mexico, was bleak, and he turned down offers to return there. Farhi is atypical, however, since most Jews have prospered in São Paulo.[27]

For the most part, the Syrian Sephardim in Latin America continued to be concentrated in commercial occupations, but in the 1950s many went into light manufacturing. "Clara Silvera's" family in Central America is an example. She was married to an Egyptian Jew and had lived in Europe shortly after World War II. They returned to Central America when her husband's cousins opened a textile mill there. The next generation, however, changed its occupations. Their son went to business school in the United States. First he worked for his father in Central America, but then he returned to the United States with his American wife. Two of Clara's daughters also live in the United States.

Clara is a native of Central America. She was one of eight siblings. One brother is a physician; another is an engineer in Central America. One lives in Colombia. Another owns and operates a food processing factory. So, even though several are not in traditional commercial occupations, only a few remain in the country in which they were born and grew up.

In 1955, Celia Stopnicka Rosenthal visited Barranquilla, Colombia, and described its Jewish community, which included Middle Easterners, East Europeans, and Germans. By the mid-1950s, most Jews had achieved a measure of affluence. Of 293 heads of family, 88 percent were self-employed (for the Sephardim, it was 96 percent). In this they were similar to the Arabs living in the town. Most of the Jews had "servant-staffed homes" in the most fashionable part of the city.

Until 1955, however, they were excluded from the city's elite social clubs. The Jews therefore formed their own clubs. The Union Club was founded in 1942 by Sephardim, although it was technically open to all Jews. The main activity of the club was card-playing, and though the club offered tennis facilities, these were rarely used. Even the weekly meetings of the only Jewish women's organization (WIZO) were occasions for card-playing. The East European Jews founded another organization, the Centro Israelita Filantropico, which promoted Yiddish culture. The second generation, however, preferred to meet at the Union Club, which had greater prestige and was 30 percent East European by 1955. The German-speaking Jews had their own center, which also served as a synagogue. Thus the community was divided primarily along ethnic lines. Class, politics, and religion played little role in these divisions.

Stopnicka-Rosenthal noted that the activities of Jewish organizations were of little interest to younger people. For a few years after 1935, the Sephardim ran a primary school, but it went out of existence when the teacher left. Later, East European Jews tried to start a school, but many parents preferred to send their children to a nonsectarian North American school. In the 1950s, there was a Sephardic-sponsored afternoon Hebrew school as well. Few kept kosher, and synagogues had a hard time finding a minyān (quorum for prayers) to hold Sabbath services.

Stopnicka-Rosenthal describes a small community that is demoralized in Jewish terms. Unlike in Mexico City or Buenos Aires, the Sephardim in Barranquilla, many of whom were of Syrian origin, did not have strong rabbinic leadership. They were too small in number to attract the kind of leaders who went to the larger centers.[28]

In Panama, by 1989 the Jewish community was primarily Sephardic. 70 percent of the nearly four thousand Panamanian Jews were Sephardic, most of Aleppan origin. They were concentrated in Panama City.[29] They were wealthy enough and interested enough to support two Jewish day schools, one more Orthodox than the other. The more moderate school, Albert Einstein, also was attended by the children of army officers. According to one former student, army officers during the Noriega period felt more comfortable having their children in the Jewish school because they were snubbed by other Panamanians.

In late December 1989, the United States government invaded Panama in order to remove Manuel Noriega. U.S. sanctions on Panama in the two years preceding the invasion and during the battles around Panama City had adversely affected much of the commerce in and through Panama, and had ruined Panama's reputation as a center for offshore banking. The invasion was accompanied by extensive looting of shops, as law and order broke down.

Jews played a prominent role in all of these events. In February 1988, Eric Arturo Delvalle, the figurehead president, attempted to oust strongman Manual Noriega, but failed to do so despite American help. Delvalle was a Jew of Caribbean Sephardic descent. After his attempt to remove Noriega, he was, in turn, removed from office. Michael Harrari, an Israeli, was arrested by American troops and it was alleged that he had been a Noriega security advisor. A professional diplomat who was appointed to be deputy Panamanian representative at the United Nations by the post-Noriega government was someone with a Sephardic surname, Leon Abadi.[30]

During the invasion, businesses, including those owned by Jews, were looted to the light fixtures and toilets. The affluent neighborhood of Punta de Patilla, where many Jews live, was assaulted by looters and Noriega supporters. The Jews formed their own vigilante unit of about thirty people, organized by Victor Angel, a native Panamanian Sephardi and owner of a chain of women's wear shops (La Casa Amarilla). Shortly after the invasion, three hundred business leaders held a meeting at Shevet Aḥim, a local synagogue, and estimated business losses at $400 million. The article from which this information was taken also claimed that Jews owned a substantial portion (between 70 and 90 percent) of the major businesses in Panama.[31]

The family of "Jaime Sutton" has lived in Panama for many years. Like others, they have family connections with Manchester and Jerusalem. The family has been involved in a number of businesses in the post–World War II period, including clothing, shoes, and electronics, both in manufacturing (or finishing) and in retail trade. In recent years, some of the women in the family have become real estate agents.

At the time of the invasion, Jaime was a student at a private American university. I do not know if he was able to return to the United States for study.

Religion and Assimilation

When we consider the general vectors of Syrian, and especially Aleppan, accommodation to their various environs, we find a mixed picture. In general, Ḥalebis see themselves and are seen by others as among the most persistent in their loyalty to traditional Judaism throughout the world. This comes through in the works of Joseph Sutton, David Laniado, and Amnon Shamosh, and in the various interviews that I have conducted over the years. Yet they are no more uniform than any other human group.

At various interviews over the years with people like Frieda Sitt, Flora Cohen, and Ralph Ades, I have met individuals who were secular in their basic orientation. Ralph and Frieda themselves had been attracted to left-wing radical ideologies. This was particularly true of a few individuals in the 1930s and 1940s, although generally Syrian Jews in Latin America have been fairly conservative politically. Intellectual Sephardic Jews, such as Victor Perera, may continue to be attracted to left-wing ideologies, but they will probably be a minority. Some, such as Flora Cohen's husband, are not religious or drawn to Asian or New Age religions.

Small communities, such as those in Barranquilla and Guatemala, were more subject to secularization and assimilation, because they did not have the depth in numbers and the cultural intensity present in larger communities. They also did not have the vigorous and sustained rabbinic leadership that was found at times in Buenos Aires and Mexico City. In the large communities, of course, many individuals also felt the attractions of the larger society, but there were more traditional alternatives. Despite the fact that there is evidence of structural and identificational assimilation in Latin American Syrian communities, the Syrian communities still stand out for their persistent Jewishness.[32]

Syrian synagogues continue to occupy an important place within the Mexican Jewish community. They have made strong efforts to maintain Jewish education and dietary laws. They have also been active in Zionist and pro-Israel activities. In Argentina, they stood out in the early part of the century for their strong resistance to secularization. The Syrians, especially those from Aleppo, were noted for respecting the authority of their *ḥakhām*, Shaul Setton Dabbah. On the advice of an Ashkenazi colleague, this *ḥakhām* issued the first ban (*ḥerem*) in the New World against Jews marrying persons of Gentile origin, whether converted to Judaism or not. That order is still in effect.[33] This *ḥakhām* also resisted educational reform in the talmud torah and adhered to the anti-Zionist position of Agudat Yisrael. One of his successors, Ḥakhām Yiktzhaq Sheheber, also aroused controversy. He continued Setton Dabbah's policy of adhering to traditional orthodoxy.[34] He had both supporters and opponents in the Aleppan community, but he was a recognized rabbinic authority.[35]

Strengthening of traditional Jewish education has occurred in other places, too. In the 1930s in Panama, Ralph Ades studied Hebrew with an old-fashioned *ḥakhām*; in the 1980s, Jaime Sutton studied at the Einstein School. This school was attractive to upwardly mobile Panamanian non-Jews as well, though Jaime also reported that there was another school in Panama that excluded non-Jews. By this time, Jews were concentrated in Panama City. The school had a Hebrew curriculum that included Mishnah and Bible. Both of the Jewish schools were Orthodox in orientation. Most of the Jews at these schools are Syrian Sephardic, so in Panama the movement educationally has been toward a more intensive Jewish variety than in the past. In Mexico City, Daniel Levy noted that women from Aleppan homes have become teachers in Jewish day schools. For many it is their first job outside the house, and it is thus noteworthy that they have chosen a job within the Jewish community.[36]

Syrian Jews as Sojourners and Settlers

As stated earlier, the various testimonies and personal histories show people who have relatively loose ties to the countries in which they live. While there are some indications that this may be generally true of Syrian Sephardim, it is also possible that because these individuals were all interviewed in the United States and elsewhere outside of Latin America, I have encountered those who were closer to the sojourner end of the continuum. Had I done a study of the communities in situ, I might have encountered many more people—especially among those born in their countries of residence—who view themselves as Mexicans, Guatemalans, Panamanians, and so on. Indeed, the Syrian Jews in Mexico, around 90 percent of whom were born in Mexico, generally saw themselves as both Mexican and Jewish.[37]

Furthermore, several of my interviews were with second-generation children of immigrants. For various reasons that generation may have had fewer roots in Latin America than others, especially in the case of the three whose parents moved to Manchester and New York in that period. The same is true of Sutton's oral histories. He interviewed several of these people in New York City. Eduard Farhi, for instance, had immigrated to Brazil from Aleppo, then immigrated to Mexico and from there to New York.

Finally, we should turn from the consideration of the sample to that of the countries in question. The nations of the world differ in their will and ability to absorb immigrants. Until recently at least, the United States was unusual in its capacity to "Americanize" immigrants and to encourage them to identify with the country. This was especially true for immigrants from Europe and the Middle East. While Syrian Jews in the United States were not as eager to participate in American affairs as others, a substantial number served in the United States military during World War II. On the other hand, Egypt had a large foreign population until the 1950s, few of whose members fully identified with the country and most of whom maintained their foreign citizenship.

Much of Latin America appears to be closer to the Egyptian model than to that of the United States. Those who sojourn in Latin America in substantial numbers include North Americans, Levantine Arabs, and Europeans of many nationalities. Maintenance of their cultures of origin varies. Some take local citizenship and some do not, although the tradition of extraterritorial rights that was present in the Middle East (see chapter 2) is not formally present in Latin America. The strength of national identification also varies. For example, national identification was initially weak in Panama, which was created by a United States-inspired coup, but it became more intense as Panamanians struggled to rid themselves of the American presence in the Canal Zone. Latin American countries also vary in the degree to which nation-states are willing to include those who are neither Spanish Catholics nor Indians into the body politic, as recent writings on the history of Latin American immigration policy show.[38]

For Jews in general and for Syrian Sephardim in particular, these generalizations apply. We should, however, recognize that they are more applicable to certain groups than to others. Intellectuals may become more committed to nationalistic political movements than are businessmen. Manufacturers have considerable investments in the country at stake. A manufacturer today can live abroad and run his factory together with an in-country manager by use of computerized telecommunications, but he still must visit his factory from time to time.

Many Sephardim, including Syrian Jews, have integrated into their country of residence and have participated actively in its affairs. Some of these individuals are not as involved in the Jewish community itself. On the other hand, the civil violence and volatility found in many Latin American societies have made exiles of citizens of all classes, especially in places such as Guatemala and Argentina. Thus, even those who are withdrawing from Sephardic commercial and kin networks might still find utility in such identities. It is therefore not surprising that Latin American immigrants have joined other Syrian Sephardim in Brooklyn and have formed subgroups within the Flatbush neighborhood (see chapter 10).

In brief, in Latin America we find a continuum of Jewish communities. Cities such as São Paulo, Mexico City, and Buenos Aires have strong religious and communal institutions, including Jewish day schools. In other places, these institutions are smaller and weaker. Individuals, too, vary. Orthodox rabbis may maintain summer residences in Jerusalem while serving communities in Latin America. Wealthy people in commerce may spend a few months of the year in a predominantly Syrian condominium near Miami. Others may see themselves primarily as Mexicans, Brazilians, Colombians, or Venezuelans. If they are nonreligious and in intellectual occupations or universities, their ties to the Aleppan web of relationships may be quite weak.

CHAPTER 8

SYRIAN JEWS IN NEW YORK IN THE LATE 1950s

The Syrian Jewish community in Brooklyn has long been seen as one of the most cohesive Jewish communities outside of Ḥasidim in the diaspora. My fieldwork there in 1958–59 and 1962–63 was devoted to understanding the reason for this (see the preface for details on the fieldwork). This chapter describes the community at that time, but the Syrian Jewish community can no more be contained by a single portrayal than any other entity.[1] The changes that have occurred in the past thirty-five to forty years will be considered in chapter 10.

JEWS IN THE SYRIAN EMIGRATION TO THE UNITED STATES

As noted in chapters 2, 4, and 6, a great emigration from Syria and surrounding Arab provinces of the Ottoman Empire began in the last decades of the nineteenth century. Increased economic opportunity was the prime motivation. After 1909, when Jews and Christians became subject to conscription in the embattled Ottoman Empire (during the period of the Balkan Wars and World War I), many Jewish young men sought refuge in the New World, arriving between 1908 and 1915. After the war, the immigrants included many women who came to wed or to be with their husbands. The main period of immigration to the United States lasted until the immigration law that imposed quotas was passed in 1924. Under this law, Syria (including Lebanon until 1944) was restricted to one hundred immigrants a year.

Some Syrians continued to immigrate illegally, sometimes as "spouses" of Mexican citizens.

Almost from the beginning, the Syrian Jews separated themselves from their Christian compatriots. Such distance was kept against the background of tensions in Syria between Christians and Jews who were commercial competitors. Many of the Syrian Christians had deep-seated anti-Jewish sentiments. The Jews reciprocated. Despite this, there were and continue to be some contacts between the Syrian Jews and the Christians. The two groups of Syrian immigrants were similar in their trades, particularly textile imports, and they maintained commercial ties.[2] Some Syrian Jews have continued to purchase Middle Eastern foods on Atlantic Avenue, the shopping center for Arabs in Brooklyn.

The separation of Syrian Jews from other Arabic-speaking immigrants is shown in their respective residence patterns. The Christians first moved to the Lower West Side, near Wall Street, and to downtown Brooklyn. Syrian Jews first lived on the Lower East Side in predominantly Jewish areas. Syrians and other Sephardim were generally concentrated on Broome and Allen Streets. Many of the Christians moved to Bay Ridge at a later date, while Bensonhurst-Mapleton Park in Brooklyn was the main center of Syrian Jewry from the 1920s until the 1960s. Since 1960, the main area of residence for Syrian Jews has been along Ocean Parkway. All of the areas where the Syrian Jews have lived are Jewish neighborhoods.

The Jewish neighborhoods into which the Syrian Jews have moved have generally been East European Ashkenazi, which is natural considering the composition of New York Jewry. It is noteworthy that Syrian Jews lived apart from the main concentrations of non-Ashkenazi Jews in Brooklyn, such as the Ladino-speaking Sephardim, Yemenites, and Bukharians.[3] In the late 1950s, however, many Egyptian Jewish immigrants, usually of Syrian origin, did move into Bensonhurst and the part of Flatbush where the Syrians lived.[4] Since 1960 the descendants of Syrians who had immigrated to Lebanon and Israel have also moved to Flatbush.

The Syrian Jews maintained a relatively high profile as a homogeneous and cohesive minority. There were Syrian synagogues in Bensonhurst and on Ocean Parkway, as well as a day school, a community center, and a ritual bath. I noted the relative cohesiveness of this community when I compared this group with Sephardim in Israel. Sanua also wrote that this community had greater solidarity than other Sephardim in the United States.[5]

The Economic Base

The occupational structure among Syrian Jews was marked by a tendency toward specialization on an ethnic basis. Both Christians and Jews from Syria began their American careers as peddlers.[6] While some of the

Damascus Jews became textile workers, Aleppan Jews generally started as peddlers or merchants. Sale of lingerie, lace, and linen were Syrian specialties. The progression was from immigration as unskilled workers to peddling. Usually the Syrians started with household linen and moved on to lingerie and linen stores. Many of the peddlers peddled at resorts.[7] Despite religious antagonism between Syrian Christians and Syrian Jews, some Syrian Jews were aided by Christian merchants in obtaining their first consignment of goods.[8] As late as 1960, many wholesalers of both groups had offices on lower Fifth Avenue.

The Depression affected most of the Syrian Jewish shopkeepers, peddlers, and wholesalers adversely. During World War II, however, many began to prosper. Few, even of the American-born, entered the professions in the postwar period, because there were few who continued in college. Many entered the infantwear line or imported cheap tourist items. In addition to these specialties, there were Syrians who had other occupations, including some in the electrical trades, candy stores, and groceries, as well as a butcher and a masseuse. By the end of the 1950s, several Syrians had become academically trained professionals, including a lawyer, a certified public accountant, a chemist, a psychologist, and a specialist in Middle Eastern studies. While the lawyer and the C.P.A. worked for firms that dealt with the Syrian business community, many of the more academic professionals no longer interacted with Syrians outside of occasional visits to kin.

The main form of economic organization continued to be the family firm, which was supported by a kin and ethnic network. Most New York Syrians were self-employed or worked in shops owned by other Syrians or in Syrian-owned wholesale houses. A young man, after completing high school, would work in a store owned by another Syrian, usually a relative, until he could afford to go into business for himself. Wholesalers or other wealthy members of the community would give loans to the younger men. Sometimes a dowry given at marriage would be used to set the groom up in business. By the 1960s, dowries were also used to further the education of the groom, as an alternative to an investment in a business. In the late 1950s Syrians hired only members of their own group as shop clerks or for more important jobs in the business. Partnerships were formed by relatives. Sometimes men would "import" relatives to be their employees or junior partners, sending for kinsmen in Syria, Israel, or Latin America.

Where the family firm predominates, branching often consists of sending forth kinsmen to do business elsewhere. Such was the case with the Syrian Jews. Different members of a family followed the same line of business in different cities, such as Washington or Chicago, and even in different countries, such as Panama and Hong Kong. In some cases, Syrian Jewish entrepreneurs invested money in building factories in those countries, especially after World War II.

The concentration in export-import trade led to a number of Syrian Jewish lines of specialization. The so-called tourist bazaars, which were located in old central business districts of major cities, were such a specialty at the time. These were shops that sold imported cameras, electronic equipment, rugs, and a variety of bric-a-brac.[9]

Familial Ties

As in many other ethnic groups, the family lay at the core of the Syrian Jewish community in New York City. Relatives were favored as business partners. People preferred to marry cousins or other members of their origin group. Men "imported" brides and partners from among their relatives in Israel, Syria, or Latin America. The connection between marriage and business arrangements was recognized. Some informants claimed that the reason the men preferred Syrian brides was that a man expected a dowry from a Syrian bride's parents. Men often deferred their marriages until they were established in business, which often meant that they were in their late twenties, while they wanted as wives young women between eighteen and twenty. Beauty, youth, and wealth were what they valued in the women.

The importance of beauty, youth, and wealth for marriage was emphasized in conversations with women or about sisters and other female relatives. One woman said that she had lied about her age for as long as she could, so that people would think that she was younger. Another woman said that despite her family's relative poverty, she had been sought as a bride because of her fair hair, a quality admired in the Levant. In several instances, the reason given for women marrying Ashkenazi Jews was the fact that they were "old maids" from poor families—that is, women in their twenties.

Syrian Jews in Brooklyn were caught between their traditional view of guarding the virtue of their daughters and the dating pattern prevalent in American society. Preferring to keep marriages within the group, they nevertheless allowed their sons to date outside the group. The young men might hang around with others on a corner or in a luncheonette.[10] It was said among the young men that if a Syrian boy went out with a Syrian girl more than two or three times, it was assumed that he would marry her. Consequently, he might turn to girls outside the group for premarital dating. Affairs with Ashkenazi girls sometimes led to marriages. Thus, in spite of strong negative attitudes toward outgroup marriage, certain pressures from within the group were leading both men and women to Ashkenazi mates. One Ashkenazi rabbi serving a Syrian congregation estimated that as many as 25 percent of weddings in the late 1950s were with Ashkenazim. This pattern continued, despite the reputation of the Syrians as a cohesive group. Hayyim J. Cohen, in his survey of American Sephardim, found that about 33 percent of the daughters-in-law and 80 percent of the sons-in-law of his U.S.-born

Syrian respondents were Ashkenazim, while nearly 16 percent acknowledged that some (possibly distant) relatives had Gentile spouses.[11]

After marriage, those young couples who continued to live in Brooklyn lived in neighborhoods close to where their parents lived. In the 1950s, many Syrians had moved from Bensonhurst down Avenue P to the Ocean Parkway area of Flatbush. This was still a short ride from the older neighborhood. Most Syrians lived in one- and two-family houses, even those who were relatively poor, unlike Ashkenazim, who often lived in apartments.[12] This was due, in part, to the large families of the Syrians.

Family ties continued to be close. There were frequent telephone conversations and mutual visitation among the women. While during the 1920s women helped out in the stores and some unmarried women worked in offices or shops prior to marriage, married women generally did not seek employment outside the home. Women were responsible for housework and child care.

In the past, Syrian families were quite large, with as many as ten children. By the late 1950s, according to one rabbi, the number of children had declined but many women still gave birth to more than two children. In some very large families, the older children might occupy one apartment in a two-family house, while the parents and younger children lived in the other apartment.

A double standard of morality was accepted by Syrians in the 1950s. Young men sometimes had affairs outside the group, and there was much gossip about the extramarital relationships of the men. When a woman's group in 1963 produced a play, they chose Clare Boothe Luce's *The Women,* a melodrama from the 1930s that addressed this problem.[13]

While women were primarily concerned with housework, some women did volunteer work for the community during the late 1950s. For instance, there was an active Parent-Teacher Organization connected to the Syrian day school. During the 1960s, some women continued their education after marriage. In general, however, the Syrian Jewish family in New York City in the late 1950s was one in which the women took care of the house and the children while the men worked and even played away from home.[14]

Communal Organizations and Volunteer Associations

In New York City, despite constant complaints about general indifference and monopolistic control by certain cliques, voluntary organizations of Syrian Jews were active. The intensity of such voluntary activity in the United States, especially among the Ashkenazi Jews, who were an important comparison group for the Syrian Jews, was a factor in this, as was the relative leisure of many Syrian Jewish women in the United States. Many of the forms utilized by the Syrians in New York had been adopted from the local

Ashkenazi Jews, including the forms and functions of contemporary synagogues.

The Syrian synagogues in Bensonhurst, Flatbush, and Bradley Beach were multifunctional and included facilities for recreation as well as for sacred learning and prayer. As noted above, a women's group had a theatrical performance in a synagogue. At Bradley Beach, the New Jersey coastal resort frequented by the Brooklyn Syrians, a synagogue building was used several times a week for social purposes. Men and women went there to meet friends, drink Turkish coffee, and play cards or backgammon. While the propriety of using a synagogue for gambling was debated by the Syrians, as it has been by American religious groups generally, the practice was allowed.

Since most of the Syrian Jews in Brooklyn were of Aleppan origin, most synagogues were "*Ḥalebi.*" In Bensonhurst, there was one Damascus, or *Shāmī,* congregation, Ahi-Ezer, only four blocks away from the largest Ḥalebi synagogue, Magen David. Each had its own rabbi and cantor. By the late 1950s, there was also a congregation on Ocean Parkway called Shaʿare Zion, which was led by Rabbi Abraham Hecht, an Ashkenazi rabbi who served that congregation until 1995. In addition to these three synagogues, services were held in other communal buildings, such as the Magen David Community Center, as well as in a number of private prayer quorums. In the 1950s, Bensonhurst was still the center of the Syrian community. The center had moved to Flatbush by the 1970s, however. By then, a permanent community had settled in Deal, north of Bradley Beach.[15]

In the late 1950s, there were other voluntary associations, including a B'nai B'rith Lodge, a religious day school (yeshiva), a Parent-Teacher organization associated with the yeshiva, and a burial society, as well as a number of social clubs. The Magen David Yeshiva PTO *Community Bulletins* of October and November 1959 give us a picture of the degree to which these organizations, at least in their public presentations, were like comparable Gentile and Jewish organizations elsewhere in North America. The contents of these bulletins show the importance of Ashkenazim as a reference group to the Syrians in Brooklyn.

The *Community Bulletin* was a standard four-page bulletin, much like that issued by synagogues and similar groups.[16] It contained news about what was going on in the school, the PTO events, religious and educational columns by the school principal and teachers, columns for the Magen David Community Center sisterhood (the Community Center shared a building with the school), other Syrian community announcements, B'nai B'rith announcements, milestones (announcements of births, bar mitzvahs, engagements, marriages, and so on), and advertisements. Analysis of each feature indicates the degree to which the Syrian community was integrated into the larger society, at the same time that it maintained a separate identity through parallel institutions.

For instance, both the English and Hebrew principals of the yeshiva were Ashkenazi Jews. The advice that the Hebrew principal gave parents in each bulletin was noteworthy. In the October issue he stressed regular home observance of Jewish ritual, especially the Sabbath, to reinforce the teaching of the day school. In the November issue, he suggested places to take the children during school holidays, particularly the attractions of Manhattan. PTO and Sisterhood activities listed are what one would expect of an American women's auxiliary during this period: cake sales, card parties, membership teas, raffle drawings, fashion shows, and gala dances. The same is true of the B'nai B'rith chapter. In the October issue, there was an announcement of the formation of a Girl Scout troop in the new congregation. It was termed the first "S-Y Girl Scout troop" (S-Y is a Syrian term for Syrian, as opposed to J-dub, for Jew or Ashkenazi). Most of the teachers in the school who were mentioned in the bulletin had non-Syrian names, such as Masters and Golubshik, while only one PTO officer listed had a distinctly Ashkenazi name. The neighborhood businessmen who advertised in the bulletin were both Syrian and non-Syrian.

Syrian Jews participated in activities at the Jewish Community House of Bensonhurst. During the 1930s, this center was used by one group of Syrians for religious services before they built their own synagogue. A community center was organized after World War II by younger Syrians in Bensonhurst. Such an organization was, however, opposed by the older leaders, and its own members became indifferent. By 1958, the Center building had become the day school building and the Center was simply another Syrian synagogue, as noted above.

With the movement of Syrian Jews to Flatbush, new efforts were made to build a separate Syrian Jewish Community Center. The Sephardi Syrian Community Center was dedicated in 1979. The tendency toward parallel organization was also present with regard to the B'nai B'rith. Some sources indicated that there had been all-Syrian Jewish Masonic and Odd Fellow lodges. In the B'nai B'rith lodge, members were generally second-generation Americans.

In addition to these organizations, which had Jewish aims, there were also several social clubs whose main activities were card playing and parties. Membership in these clubs was reputed to be on the basis of wealth and was considered to be an exclusive privilege.

The "umbrella" organization of the Syrian Jews was headed by self-appointed leaders. This was similar to the situation in Jerusalem in the 1940s, 1950s, and 1960s.[17] Fund-raising took place on behalf of new synagogues, the day school, the Sephardi Porat Yosef Yeshiva in Jerusalem (a rabbinical seminary, see chapters 5 and 6), general Jewish philanthropies, and special funds set up for New York Syrian Jews. Another charity was Otsar HaTorah, which established Jewish religious schools in a number of Muslim countries after World War II. The leaders were said to be the main contributors. They were wealthy religious men, generally of the immigrant generation. One rabbi, Jacob Kassin, was called ḥakhām bāshī (the old Ottoman term for the chief rabbi, see chapter 2). The use of this title gave Syrian Jews a sense of continuity with the past. He was, however, considered to be only primus inter pares by the other rabbis. At various times he presided over a rabbinic court, which handled cases involving Syrian and other Sephardic Jews in New York and elsewhere.[18]

Unlike the American Jewish community, in which private morticians have played an important role, the Syrian Jews in Brooklyn maintained a Burial Society. If the deceased individual was a member of the society and the community, the society would bury him or her without extra cost. In this, they continued a medieval tradition that was common to most Jewish communities. Most Syrian Jews have been members and the society has not given preference to rich or poor.

For women who practiced the restrictions placed on them during their menstrual period, which required them to refrain from sexual activity for a long period each month, the community had built a *mikveh* (ritual bath). In the 1970s, a new *mikveh* was built in the Ocean Parkway area.[19]

Religion

Syrian Jews in Brooklyn and in Bradley Beach were considered "very religious" or traditional by their Ashkenazi neighbors. In both places, there was good attendance at the synagogue by men, including those in their twenties and thirties. The attendance was better than one would find in equivalent Ashkenazi Conservative and Orthodox congregations in the 1950s. On the other hand, many Syrians kept their shops open and worked in them on the Sabbath. Many younger men went to dances and parties on the Sabbath. In Bradley Beach most Syrians went to the beach on Saturday afternoon, even some who were conscientiously Orthodox. Observance of the dietary laws in the home was prevalent among Syrian Jews, although some ate nonkosher meat away from home. Daily prayer quorums (*minyānim*), sacred study sessions, and the singing of *pizmonim* (sacred Hebrew songs) continued in Brooklyn. In the 1950s, the main participants were older men and a small group of younger "ultra-Orthodox" individuals. After-school classes for girls who attended public school and needed instruction in Judaism were given in addition to Hebrew classes for boys.

The impact of outside influences on the Syrian Jews in Brooklyn can be seen in their transitional rites. In one wedding that I observed in 1963, the wedding ritual itself followed the Sephardi rite. In the reception, however, the American and Ashkenazi influences were quite evident. The wedding was held in a New York-style wedding hall, and the caterer served Ashkenazi-style hors d'oeuvres and food at the dinner.

Religious observance in Brooklyn ranged from rebels who were identified as atheists through those who were indifferent or casual, to those who were conscientiously Orthodox or even ultra-Orthodox. All the Syrian congregations were and still are Orthodox in affiliation. Movements of rebellion among Syrian Jews expressed themselves in religious terms. A number of young men identified themselves as Communists during the 1930s. They were said to have read left-wing pamphlets in the synagogue, hidden in their prayer books. They were jokingly called "*laḥimajin* Communists." *Laḥimajin* is a Syrian and Armenian equivalent to pizza, consisting of flat Syrian bread with some meat and tomato sauce on top. The young men in that group remained in the community and became businessmen, although some other Syrians who became leftists left the community.

In the late 1950s, a group gathered around Rabbi Jose Faur, a young rabbi who was the assistant in one of the congregations. He had come from Argentina, and had studied in an Ashkenazi yeshiva. He taught his followers that they should observe Jewish law much more strictly, and understand the "greatness of Sephardi heritage." His message contained religious, ethical, and ethnic themes. His followers were men in their teens and twenties, although there were also a few middle-aged men. He encouraged his followers to study both traditional texts, such as the Talmud, and secular subjects, particularly philosophy. The group was critical of the business and recreational practices of Syrian Jews, including the celebration of the secular New Year's Eve, as pagan. The older leaders of both the Ḥalebi and Damascan communities opposed this young rabbi and eventually he became peripheral to the community. When I first met him in 1958, I thought of him as "ultra-Orthodox," a perception that was mistaken. This rabbi's style, however, stressed "Sephardic pride." It was far from the "black hat" Ashkenazi pattern that has become so prominent in recent years. Faur went on to teach at the Jewish Theological Seminary of America, a Conservative institution.

Certain realms of folk religion persisted for a time in America. The Ḥalebi and Shāmī Jews brought their traditions of magic and medicine to America. In the late 1950s rabbis still said prayers over boys who were diagnosed as having become ill on account of "frights." In 1961, a wealthy Ḥalebi in Los Angeles requested an amulet from a saintly rabbi in Jerusalem for the cure of a neighbor's son.[20] Younger Syrians view these traditions as superstitions.

Syrian Jewish religious life was greatly influenced by the American Ashkenazi environment. Still, religious Syrians from Jerusalem expressed surprise that their American counterparts still believed that "the Torah came out of Aram Ṣōbā" (Aram Sōbā-Aleppo), since these Israeli rabbis felt that Ashkenazis were superior in their command of the Talmud. In New York, the opinions of Syrian rabbis were still preferred over those of Ashkenazim, and many would rather send their children to the Syrian day school than to Ashkenazi yeshivot. The Israeli Ḥalebim who expressed these views had themselves been educated in both Porat Yosef Yeshiva and Ashkenazic yeshivot (rabbinical academies). But this was only a superficial impression, because Ashkenazi influence in New York was strong. Several Syrian synagogues, as well as the Syrian day school, had Ashkenazi rabbis, principals, and teachers. Many Syrians sent their children to Ashkenazi day schools. Most of the younger Syrians who received higher religious education did so at Yeshiva University and other Ashkenazi-controlled institutions. As indicated above, the synagogues in Brooklyn acquired the traits of American synagogues.

"Secular" Tastes and Leisure

The New York Syrian Jews were subject to several influences in their tastes. Eastern music in both Arab and Hebrew forms was extant in New York City. Around 1960, there were several Greek and Armenian cabarets where one could see belly dancing. Some of the tourist bazaars sold records of Arabic music. At one time one of the Bensonhurst movie houses exhibited Arabic films. In the late 1950s, some Jews went to the Brooklyn Academy of Music to see Egyptian films. The Academy of Music is near Atlantic Avenue, which was the center of the Syrian Christian community and has continued to be an area of Arab restaurants. Arab music was an ethnic symbol for the Syrians. At a party some women would perform belly dances. In the PTO *Bulletin* (cited above), one Ḥalebi offered "Music of Distinction Orchestras Large and Small Custom Made to Your Affair." Syrian Jews, however, appreciated popular American music as well as that of the Middle East.

The Brooklyn Syrians were familiar with the films, nightclubs, and social dancing as they existed in New York City. Some attended "legitimate" theatrical performances. A few even attended the opera regularly. Card playing was a popular activity. Certain card games, one informant said, were known to him only in a Syrian context. Backgammon was played in the 1960s primarily by older men before its American revival. Card playing was as popular among women as among men, in both homes and clubs.

Israeli Ḥalebim in New York said that Syrian foods were better in New York than in Jerusalem. The Syrians in New York were richer than those in Israel. Ingredients such as pistachios were easier to get in New York City than in Israel at that time. One Syrian woman published a cookbook of Syrian Jewish dishes. In the 1960s, Claudia Roden, an Egyptian woman of Syrian Jewish descent, published the popular *Book of Middle Eastern Food,* which contains some distinctly Ḥalebi recipes. The Deal Sisterhood's cookbook contains many international recipes and shows the influence of Ashkenazi and general American cultures on Syrians.[21] Some Barton's Confectionery branches (a candy store chain that was kosher and closed on the Jewish Sabbath) in Brooklyn were owned by Syrian Jews. One Syrian Jew owned a typically American Jewish delicatessen in a Syrian neighborhood and he had many Syrian customers. The menu included corned beef and pastrami on rye bread, chicken soup with noodles, and salami, but no Middle Eastern dishes. An Egyptian Jewish immigrant owned a pastry shop that also served food, all in Middle Eastern style. Syrian bread (pita) was available; some was packaged by Syrian (Christian) firms on Atlantic Avenue.

School Performance and "Intellectualism"

In the late 1950s, relatively few Syrian Jews graduated from colleges and universities. Those who did were often among the alienated. While this information was derived from both Syrian and Ashkenazi informants, there was general agreement about the fact. By that time, the Brooklyn Syrians were sufficiently prosperous to be able to afford to send their children to college. It appeared that Syrian Jews had not chosen the "educational" route of social mobility.

Lillian Herling, a sociology student at Columbia University, carried out a study in Bensonhurst in 1929 on why a large number of Syrian Jewish students in that neighborhood were not promoted in school. This was called "school retardation" at the time. This study showed that the educational performance of Syrian Jews was lower in the 1920s than that of their Ashkanazi neighbors, although not unlike that of their Italian neighbors. Their rate of being held back or flunking was 44.0 percent, while that of an American-born was 17.8 percent, and that of the Italians was 59.3 percent. Ashkenazi origin groups, such as "Poles," had retardation rates that were far lower than even those of the Americans.[22] Since 1960, the number of Syrian Jews going to college has steadily increased. Still, business success, rather than educational attainment, was seen as the ladder to prosperity and happiness.

The Alienated and the Assimilating[23]

While there was an ethnic entity in which any Syrian Jew could participate, there were those who for a variety of reasons had left the Syrian community and lived outside it. Even in Brooklyn, in the neighborhoods where the Syrian Jews resided, some Syrians kept their participation at a minimum.

Some of those who were assimilating into American society had never been part of the Brooklyn Syrian Jewish group. Many Syrians opened businesses in such far-off places as Chicago; Laredo, Texas; and Saint Petersburg, Florida. While some of these Syrians later moved to Brooklyn so that their children would be reared in a Sephardi Jewish environment, some did not. Their children married Jews of other origins or even non-Jews (see chapter 9). Similarly, the paths of immigration for some Syrian Jews were idiosyncratic.

"Albert Harari," for example, was born in Istanbul of Ḥalebi parents. After his emigration to the United States, he joined the Marines. Later he married a Jewish woman from Poland. He lived in Manhattan for most of his adult life. Although he was Syrian, he never settled among the Syrian Jews of Brooklyn, and he had little to do with them. His daughter, "Joan," knew that her father was Syrian or part Syrian, but she never lived in a Syrian Jewish context. She had some identification with the Syrians and would speak about the "Syrian personality."

Among the Syrian Jews in Brooklyn, there were those who were alienated from the dominant ways of the community and from its leadership. The "*laḥimajin* Communists" and the "ultra-Orthodox" group were examples of young men of this variety, although most of them remained within the community and continued to participate in it. Some stayed on the periphery. One man in his twenties in 1960, for instance, went to college and to graduate school. Although he continued to live in Brooklyn, he generally went to Ashkenazi synagogues.

Some left the Syrian Jewish group entirely, although they maintained ties with their kin. "Ralph Abbady" grew up in Brooklyn. In his teens he rebelled strongly against Syrian attitudes toward intellectual activity and commerce. In fact, he developed a strong aversion to commercial activity. After he served in the army in World War II, he went to the university, where he earned a doctoral degree. After that, he lived away from the Syrian Jews in New York. His wife was of European Jewish background. He saw his siblings mainly on the occasion of rites of passage, such as weddings. Ralph was assimilating into a general American intellectual group and had broken with the Syrian group, but he did not try to "pass." He remembered and identified with his Middle Eastern background. For instance, he bought records of Arabic music. He gave his son a name that he occasionally Arabized. Nevertheless, he did not participate in Syrian activities.

"Gladys Mizrahi Jacobs" was born to a relatively poor family in Panama. After her family moved to Brooklyn, she suffered from their poverty. Because she was considered beautiful, she received a marriage proposal from a wealthy, but older, Syrian Jew. She rejected this offer, and instead broke with her family and married an Ashkenazi Jew. She moved away from Brooklyn and maintained few ties with her family.

"A Minority within a Minority"

The Syrian Jews in Brooklyn were connected to other Jews in the United States; yet they were (and are) identifiably separate. Michael Steinhardt termed them "a minority within a minority." They had a separate set of names for themselves: *Ḥalebiye*, Syrians, *S-Ys*, Sephardim. They called the Ashkenazim Jews, yiddish, Itchies, and J-dubs (J-w). The simple term *Syrian* referred to the dominant Ḥalabi group. A Ḥalebi would refer to the Damascans as Shāmīs or *Shawām*. Lawrence Plotnik noted that the Spaniole Sephardim of New Lots similarly differentiated themselves from the dominant Ashkenazi group, although his report aroused indignant censure by Sephardim at the time it was published.[24] The Syrians were recognized as a separate ethnic group in the Brooklyn neighborhoods, as well as in Bradley Beach (New Jersey), which was also an Ashkenazi resort. If one asked people in Bensonhurst what "nationalities" lived in the neighborhood, they would answer: Jews, Italians, and Syrians. However, if one asked the religion of the Syrians, one would be told that they were Jews—in fact, Orthodox Jews.

It is difficult to explain the reasons for the disengagement of the Syrians and the Sephardim from the East European Jews. A number of factors may account for this. Ashkenazi Jews did not give Ladino-speaking and Arabic-speaking Jews full recognition as Jews because of their exotic ways. One Syrian Jew was praying on a weekday morning in a Chicago synagogue around 1914, I was told. He was wearing, as an Orthodox Jew would, his prayer shawl and phylacteries, when a fellow worshiper started speaking to him in Yiddish. He replied that he did not understand that language and the man then asked him if he was a Jew.[25]

The Ashkenazim had preempted the term *Jew* for themselves. "Jewish" as a language meant Yiddish, and "Jewish food" was East European in origin. The Syrian Jews were probably soon aware of the negative, anti-Semitic stereotypes that the Christian Americans held of the East European Jews, and they may have preferred to identify themselves as other than Jewish for public purposes. Syrians were a less important target as scapegoats than were Jews.

The local Jews of East European descent were the most significant ethnic group for Syrian Jews. Other Sephardi groups were separated from them by neighborhood and language of origin. Most other Sephardim were Ladino-speakers, though there were also some Persians. In Bensonhurst there were some other Sephardim. By 1960 the latter included a number of recent Egyptian refugees, some of whom were Ḥalebis, but they were "more French" than the American Syrians.[26]

Relations with Arabic-speaking Christians were very distant. In this they were similar to what they had been in Syria, except that there was less interaction in Brooklyn. The attitudes of Syrian-American Christians toward Jews were complicated. While some were very sympathetic to the Arab cause, others, particularly the Maronites, viewed pan-Arabism as a threat to Middle Eastern Christians. Syrian-American Christians were sometimes mistaken for Jews and even called themselves "Christian Jews."

The main Gentile group in the neighborhoods where Syrian Jews lived was the Italians. Otherwise the two neighborhoods were predominantly Jewish. Many of the teachers in public and religious day schools were Ashkenazi

Jews, as were the professionals (doctors, lawyers, accountants) and the politicians. In the U.S. Army, a Brooklyn Syrian had an opportunity to meet members of other groups, but that was an experience separated from civilian life.

The integration of Syrian Jews into American life showed some distinctive features. All went to schools that taught American values. They paid taxes and served in the armed forces when conscripted. The second generation spoke English as its mother tongue. Some said that they could tell a Syrian Jew in Brooklyn from an Ashkenazi, but both spoke with New York accents.

One major difference between the New York Ashkenazi and the New York Syrian Jews was the apolitical attitudes of most Syrian Jews. According to one Ḥalebi who was active in local politics, few Syrians, even among the American-born, bothered to vote, whereas, he said, 90 percent of the Ashkenazim did vote. There were, however, some exceptions to this nonparticipation in politics, such as the leftists of the 1930s. In the 1950s, one rabbi's son was a member of a Zionist youth group and a lawyer and was active in local Democratic politics. Some older leaders in the community were active in Jewish fund-raising, including campaigns on behalf of Israel and of non-Zionist yeshivot.[27]

The Ashkenazi stereotype of the Syrian Jews in Brooklyn, as elicited by Steinhardt and me, is that the Syrians were considered "thieves and swindlers," big spenders, and big gamblers. The Syrians were seen as foreign and as having a false sense of superiority. Steinhardt's interviews with middle-aged Syrian women in Bensonhurst brought out responses of indifference toward the Ashkenazim. They felt that the latter were jealous of their (Syrian) success in America. The Syrian Sephardim had a stronger identification as Sephardim and Syrians, while the Ashkenazi women felt more American. The Ashkenazim identified themselves simply as Jewish, rather than as Ashkenazi. They used the word *Turk* for the Syrians in a derogatory manner. They believed that Syrian marriages were prearranged by the parents. On the whole, the Ashkenazi occupational structure in Bensonhurst was more diversified than the Syrian. It included postal workers, jewelers, and furriers, as well as retailers and wholesalers. On the other hand, Steinhardt found that richer Ashkenazim moved to the suburbs more readily than the equivalent Syrian group.[28]

The Syrian stereotype of Ashkenazim was more difficult to elicit. The fact that the interviewers (Steinhardt and I) were Ashkenazim may have been part of the difficulty. Some younger Syrians were concerned about the fact that there were more Ashkenazi professionals and college graduates. On the other hand, Steinhardt found that the goal of wealth was pursued with more openness among the Syrians than among other Americans. Syrians tended to underestimate their wealth in response to questions more than Ashkenazim did. I found that Syrians felt that Ashkenazi women were too independent.

One informant said that one reason more Syrian women married Ashkenazi men than vice versa was that Ashkenazi men were better around the house, while the women were too free. Steinhardt found that while Ashkenazim said that Syrians had four, five, or six children, above the average, Syrian women claimed that they had no more than average. This finding may have been the respondents' reaction to the interviewer rather than their belief. Steinhardt found that Syrians and Italians in Bensonhurst tended to live in homes or two-family houses, whereas Ashkenazim were apartment-dwellers. This trend had already been noted by Herling in 1929.[29]

Steinhardt's main finding was that the Ashkenazim were the main reference group in American society with which the Syrians had contact. On the other hand, the Syrians had a feeling of indifference and self-confidence toward the Ashkenazim, in their own way. To the Ashkenazim, the Syrians were of little concern. From the discussion of Syrian Jewish institutions in Brooklyn, however, it is clear that the indifference to the local Ashkenazim was only partial.

Conclusion

Elsewhere I have written about this group as an example of a "sojourning" middleman minority. The first two generations of Syrian Jewish immigrants did not necessarily see America as a permanent home, any more than those who settled in Latin America. In fact, there were families who moved easily between different localities across national boundaries. Their disinterest in local politics was another sign of their sojourning.

The association of a disproportionate number of Syrians in a number of related lines of trade, their strong family and kinship system, their family firms, their worldwide familial and commercial connections, and their maintenance of distinctive synagogues were part of a single picture that also was related to sojourning. Their cohesiveness and their occupational specialization were connected, as I showed in contrasting them with Israeli Ḥalebim where this linkage was broken (see chapters 5 and 6).

While Syrian Jews have maintained a high degree of ethnic solidarity, their culture has been affected by the surrounding society, and there is considerable intermarriage with other Jews. A new occupational structure has arisen out of the old, which will be discussed in chapter 10. The Syrian Jewish community in Brooklyn has changed considerably since 1960, but a portrait of its past will help in understanding this community in the present.

CHAPTER 9

SYRIAN SEPHARDIM IN THE UNITED STATES: THE OUT-OF-TOWNERS

Studies of ethnic groups should take into account those who live outside places where the ethnic group is concentrated. Small groups like Sephardic Jews in the United States must often live in places where they are not only a minority but also isolated individuals and families. Some may be able to join Jewish communities that are dominated by Ashkenazim. Others may be the only Jews in a particular town. Here we will generally consider those who must join Ashkenazic communities, either because there are too few Sephardim, because the Sephardim are too disparate to form a community, or because the Sephardic congregation has disintegrated.[1]

This chapter deals with those Syrian Jews in the United States who have lived outside of what Joseph Sutton has called "Aleppo-in-Flatbush" or "Aleppo-in-Deal." These people have a variety of personal histories, but they share the destiny of being "out-of-towners." Some of the "out-of-towners" are those who have come directly from abroad. Others lived first in New York City, while still others were born and bred in these smaller communities. Some of the latter have chosen to live outside the Syrian Sephardic community while others have returned to it at some point. This chapter presents biographical information on both early immigrants and their descendants and some recent "emigrés" from the New York City area.

Certain aspects of the Syrian experience in the United States are magnified among the "out-of-towners." While the neighbors of Syrian Jews in Brooklyn have some familiarity with Sephardim, most Jews and Gentiles elsewhere are unfamiliar with non-Ashkenazic Jews. On the other hand, the pressures of being part of a tightly knit community are not felt as much when one leaves Ocean Parkway. The farther one goes, the lighter the pressures to conform become. The "out-of-towners" are split between those who did not move to Deal or Brooklyn for short-term economic reasons and those who deliberately moved away to escape what they perceived as the restricted community that marks these places. The ones who ended up outside of Brooklyn solely for economic reasons sometimes moved to Brooklyn later in their lives.

Moving Out of Town

Early immigrants migrated primarily because of a need for economic opportunity. The history of Sophie Ashkenazi's family illustrates this. Her father left Syria for Mexico in 1908, in order to escape conscription into the Ottoman army (also see chapter 8). She arrived in Mexico with her mother a year later and went to school there. When she was fifteen (c. 1916), her father arranged a marriage for her with Ezra Ashkenazi. He had immigrated from Aleppo a few years before. He had gone first to New York, but had decided to seek better opportunities elsewhere. First the Ashkenazi family tried peddling in the vicinity of New York City, but then they went to Puerto Rico. They were invited home by some Christian Syrians there who gave them pork to eat. This made them sick. They then decided to leave and found transportation to New Orleans. They prospered there until a postwar depression hit. They were among the first Syrian Jews in New Orleans, but later there were about sixteen Syrian families there. When they were close to bankruptcy, the Ashkenazis left New Orleans for Ilton, Georgia, where Ezra bought a store. They stayed there until one of their children died.

The Ashkenazis then moved back to Mexico City, where Ezra became a peddler. He became ill, and they returned to the United States. First, Ezra became the partner of another Syrian Jew in Houston, Texas. After he quarreled with his partner, the Ashkenazi family bought a store in Birmingham, Alabama. They then moved, first to Atlanta and then to Charlotte, North Carolina. In that area they had two shops: one in Charlotte, which Sophie ran, and another in Winston-Salem. Even though they prospered, the Ashkenazis returned to New York at the time of the Second World War, because they did not want their children to marry Gentiles. In fact, they wanted them to marry other Syrian Jews.[2]

Barbara Freed's father, Joseph B. Hai, was an immigrant from Damascus. His father was a tailor. As she related it:

> My father and his first cousin [on Joseph's mother's side] grew up in the same household. The eldest Flah brother, Albert, came to the United States around 1909. My father arrived then in 1911, when he was sixteen years old. . . . My

> father traveled a bit on the way here. He stayed in Cairo for a bit and came to the United States via Marseille. . . . He and Albert lived in Bradford [Pennsylvania] for several years. They peddled . . . linens. In 1915, they opened the first Flah's & Co. store in Syracuse as a lingerie shop. Then they brought over Paul Flah, the next oldest brother, and the three of them lived in Syracuse. Then, when the First World War came, my father and Paul Flah were drafted. . . . My father was drafted in 1917 and served until the war ended. . . . When he was discharged from the Army, he did not go back to Syracuse to live, but he came to Albany in 1919. He opened the first Flah's store in Albany at the Ten Eyck Hotel; it was also a lingerie shop. The name Flah was the name on the business.
>
> Joseph Hai married my mother in 1927. My mother's family is from Central Europe; she was Ashkenazi. My father and all three of the Flah brothers married out of the [Syrian-Sephardic] community. The third brother, David Flah, was brought over later. He was young and the brothers didn't know what to do with him, so they sent him to a school in Manlius [near Syracuse]. . . . The youngest brother married somebody who was not Jewish. The other two married Jews. My uncle, Paul Hai, came over in 1922 and subsequently he married Edith Braun, from the Albany Braun family, in 1935. He was in the business also.
>
> In 1930, my father brought my grandmother, Jamila, and his baby sister, Rachel, to the United States. They lived in Albany for a brief period. My grandmother found it particularly hard to adjust, as she spoke only Arabic. Subsequently she and Aunt Rachel went to live in Brooklyn. Rachel married a Sephardic Jew there. . . .

From 1956, Flah stores in Syracuse and in Albany were independent of each other, although they would purchase goods together as long as the Flah and Hai brothers respectively ran the business. In 1970, Flah's of Albany bought the Flah stores in Syracuse. The stores by then had expanded into general women's clothing and later into infant- and menswear. Flah's became a public company in 1971 and Barbara Freed became president of Flah's, a position she held until it was sold in 1984. Whereas the first stores had been in downtown locations, by the 1980s, most were in suburban locations.[3]

The Flah and Hai brothers joined Reform temples. In some ways, Joseph Hai, Barbara's father, was still traditional, as shown by his staying in temple all day on Yom Kippur. Barbara Freed still follows this tradition. Joseph Hai was also a member of both Jewish country clubs in Albany. As with most new immigrants, the old German Jewish Colonie Country Club did not originally accept him, until they found out that he was a Sephardi and not an East European Jew. Then they actively sought his membership. Through his marriage to Mae Doling and the marriage of his brother to a woman also from Albany he became related to many of the families in the Albany Jewish community, of which he became a valued member.

Businesses

As these two biographies indicate, Syrian Jews moved to a wide variety of localities throughout the United States. These included urban communities like Chicago, Troy (New York), Bridgeport (Connecticut), and Providence (Rhode Island), but many moved to resort communities, including Myrtle Beach (South Carolina), Narragansett Pier (Rhode Island), Saratoga (New York), Old Orchard (Maine), Estes Park,(Colorado), Florida, and Atlantic City.[4] Selling table linen and souvenirs to vacationers had become a Syrian Jewish specialty by 1930, as noted in chapter 8. The movement of New York Syrians into the importation and manufacture of infantwear caused some to open children's stores in places like Washington, D.C., Troy, N.Y., and Chicago.

Some of the out-of-towners were in touch with Syrian importers in New York. Eli Hedaya discussed the problems that linen and lace importers, who were both Jewish and Christian, had during the Depression in selling their merchandise. He pointed out that there were linen shops in places like Atlantic City's famous Boardwalk that were owned by Syrian Jews and Christians. The business was unstable and there were many bankruptcies, both "genuine and contrived." Goods were often sold by auction. For tourists and others, auctions were a form of entertainment.[5]

Max Sutton, who was about eighteen in 1930, described the way young Syrian Jews would go on trips to various places. He and some of his friends went to the New England coast, visiting Cape Cod and Plymouth. At Narragansett Pier, a popular resort, he rented an empty store for the rest of the summer, ending up with a profit of $340. Then he worked in Miami for the winter and spent the next summer in a resort in New Jersey, selling tapestries, bedspreads, and the like.[6]

In the second generation, there was more diversification. This is strongest among those who never lived in New York. For instance, one individual who was born in a resort town started by opening a business in another resort. Then he opened an infantwear store in a small Northeastern city. When that city's downtown area began to decline, he found that he had valuable investments in urban real estate. He is now a partner with two other Jewish real estate investors in a company serving the whole metropolitan area. Another couple went into the jewelry business.

More recent immigrants also established themselves in resorts. Gabriel Shehebar, who immigrated to the United States from Egypt via Cuba in the 1960s, rented a store in Old Orchard, Maine, where a number of Syrian Jews had stores as late as the early 1990s. Since he did not speak English well at the time, he dealt primarily with French-speaking Québecois tourists.[7]

Other out-of-towners of the second and third generation moved out of the traditional Syrian business lines as early as the interwar period. In Chicago one opened a hot dog stand and another became employed by a large utility. One became a well-known car dealer.

The diversification continued in the third and fourth generations of out-of-towners, accompanied by assimilation into the American Jewish and general communities. A decreasing number went into their parents' businesses or returned to Brooklyn or Deal. They chose a variety of careers, such as psychotherapist, accountant, manager of a television station, and attorney. An increasing number of women entered small business and the professions. They lived far from their home communities and did not interact much with other Sephardim, other than family members.

Integration into the Local Community

In most of the places outside of New York City where Syrian Jews moved, they were among the few Sephardim. In a few places, such as Washington, D.C., Chicago, and Atlantic City, there were a fair number of other Syrians or Sephardim. In Chicago (as will be discussed in the following), Syrians for a time had their own congregation. When that failed they had the choice of either another Sephardic congregation or one of many Ashkenazic synagogues. Atlantic City had a Sephardic minyān at one time, but this was gone by the 1950s. At least one Syrian family there belonged to a Conservative synagogue. Syrians living in smaller communities in Upstate New York or New England joined Conservative or Orthodox synagogues. As noted previously, at least one family joined a Reform temple. Their children learned Hebrew with an Ashkenazic accent and Ashknazic melodies in Hebrew school. Another, a Syrian who had been raised in Brooklyn, said that he could only read Torah using the traditional Syrian cantillation. Some of these Syrians were active members of their synagogues. Out of necessity, most of the Syrian out-of-towners have accommodated themselves to the Ashkenazi majority. In this way, they resemble other Sephardim.

On the West Coast, San Francisco has had a small cluster of Syrian families, with an estimated one thousand to two thousand Syrian Jews there. They maintain a synagogue and school, but the community is widely scattered, unlike the situation in New York City. Syrians who move to Los Angeles are said to lose their "Syrian-ness" rapidly (in a month or so, some say).

Montreal represents a special situation for Sephardi Jews in North America, since many Francophone (French-speaking) Sephardic Jews have found it to be a favorable environment, but with its own troubling features. This is because of the intense xenophobic character of some forms of Québecois nationalism. Some Syrian and Lebanese Jews settled there, though the majority of Francophone Jews are North Africans (especially Moroccans). Fred Anzarouth moved to Montreal in the 1970s. When he first arrived he registered his children in a French school, but found its atmosphere too Catholic for his taste. Then he enrolled them in a Jewish day school that was dominated by Ashkenazim and used Ashkenazi Hebrew. Sephardi Jews, he felt, were well regarded by the French. In part, this was because many Sephardim were Francophone, as opposed to the Anglophone Ashkenazim. The differing Jewish origin-groups also expressed a variety of prejudices toward one another. Ḥalebiyeh (Aleppans) were looked down upon by the Lebanese. Both the Aleppans and the Lebanese got together to play cards and gossip. But by 1988, Fred felt that the Ḥalebiyeh were fully accepted by the Ashkenazi community.[8]

Generally out-of-town Sephardim have accepted the Ashkenzic ritual practices in the synagogue. One exception occurred in Albany in 1991. An Iraqi couple sent their daughter to a Sephardi cantor in Manhattan once a week to prepare for her bat mitzvah. When the son of a Jew of Greek origin had his bar mitzvah, he learned to read the Torah using the Greek (Romaniot) cantillation from a cantor in New York City. Other Jews are often ignorant of the existence of Jews who are not Ashkenazi. The problem of proving one's Jewishness is constant. While rabbis and other functionaries of the Jewish community know of the ethnic diversity of non-Ashkenazim, their knowledge of Sephardi custom is often negligible.

Those who have gone out of town recently must adapt to a smaller metropolitan area than New York City. "David Levy," a Aleppan lawyer in western New England, has lived away from New York for several years. As a single person, he found the Jewish community in general limited for social purposes, since in that city the Jewish community is very much oriented to married couples. On the other hand, he did find that by living away from New York, he was able to discover secular American life, through such activities as participating in folk dances and volleyball games with Americans who are not Syrian Jews. For socializing with Jews, he tries to spend time on weekends in larger cities like Boston. His problems are not specific to Syrian Jews, but are common to single Jews of all origins.

Most of the Sephardi Jews living in one small metropolitan area were aware of other Sephardi Jews living in the area. They were not always aware of the same ones, however. One young man had been fixed up with the daughter of one of the other Sephardi families in the area. Another knew a Sephardi divorcee, because they had grown up in the same community before they moved to this area. One old-time Sephardi resident knew of a relative newcomer to the area, but he did not remember meeting her. Some also knew of a Sephardi who had married a non-Jewish woman in the area.

Out-of-Towners and Intermarriage

The communal ban on intermarriage, which is enforced by the Syrian Sephardic rabbinate in New York City (see chapter 10), has much less power on out-of-towners, especially in the younger generation. In fact, one can find early instances of intermarriage among this group. Writer and politician William Haddad grew up in the South. He went to graduate school at Columbia. His wife is a Roosevelt. In his career as a journalist, he did not stress his Jewishness, but in 1964, he decided to run for Congress in a primary against a Jewish politician in a predominantly Jewish district in Manhattan. When his opponent began to claim that he was an Arab and would presumably promote the Arab cause against Israel, Haddad appeared as a Jew and tried to convince voters of his pro-Israel stance.[9]

A Syrian Jew who was raised in the Middle South, near Washington, D.C., became a doctor and did his residency in the Northeast in the 1980s. He married a woman who converted to Judaism. Sanctions by New York City rabbis had little effect on his decision. On the other hand, when another young professional from Brooklyn was in Pennsylvania and was rumored to be dating a Gentile woman, rabbis and other community leaders sent him messages warning him to break this relationship or face excommunication.

Max Haddad, in an interview with Joseph Sutton, contrasted the situation in Brooklyn, where there was little intermarriage with Gentiles, to the situation elsewhere. He said that his teenaged son had been staying with a family with a Syrian surname in Atlantic City when he noticed his friend's mother's sister was wearing a cross. He thus found out that his friend's mother was not of Jewish ancestry but was Italian. He noted that one of his out-of-town cousin's daughters was married to a Protestant. Max Haddad felt that marriage with Ashkenazim was actually "welcome."[10]

Syrian Sephardim in Chicago

Much of what has been written in the preceding also applies to the Syrian Jews who settled in Chicago. In Chicago, as in Atlantic City, there were a substantial number of Syrian Jews, though for a long time not enough to maintain a congregation.[11]

The history of the Syrian community in Chicago can serve as an example of an out-of-town community. Sephardic Jews from the Balkans and the Middle East arrived in Chicago prior to World War I. They were small in number compared to the nearly three hundred thousand Ashkenazic Jews, mainly from Eastern and Central Europe, who had flocked to this Midwestern center. Three small groups formed congregations and other organizations. Probably they were under 1,000 to 1,200 people in all. They were divided linguistically between the Ladino-speakers from the Balkans and Turkey, Aramaic-speakers primarily from Iranian Azerbaijan, and Arabic-speakers from Syria. Many went to work as peddlers or lingerie merchants. They settled among the more numerous Ashkenazim on the Near West Side and later followed them to Lawndale and to other neighborhoods.

In the case of the Ladino-speakers, the congregation was intimately connected to the Portuguese Israelite Fraternity. This congregation continues today as the Sephardic Congregation on the border of Evanston and Chicago.

The Aramaic-speakers, known as Persians or Iranians, have also maintained their congregation, which is now located in Skokie.

A Syrian Sephardi congregation (*Ḥevrat sephardim shel Suriya—Shikago*) existed during the interwar period on Douglas and Homan Streets. The only documentary evidence I found of this congregation's existence was the name imprinted in a *ḥumash* (Pentateuch) that is now owned by the Sephardic congregation in Evanston. The congregation may have lasted up to 1940. Some Syrians came to Chicago for the Century of Progress Exposition in 1933 and a few may have stayed. One interviewee said that at its peak the congregation included about fifty families. As families moved away, intermarried, or left the neighborhood the congregation disappeared, leaving barely a trace. A few families of Syrian origin—the Beydas, the Haras, the Hazans, and the Seruyas—remain in the metropolitan area. Like most other Jews in the Chicago metropolitan area, they now live on the North Side or in the northern suburbs.

When all three groups lived on the West Side, first near Maxwell Street and later in the Lawndale area, they seem to have cooperated. Sometimes people who read Torah for one did the same for the others. Still the members of the different Jewish groups had conflicts and negative stereotypes of the other groups, which prevented a merger.

All of the Sephardic groups felt that they were not recognized as full Jews by the Yiddish-speaking Ashkenazim. As elsewhere, people had anecdotes to illustrate this point. One example is the anecdote reported in chapter 8 of the Syrian Jew wearing his *tefillin* (phylacteries) and *tallit* (prayer shawl) in a synagogue who is asked if he is Jewish.[12]

A Persian Jew recalled that in an English class at a Jewish community center, a teacher would speak Yiddish with the other students until he protested. Some Ladino-speakers years later recalled that Ashkenazim would refuse to lease them apartments.

An Ashkenazi woman told a story which she placed around 1930 that showed how in some sensitive areas, Jews found it difficult to know for sure who was Jewish. When she was in her late teens, she had dated a young man who called himself Joseph Cohen. One day, he came to her house asking for help from her brother, because his father had had a heart attack. When her brother got to Joe's house, he found out that Joe Cohen was really Joe Rossi, an Italian Catholic. He had used a Jewish name so that he could date Jewish girls.

The non-Ashkenazi Jews also held negative stereotypes of the other Jewish groups, although they cooperated with them as well. The Persians were seen as miserly, while Ladino-speakers were seen as snobbish, lording it over the others. The Syrians and the Persians were seen as unscrupulous in business by the Ladino-speakers.

The various Sephardi groups did receive help from Ashkenazi institutions. They also cooperated in forming a Talmud Torah to teach Hebrew after school to their young people. The teachers came from a number of different groups. One man (in 1988 he was in his fifties), however, remembered how one Talmud Torah picnic that he had gone to broke up in quarrels over money when the men from the three groups could not agree.

The most visible group of Arabic-speaking Jews during the interwar period were the Syrians, mainly from Aleppo. One Syrian Jew recalled how his family came to Chicago:

> My father came from Aleppo in 1902. . . . He was born in Turkey. He went to Syria. I think he met my mother there. I told you of my cousins whom my dad brought over. They lived with us. They came over after the First World War. Their mother and father got killed from a bomb. Dad got together with my uncles [also in Chicago] and brought them here. . . . He was the guardian of them. . . .

Some of the Syrians made and sold ladies' undergarments. But they went into other businesses as well. A Lebanese Jew who had lived in Chicago described his ups and downs in business as follows:

> First I was in peddling. I was ashamed to knock on [the] door. . . . Then I was a package and stock boy in a tailor shop. Then I start to learn [the] design and cutting business for ladies and children. . . . 1925—big strike. I become "policeman" to protect myself. Next year I went to Lebanon for my health for a year and I lost my business in Chicago. I come back to America and work in manufacturing ladies wear up to 1932. I bought land in Israel in 1925 and I went back in 1932 and lost land. I start to work as workingman up to 1940. Then I went back into business—sportswear. 1947 I go back to Lebanon for my health. 1948—I come back. . . . I stay in Chicago for two years and dissolve my business. In 1950, I go to New York.

Several Syrian families left the lingerie business and went into other lines of trade, similar to those of Syrians elsewhere, such as importation of household linens and later the sale of infantwear. Some families have continued in those lines of trade. These businesses involve Syrians in other cities, and lines of communication between the Chicago Syrians and others continue.

Some Syrians, however, went into other occupations. One became a bus driver. Others became professional soldiers, car dealers, corporate executives, and lawyers. Some who remain in the traditional lines of trade now have shops in the suburbs, while a few have maintained traditional linen and tourist shops in downtown Chicago. The newest Sephardic congregation in the Chicago area was founded by Eli Abadi, a Mexican-born Syrian Jew. He is a rabbi who also decided to go medical school. Before he came to Chicago, he had been the spiritual leader of a Syrian Sephardi minyān that met in an Ashkenazi synagogue building in Bell Harbor on Long Island.[13] When he came to Chicago for his medical studies, he found that he lived far from the nearest Sephardi synagogue. He met some other Jews of Sephardi origin, from places such as Israel or North Africa. Through them he found there was interest in starting a congregation. They put up notices in supermarkets and elsewhere and rented space in an Ashkenazi synagogue. The congregants came from a variety of backgrounds, including at least one Ashkenazi who wanted to pray among Sephardim. Even though Abadi returned to New York City after a year, the congregation continues. By 1996. the congregation rented its own space.

While the Syrian Jews do not form a major presence in Chicago, they have played significant roles. In addition, the situation of Sephardi Jews in Chicago also shows the problems that Sephardim have had in maintaining their particular form of Judaism in North America.

Academics, Bohemians, and other Rebels

Those who are alienated from the Syrian community in Brooklyn and Deal often move out of town. They often have rebelled against the constraints of the Syrian community in a number of ways, including rejection of commercial occupations, rejection of orthopraxy, and intermarriage with Ashkenazim or Gentiles. Several such individuals have become doctors, lawyers, and academics. One is the poet Jack Marshall. He is the only Jew whose work is included in an anthology of Arab-American poetry.

That anthology includes a brief biography. His father was born in Baghdad and immigrated to the United States via Manchester. His mother was of Syrian origin. He was born in Brooklyn in 1937. He worked in his father's business while studying literature at Brooklyn College and for a while after he graduated. Then he left the community, first by working on a freighter and then as an advertising copy editor in New York. After he left New York, he worked at a variety of jobs, including house painting, as a longshoreman, and managing a clothing store. He moved to San Francisco in 1967. In 1960, he had married another poet, Kathleen Fraser, with whom he had a son. He had published eight books of poetry by 1993 and had written several plays. Jewish and Middle Eastern themes abound in his work.

Stanley Sultan, a native of Brooklyn, went to Cornell in 1945, when he was seventeen. He claims that he was the first Syrian Jew to attend college outside of New York City. He became a literary critic and professor of English at Clark University in Worcester and has resided in Boston. His novel, *Rabbi,* is discussed in chapter 10. As in the works of Marshall and some younger authors descended from Aleppan Jews, the exotic nature of Syrian identity is discussed in his work.[14]

Continued Ties with Brooklyn

The out-of-towners sometimes expressed mixed feelings about their economic success. One said that they had been "chicken" about returning to

New York. If they had returned, they might be much more wealthy than they are now. Still, the competition in New York is much more fierce than it is out of town.

They also adjusted to a less ghettoized situation than those in New York City had. The New York City Syrians have lived in Jewishly dense neighborhoods. Those elsewhere found themselves in mixed neighborhoods. They might have Gentiles living next door or they might become friendly with non-Jews on the block. They were much less isolated. It is not surprising that at least one such Jew of Syrian origin was a leading figure in the United Way campaign of his community.

First- and second-generation out-of-towners, especially those in New England and the Middle Atlantic states, often had close ties to Brooklyn. After all, New York City was only a few hours away by car or train. Frequent circumcisions, bar mitzvahs, and weddings in the growing Syrian families provided the occasion for many visits. Through such visits those born in places like Niagara Falls, Bar Harbor, or Atlantic City could get acquainted with their Bensonhurst or Flatbush cousins.

Getting to know the Aleppan way of life, however, could be a negative as well as a positive experience. One woman who was born and raised out of town reported that she always disliked the princely fashion in which Syrian women served their menfolk. When the time came for her to go to college, she insisted on going away from home and living on campus. On the other hand, some out of town women, despite Americanization, married into Brooklyn families and accommodated themselves to the more restricted ways of "Aleppo-in-Flatbush." An example is Rachel Cohen, who was raised in Providence and who went to Syracuse University before marrying a Brooklynite.[15]

Since most families in the first and second generations were in Syrian-linked businesses, these visits were related to work. If one was in infantwear, for instance, one might make contact with Aleppo-owned infantwear dealers and manufacturers. The same was true of those who owned shops selling lace, household linens, and imported electronics. Thus visits to New York City could serve more than one purpose. Third-, fourth-, and fifth-generation Syrians from New York who have moved out of town generally continue to visit their families in Brooklyn and Deal. This is their primary contact. One who is single may find that relatives with whom they had distant contacts in the past may try to fix them up with Syrians of the opposite sex who live outside of the main Syrian communities. It is not surprising, however, that those in Brooklyn may often feel that those who were brought up "out of town" are not really "Syrian" or S-Y.[16]

Resorts have always been important for the out-of-towners, since Syrians would gather there during the off-season. I recall visiting Bradley Beach in 1958 and meeting a man who had a store in Milwaukee.

Resorts in the area north of Miami Beach serve such a purpose today. One such place is Hallandale. Many Jews, both Syrians and others, own apartments in the condominiums there. They occupy them primarily during the period from December to April. The Syrians who go there include New Yorkers and out-of-towners from New England, the Midwest, and Latin America. Since their numbers are large enough, a Sephardic minyān is held each Sabbath, and they are able to celebrate holidays, like Purim, together. Ties between old acquaintances are renewed.

In this setting, the Syrian Sephardim find some aspects of their situation in North America comes to the fore. There is some tension between the Sephardim and the Ashkenazim. The latter find the former somewhat exotic and do not fully accept them. The New Yorkers, in particular, do not interact much with them, although the out-of-towners are more outgoing. The latter also find that they have in some ways grown apart from those who never left "Aleppo-in-Flatbush" or "in-Deal." Since long vacations in such winter resorts are more for the middle-aged and the elderly, the younger offspring of Syrians who grew up outside of the metropolitan area are less likely to participate in such ethnic renewal. They are less likely to be involved in international ethnic networks.

In general, the unique resilience and cohesion of the Brooklyn and Deal communities do not spill over to the out-of-towners. While some maintain their specialization in Syrian lines of trade, many do not. They are much more like other American Jews in their general orientation, with the strengths and weaknesses shown by this Jewry. Still, as individuals, many have contributed to their local communities.

CHAPTER 10

BROOKLYN'S SYRIAN SEPHARDIM IN THE 1990s: DIVERSIFICATION AND ETHNIC PERSISTENCE

BY WALTER P. ZENNER AND MARK KLIGMAN

SIGNIFICANCE AND BACKGROUND

This chapter describes aspects of the Syrian Sephardic community of the New York metropolitan area in the 1990s. By "metropolitan area," we mean something much larger than the "Standard Metropolitan Area" used in censuses, since we include Syrian permanent and summer residents of the Monmouth County, New Jersey, area. This area includes Deal and Bradley Beach. The chapter concentrates on changes in the community since the early 1960s. While we describe this community as "Syrian-Sephardic," one part of its diversification has been the increasing numbers of Sephardic immigrants into the community from Egypt, Lebanon, Israel, and Latin America. Many immigrants from these places, like the Brooklyn Syrians, are also one or two generations removed from Syria.[1]

Longtime residents and their descendants remain distinct from these Sephardic newcomers, as well as from Ashkenazic and non-Jewish residents. What "Syrianness" means in this situation is not always clear, since an increasing number of individuals are of mixed ancestry and references to Aleppo, Damascus, and other Middle Eastern locales are infrequent, except among recent immigrants. Still, Syrian Sephardim are perceived and see themselves as distinct.

In the early 1960s, the Syrian Sephardic community was more concentrated in a few locales than it became in the 1990s. Most businesses were located in New York City, particularly near Times Square, but also in other areas, including Union Square (14th Street), Harlem, and the Upper West Side. Infantwear and the importation of Asian electronics were common specialties. Most continued to live in Brooklyn, particularly in Bensonhurst, Mapleton Park, and Sea Beach. Many others moved in the 1950s to the Ocean Parkway area (Flatbush/Gravesend). In less than half a century after their arrival in America they had prospered greatly, and other changes were taking place.

What is significant about the Syrian Sephardim in the 1990s is that they represent a prosperous ethnic group which is not assimilating into the mainstream elite of American or world society. Unlike others, such as the Ḥasidim, Syrian Jews maintain their separate existence without distinctive dress. They are acculturated in terms of the language they speak on the street and the clothes they wear. Social and familial insularity is maintained with outer assimilation in fashion and entertainment. We examine factors that contribute to this separateness, such as the level or depth of religious practice or Arab musical practices.[2] What follows is a description of Brooklyn Syrians' residences, schooling options, occupations, interaction with non-Syrians, and religious orientations.

The theme that characterizes the period since 1960 is a continuance of ethnic persistence, but the community is marked by diversification in a number of realms.

Residence: Movement Out

Deal

In the 1950s, most Syrian Jews in the New York City area continued to live in two Brooklyn neighborhoods: Bensonhurst and Flatbush/Gravesend. By the late 1970s, a substantial number of families had become permanent residents of Monmouth County, particularly Deal. The migration in that direction had been preceded by the use of Bradley Beach, south of Asbury Park, as the locus of Syrian summer homes, as noted in chapter 9.

Deal, which is the primary center of the New Jersey community, was once a place for summer cottages for wealthy German Jews. It once had and still has the appearance of a place like Newport, Rhode Island. Quite sumptuous mansions, especially near the beach, are now owned by Syrian Jews. Many Syrian families live in nearby West Deal, South Deal, and Longbranch. A few still live in or go for the summer to Bradley Beach. The business center for the area is on Norwood Avenue in Deal. This is where the Synagogue of Deal is located. The area includes several restaurants and food stores, as well as other businesses that serve this community.

The cost of living in Deal, especially for housing, is somewhat higher than in Brooklyn, though this may be offset by lower New Jersey taxes and other costs of living. The movement out of Brooklyn to Deal has been gradual. Some maintain two residences, one in Deal and another in Brooklyn. During the week these people reside in Brooklyn, with easy access to Syrian-Jewish schools, such as the Magen David Yeshiva, for their children. On the weekends, they live in Deal. As the schools and synagogues in Deal have taken on a more active and permanent role, some people are choosing to live in Deal full time. Retirees have been attracted to Deal as well. In addition, the former summer resort of Bradley Beach has been replaced by the newer areas to the north as sites for Syrian Jews' summer homes. Gradual movement out of Bradley Beach and to Deal has developed. As of the summer of 1995, there was still a synagogue in Bradley Beach, but it looked somewhat old and rundown, especially when compared with the newer and more solid-looking synagogues in Deal.[3]

Other Suburbs and Manhattan

Some Syrian Jews lived outside of Brooklyn in the 1950s. These included some who were disaffected from the community. Others wanted to live near to their places of work or wanted to live in the suburbs. Like out-of-towners (see chapter 9), these individuals did not have a close interaction with the community. They were less subject to scrutiny than were those who lived in Bensonhurst or Flatbush, where social affiliations and religious practices would be common knowledge. Several families have moved out after their children have completed high school and/or married. Some have chosen a more suburban lifestyle and have not felt there has been any advantage to living in Brooklyn other than school for their children.

This trend has grown. Substantial numbers now live in Manhattan, as well as in Bell Harbor, Westchester, and other suburban areas. They include people who are somewhat removed from the community, such as those married to Ashkenazim. They also include some Syrian Jews who immigrated to the United States from overseas and have never lived in Brooklyn or Deal. One professional who was born in Brooklyn but does not live there currently divided them into "exiles," who had left the "reservation" (Brooklyn/Deal, which Joseph Sutton called "Aleppo-in-Flatbush" and "Aleppo-in-Deal"), and "transplants" (from outside the United States). An example of a transplant is Yvonne Tabboush, who was born in Manchester and has worked for United Nations agencies. She has generally lived on the Upper East Side.[4]

A Manhattan Syrian *minyān* has been meeting in the Fifth Avenue Synagogue, an Orthodox congregation on the Upper East Side. It is a small gathering of between twenty and thirty men. According to one participant, most are Syrians in their twenties to thirties who temporarily live in Manhattan for work or social purposes, particularly while they are single. Others live permanently in Manhattan, such as a divorced lawyer. When these men marry, they tend to move back to Brooklyn. Unmarried Syrian women also live in Manhattan. They find the circumstances there less restrictive than in Brooklyn, where there is little room for women in their late twenties and older.

Changes in the Brooklyn Neighborhoods

The center of Syrian Jewish communal activity has quite markedly shifted in the period from 1950 to the 1990s. Presently the Ocean Parkway/Kings Highway area serves as the main center. Some schools and synagogues continue to exist in Bensonhurst, such as the Magen David Yeshiva, which is a short ten- to fifteen-minute ride from Flatbush. Schools in Flatbush include the Flatbush Yeshivah (presently estimated at 50 percent Syrian and 50 percent Ashkenazic) located at the western end of Flatbush at Avenue J; the Sephardic High School at Avenue R; and Yeshivah Ateret Torah, a more strictly observant yeshiva located close to Kings Highway. Other smaller yeshivot are located between Avenue J and Kings Highway on Ocean Parkway or Coney Island Avenue. An elaborate private busing system for children connects the residents to the schools throughout Flatbush and between Flatbush and Bensonhurst.

The Kings Highway shopping area from McDonald Avenue to Coney Island Avenue, covering the length of five blocks on either side of Ocean Parkway, includes a variety of stores: *glatt kosher* (ultra-kosher) markets and restaurants, *shomer Shabbat* (closed on the Jewish Sabbath) bakeries, Middle Eastern specialties of dry goods and foods, travel agencies, beauty shops, discount stores, children's clothing stores, party stores, wedding planning boutiques (offering gowns, photographs, and the like), and shops offering decorative gifts. Proprietors and salespeople in these stores include Syrians, other Sephardim, and some Ashkenazim. Some are immigrants from Israel. Shops offer free delivery to anywhere in Flatbush and Deal, thus connecting the community over a great distance.[5]

In terms of housing, Syrians have long preferred to live in one- or two-family houses, although many have lived in apartments. This pattern continues. Many families live in close proximity. A married sibling may live in an attached house or separate residence on a different floor. People who own homes still seek to expand or renovate them. Often this renovation may include gutting or demolishing the previous house built in the 1940s–1950s and replacing it with a newly constructed, more modern, and more spacious new residence. Zoning and expansion of existing homes is an issue that involves Syrian Jews in local politics. Issues pertaining to pending legislation are occasionally discussed by a community member during Sabbath services. Often task forces are formed to maintain contact with city council members.

In the past, Syrian Jewish influence has been limited, because many Syrian Jews did not register to vote or contribute to election campaigns. On the other hand, some individuals have participated actively in politics. Robert Chira, a Harvard Law School graduate, was active in Reform Democratic politics in the early 1970s. He ran for Congress from a Brooklyn district in a three-way primary and lost. Like William Haddad in the 1960s, Ashkenazic voters did not recognize him as a Jew, because of his surname. This was in spite of the fact that he was running in a district with a substantial number of Syrian Jewish residents. He did gain some Italian votes because his family name sounded Italian.[6]

David Eliahu Cohen became involved in local politics during the 1960s. He was no longer a retailer, as he had been beforehand, and his real estate business gave him some leisure time. He was opposed to the Vietnam War and was also opposed to the local machine, so he ran for district leader. He also did not win, but later he ran the campaign of Sebastian Leone in his bid to become Brooklyn borough president. When Leone won, Cohen became his deputy.[7]

In the 1990s some Brooklyn Syrian Jews have gotten involved in the local community school boards, which were established in the 1970s as part of a plan to decentralize the public school system. Dr. Eddie Sutton served on such a school board in District 21. In 1996, a group calling itself the "Sephardic Voters League" made an effort to elect a slate in other school districts. It appealed to Jewish voters, including students and parents in Sephardic and Ashkenazic day schools in the area.[8] In any case, this school board election campaign illustrates how school decentralization in New York has given well-organized blocks of voters an important voice in the public schools, even when many of those voting do not send their children to such schools. In Deal, Syrian Sephardic voters have been active enough to elect a Sephardic mayor. This is an indication of how important they have become in that Monmouth County community.

Secular and Religious Education

In the 1950s, most Syrian children still went to public school, although the number attending Jewish day schools was increasing. Since then, white, middle-class families have become disillusioned with the public schools in general. Today most Syrian families send their children to the Jewish day schools.

Since the 1960s, more and more Sephardim, especially men, have gone to New York City colleges for undergraduate education. Brooklyn College has been favored. In the 1980s, many young women went to Brooklyn College for a few years; some did not graduate, because they had married. The more venturesome went outside of Brooklyn or out of town. Some went to graduate school, again often in New York City, but also elsewhere. Syrian Jewish students have attended State University of New York campuses, New

York University, the University of Wisconsin, Chicago-area schools, and several Ivy League institutions, both as undergraduates and as graduate students.[9] Syrian men also attend Yeshiva University, which has a Sephardic program. Several leaders in the community, such as Rabbi Lieberman, who also teaches part time at his alma mater, were trained at Yeshiva University.

College has not been part of the general pattern among Syrian males. Kligman has observed that among Syrian Jews in their twenties and thirties in the 1990s, many of those who go into business get M.B.A.'s, sometimes after they have had experience in running a business. The desire of many second-generation immigrants who have built very successful businesses is to leave the business to a son who has an M.B.A. Others continue to feel that business school is a waste of time and money.

Touro College has been particularly attractive for some Syrian Jews. Touro is a Jewish-sponsored private college with campuses throughout New York City. It offers programs for those who are interested in combining college study and yeshiva learning while staying in New York City. The main campus is in midtown Manhattan. A branch of Touro College is located across the street from the Flatbush Yeshiva on Avenue J, providing convenient access to those who do not want to leave Brooklyn.

Another significant difference since the 1950s is the custom of spending a year in Israel after high school. This is a very common practice for Orthodox Ashkenazic men and women. Many who go to Israel for a year can combine religious and college study by receiving college credit for their studies in Israel. For Syrians, the practice of attending school in Israel for a year is an increasing phenomenon. Several schools in Israel have been designed to accommodate American Syrian students. Several older members of the community have commented that the practice of sending Syrian children to Israel has had a significant impact on the increase in religious observance. Many Syrian children come back to Brooklyn more "energized" in religious practice.

Occupations

In the 1950s the occupational distribution among Syrian Jews was relatively narrow, with only a few professionals. By the 1990s, the distribution of occupations was broader. Both within the community and among descendants of Syrian Jews from the Brooklyn community, people practice a wide variety of occupations. A small number of doctors and lawyers, in particular, are found in the community. There also are real estate agents, accountants, and chiropractors. Some of these occupations are reflected in the advertising in *Jewish IMAGE Family Magazine,* a monthly publication oriented to the Syrian Sephardic community in Brooklyn and Deal. While not all of the advertisers are Syrian Jews, some have Syrian-Sephardic surnames and they give us some sense of the diversification. They include financial planners, a mortgage agency, a confectionery, five dentists, and three physicians. Women are the proprietors of a number of businesses, as discussed in the following.[10] Individuals who are professionals or academics mention that their relatives still feel that they are not in sufficiently lucrative occupations.

Many close-out stores, once a Syrian specialty, are now in the hands of proprietors from other ethnic groups. Some Syrian Jews have moved from the close-out stores into the antique trade. Yet, many continue to work in areas where they are able to maintain their traditional privacy, keep their assets relatively liquid, and make easy profits.

Several companies that have a Syrian Jewish connection have been among the New York area's top privately held companies. In 1995, these included the Bonjour Group, a licensing company; Century 21 Department Stores; SDI Technologies; and A and E Specialty Shops. Jordache, headed by an Israeli, Joseph Nakash, was considered "Syrian" because Nakash has participated in the community and is of part-Ḥalebi descent. The Duane-Reade chain of drugstores was formerly owned by a Syrian Jew.

A Syrian Jewish businessman whose advertising for his company's spectacularly low prices made him a metropolitan-area celebrity was Edward Antar. His fall from grace was equally spectacular, as well as embarrassing to family and friends. He was convicted of stock fraud during a battle over control of the "Crazy Eddie" chain. He then became a fugitive in Israel before extradition to the United States. While the "Crazy Eddie" stores are no more, another chain called "The Wiz," owned by Syrian Jews, appeared in shopping malls outside the New York Metropolitan area as well as within it. In 1997, however, they were forced into bankruptcy and sold their stores.[11]

Another highly visible enterprise associated with a Syrian Jew is Republic National Bank, which has been headed by Edmond Safra. While Safra has relatives in the New York City area, he himself does not live in New York City, but in Geneva, while other family members are in Brazil and elsewhere. He has, however, contributed to various synagogues and other institutions in Brooklyn.[12]

Among the newer immigrants, many are not so affluent. If they have enterprises of their own, their businesses are likely to be more modest than those of the better-established residents. Some have run groceries and other service businesses serving the community.[13]

Despite the rewards for those who remain in the community and follow their parents into family enterprises, there have always been those who reject this pathway. One of them is the actor Dan Hedaya. His family expected him to enter its import-export business, but he fled Brooklyn as a teenager as a merchant seaman. He began acting in plays in college. A newspaper article quotes him: "I had to get away from the Syrian community, because it was asphyxiating to me. . . . Had I stayed I probably would have become a wealthy but very unhappy businessman importing stuff from Taiwan."[14]

Others leave the community for a while, but in the end return, after having experimented with other projects. David Cohen's son experimented with television production and teaching mountain climbing in the mid-1970s. His father described these activities as "foundering around, getting no place." By the late 1980s, this son had two stores in midtown Manhattan, a situation that satisfied his father.[15]

Women in this community characteristically marry in their late teens or early twenties. They often marry men who are ten or more years older. Since the community has prospered, stay-at-home wives often have little to occupy their time after their children have gone to school, especially if they can afford maids and other household help. In the early twentieth century, card-playing was apparently the major leisure time activity for women. Now exercise has come to play a role. Some drug abuse by these women has been reported.

There are indications of other preoccupations as well. Beginning with the *Victory Bulletin* in World War II through the *Parent-Teacher Organization Bulletin* of Magen David Yeshiva in the 1950s and *IMAGE* in the 1990s, we find that Syrian women have been quite active in voluntary group activities (see chapter 8). Women run many fund-raising activities, such as Chinese auctions. One woman interviewed by Joseph Sutton in 1983 described such fund-raising activity for the United Jewish Appeal. She had arranged a tennis tournament with only Syrian contestants at the Racquet Club in Deal, while also organizing a "huge flea market" in Brooklyn.

This woman, Rae Cohen, was born in Brooklyn, but she was not raised there. She grew up in Providence, Rhode Island, and went to Syracuse University (see chapter 9). After marriage to another Syrian Jew, she quit school and went to live in Brooklyn. She describes herself as an organizer. She helped organize a B'nai B'rith women's chapter that, she says, had 350 members at its height despite opposition from another women's group in the community. Part of the opposition came from those who did not want activities oriented outside the Syrian Sephardic community, where Syrian children might meet non-Syrians, even if they were Jewish. While her children went to public school, she helped organize an afternoon Hebrew school for girls. She herself went back to college as an adult, attending Brooklyn College. Her daughters include a graduate of the Wharton School of Business (University of Pennsylvania) and a lawyer.[16]

Advertisements and articles in *IMAGE* point to a number of women who have gone into business for themselves. The women who advertise in *IMAGE* include proprietors of stores, a psychotherapist, and real estate agents.[17] There are also some Syrian women who are doctors.

Undoubtedly women's activities have diversified, including opening small businesses. For some families whose means are relatively modest in this affluent community, the woman's income is necessary to maintain the expensive lifestyle. Most, however, continue to be full-time homemakers. Many men feel threatened by women who receive a higher education or go into business for themselves. Some women who have pursued higher education have left the community.[18]

New Immigrants

Since the 1950s, Lebanese, Israelis, Egyptians, Brazilians (and other South Americans), and "new Syrians" have immigrated into the community. Many of these Sephardic Jews, if not most, have some Syrian ancestry. Each group varies in size and in its "experience" before and after immigration to America. Except for the "new Syrians," these groups have formed congregations on the basis of the languages of the countries from which they came, as well as on the basis of other common experiences.

The Egyptian Jews are of particular interest. Many of the Egyptians living in Brooklyn immigrated after the Israeli War for Independence, especially after the Suez-Sinai War, when President Gamal Abd-el-Nasser expelled foreign nationals. Many, if not most, Egyptian Jews were nationals of countries other than Egypt. Most had French secular educations, and French for many was the domestic language of choice. While many of those who settled in Brooklyn had some Aleppan ancestry, they also were often descended from Jews of other origins.

As noted in chapter 4, Egyptian Jewry as it re-formed in the nineteenth century was a community of recent immigrants. Many of the Jews, while arriving poor in Egypt, had prospered. When the various defeats that Egypt faced under Farouk and Nasser redounded on them, they were forced to leave an often comfortable existence for a new exile, which has been called "the Second Exodus." The story of how these people left Egypt in the 1940s, 1950s, and 1960s has been a defining experience for them. In December 1997, a group of Egyptian Jews, aided by the Brooklyn-based Sephardic National Alliance, held a conference at Columbia University on the history of Jews in and from Egypt.[19]

The congregation the Egyptian Jews founded in Brooklyn is called "Ahavah ve-Aḥvah" after a synagogue and school in Cairo founded by Aleppan Jews. In 1994 they formed a "Historical Society for Jews from Egypt." At the same time, the orthodoxy of the Syrian community in Brooklyn has affected them as well, and many have become more observant than they were in Egypt.

There has always been a circulation of Syrian-Sephardic Jews between the various communities of Latin America and Israel, as noted in previous chapters. After all, Rabbi Jacob Kassin, the longtime *ḥakhām bāshī* (chief rabbi) of the community came to Brooklyn from Jerusalem. Eliezer al-Beg, who was cantor of the Damascene synagogue, Ahi-ezer, for many years, was an Iraqi-born Jew who immigrated from Jerusalem.[20] This continues to be the case today. Rabbis Abraham and Joseph Harari-Raful are both Jerusalem-born Ḥalebim, while Rabbi Alouf, who was the high school principal at the Magen David Yeshiva and rabbi at the Egyptian synagogue, is of Iraqi descent and immigrated from Israel.[21] It is also obvious from Alouf's resumé and from other biographical data of community residents that the community contains many who are not necessarily Aleppan or even Syrian by origin. Some of these non-Syrians are leaders of the community.

Interaction with Non-Syrians

Obviously Syrian Jews interact with people who are not members of the community. Interaction with non-Jews occurs in the neighborhood, where Syrian Jews have non-Jewish neighbors, and in the business sphere, where there are clients and employees who are not Jewish. Even synagogues have non-Jewish employees. One congregation, for instance, has an Arabic-speaking Muslim caretaker. Like other affluent New Yorkers, most Syrians employ domestic servants. These employees come from a variety of different backgrounds. A fair number of Syrian Jewish women are able to speak Spanish with their employees. In other ways, their interaction with these employees has all the ambiguities of relations between employers and employees. As will be noted in the following, non-Jewish Arab musicians frequently play at Syrian-Jewish parties.

Ashkenazic Jews are still one of the most salient reference groups for Syrian Jews. This is especially true when one focuses on Jewish institutions. Several rabbis and other teachers at Syrian day schools are Ashkenazim. At Yeshiva of Flatbush, separate religious services are held for Ashkenazic and Syrian students. Syrian children there are aware of non-Syrian life and religious practices because of their interaction with Ashkenazic students. One Ashkenazic rabbi who has been with the community is Rabbi Abraham Hecht, rabbi emeritus of Shaʿare Zion, the largest Syrian synagogue. According to someone who grew up at Shaʿare Zion, Hecht has been very successful and is regarded "practically Syrian" (see following discussion). Similarly, Rabbi Zevulun Lieberman of Congregation Beth Torah is an important leader in the Syrian community. Mark Kligman has suggested that the political concerns of the rabbis are not necessarily those of the laity. In Kligman's fieldwork at Syrian synagogues he found it common to hear Ashkenazic rabbis who drew from their Ashkenazic rabbinic heritage. The Syrian respect for rabbis transcends their concern about rabbis' ethnic origins. Ashkenazic-born rabbis in the Syrian community are given respect and honored as religious and spiritual leaders, but this does not necessarily result in lay political activity. In addition to the rabbis as spiritual leaders, Ashkenazic religious influence is important in schools, since many Ashkenazim teach in Syrian schools.

It is also clear that older Syrian Jews, like their Ashkenazic counterparts, are attracted to the Likud approach, which involves distrust of Arab motivations in the Arab-Israeli peace process, and to groups that give support to this position. Sephardic immigrants from Israel often favor Likud and similar parties. Younger Syrians generally favor this orientation, too, but are less involved and less informed politically.

Brooklyn rabbis have been involved with local and international politics, with mixed results. One rabbi regularly spends his summers teaching at a yeshiva in Judaea-Samaria (the West Bank). Upon his return to Brooklyn, he has frequently commented in his sermons on Israel's right to retain the land rather than relinquish territory for peace with Arabs. The congregation is mixed in their support of this rabbi. In regards to local politics, a rabbi was seen as overstepping the boundary of propriety by endorsing and campaigning for a Syrian councilman in Deal. Various politicians do come to Syrian Sephardic synagogues, but they generally do not campaign directly.

The rabbi who has been most involved in both local and international politics is Rabbi Abraham Hecht. His political statements gained prominence in the news in 1995, after the assassination of Israeli Prime Minister Yitzhak Rabin. In addition to being the rabbi at Shaʿare Zion, he was a leader in the Rabbinical Alliance, whose members might be described as "moderately *ḥaredi*." This organization has been fairly active in endorsing candidates. The Rabbinical Alliance of America issued an opinion in June 1995 that ceding land in Eretz Yisrael was by rabbinic law tantamount to a capital offense. After Rabin's assassination, this statement was seen as a justification for that act. Calls for Hecht's removal as rabbi of Shaʿare Zion were published in both Jewish and general newspapers. During the late fall of 1995, after the Rabin assassination, the synagogue and community was in turmoil. Hecht was not present at the synagogue through the end of 1995, but he returned in early 1996 and spoke from the *bima* (podium) at Shaʿare Zion. Hecht claimed that he had never intended that Rabin be assassinated and that in any case he had retracted the call for execution prior to the killing of Rabin. He retired as rabbi emeritus. Both camps (pro and con to Hecht) have claimed victory.[22] This incident was an embarrassment for the community and demonstrated how the attention of the press can be a curse.

In Manhattan and in suburban communities such as Bell Harbor and Westchester, Syrian Sephardim interact much more frequently with Ashkenazim. Some of the Syrians are, in fact, individuals who have left the community. For example, "Morris Beyda" went away for medical school, returned for a residency, and then left New York City to practice in Pennsylvania. While away from New York, he began to explore the American secular world.

For a long period, most of his social ties were with non-Jews. As he matured, he realized that he wanted to raise his children as Jews. He began to observe the dietary laws and holidays, although he was not fully *shomer shabbat* (strictly observant of the Sabbath). Because of the difficulties of being a single Jewish person where he lived, he began to come to the New York metropolitan area on weekends to socialize, joining a singles group in a Conservative synagogue. In that synagogue, most of his fellow worshippers are Ashkenazim. He still, however, prefers to go to Syrian synagogues for the holidays, because he finds that the music there speaks to him more strongly.

Many of the Syrians who live in Manhattan and the suburbs are married to Ashkenazic spouses. Some Syrians attend Ashkenazic congregations. In recent years, however, Sephardic Jews, often led by Syrians, have formed separate *minyānim,* as was noted with regard to those living Manhattan. Often the practice is to hold a separate service in unused rooms of a Sephardic day school or an Orthodox Ashkenazic synagogue building. Among the rabbis who serve these small communities are Rabbi Michael Serells, director of the Sephardic Studies Program at Yeshiva University, and Eli Abady, who has led such groups in Bell Harbor and Chicago.

Certainly since the 1950s, a substantial number of intermarriages with Ashkenazim have taken place (see chapter 9). Social interaction with Ashkenazim occurs in the Flatbush Yeshivah, through study in Israel, at college, and just by living in the same milieu. Some men in their forties told Kligman that when they went to Brooklyn College in the 1970s and 1980s they participated in Hillel events that included Israeli dancing. Two men met their Ashkenazic wives in this way.

Syrian girls who attend the ultra-Orthodox *(ḥaredi)* Ateret Torah School (which is like a *ḥaredi* Ashkenazic school for girls) are taught to marry a rabbi or someone who learns. These girls may marry "religious" Ashkenazic men. Several Syrian rabbis in their thirties and forties have Ashkenazic wives. This may be because the more religious and less materialistic existence of a rabbi's wife may not have appealed to Syrian women ten to twenty years ago.

Whereas in the 1950s secularized Ashkenazim were the more significant reference group for Syrian Sephardim in Brooklyn, now Orthodox Ashkenazim have grown in importance. More and more of the secularized, non-Orthodox Jews have left the Five Boroughs for the suburbs. On the other hand, the most conservative Orthodox groups, such as the Ḥasidim, have grown in numbers. This is especially true in the Borough Park area of Brooklyn, but it is also evidenced by the many yeshivot and the Orthodox institutions on and near Ocean Parkway. In addition, as the white population of New York has deserted the public schools, Orthodox day schools have grown.

Religious Orientations

The pursuit of monetary gain in this community is quite apparent. One force spurring Syrian Jews in this direction is their perceived need to emulate their neighbors in conspicuous consumption, especially in lavish celebrations of rites, such as weddings and bar mitzvahs. In some ways, this helps define one as a Syrian Jew. Religious institutions, including synagogues and schools, have remained central foci of the Syrian community. The synagogues are well attended.

The religious observance of Syrians varies. Based on his fieldwork in Brooklyn in the late 1950s and early 1960s, Zenner designated the range of religious observance as follows: atheists and rebels (who do not affiliate and many of whom live in Manhattan, outside the metropolitan area); indifferent or casually observant; conscientiously Orthodox; and ultra-Orthodox (see chapters 8 and 9). While such variation appears in American Ashkenazic and Sephardic communities as well, there have generally been more who adhere to traditional Jewish practice among the Syrians. This categorization may also be used to describe the present level of religious observance, with each level becoming more intense than it was in the past. The *ḥaredi* (ultra-Orthodox), largely young Syrian rabbis trained at Ashkenazic yeshivot (in this instance, advanced centers of religious learning), are not part of the mainstream, but their influence is increasing. One wonders if Sutton's description of normative religious practice in "Aleppo-in-Flatbush" as "middle-of-the-road Orthodoxy" will continue into the next generation.[23]

For some in recent times, the initial purpose of synagogue attendance, as it was for early immigrants, is an opportunity for socialization. However, in recent years a more substantial religious desire motivates many younger members of the community to attend and participate in synagogue services. Several observers of the community note that all Syrian synagogues are affiliated with Orthodox organizations. According to Daniel J. Elazar, members of the community take great pride in their "religious orthodoxy . . . different from the more mainstream Reform and Conservative wings of American Jewry." He notes that the Syrian community is the most religious of the Sephardic communities in America.[24]

A factor that influences religious observance is the religious organization of the community. Each synagogue is led by a senior rabbi who has a great degree of autonomy in decision making. For example, Aleppo synagogues follow their own rite, as do the Damascus, Egyptian, and Lebanese synagogues. However, major issues that affect the community kashrut (religious dietary laws), marriage laws, and educational goals of the schools are decided by one organized religious court, the Sephardic Rabbinical Council, which is led by Chief Rabbi Saul Kassin. His father, Rabbi Jacob Kassin, who died on December 9, 1994, is credited with guiding the growth of the community.[25]

Syrian synagogues in Brooklyn have acquired many characteristics common to American synagogues, as noted in chapter 8. These structural changes include professionalization of the positions of the religious leaders rather than leadership that is lay-driven; formality and organization of the synagogue service, including the wearing of a robe by the cantor; and a prepared sermon by the rabbi. The black hats worn by rabbis reflect the influence of Ashkenazic religious observers.

Some people in the community still use traditional forms of magic and medicine. This supplements the reliance on modern medicine. Such practices include special prayers for ill family members and amulets from saintly rabbis that are used for cures. The teaching of the kabbalah (Jewish mystical literature) is part of the religious curriculum in Brooklyn. This teaching marks the continuity of traditional Ḥalebi religious life.[26]

Among New York City Orthodox Jews, stricter observance of the tradition has become the norm. For instance, the Flatbush Yeshiva (a middle-of-the-road day school) used to have cheerleaders with short skirts; now this is unheard of.[27] This follows the trend of Orthodox in America in general. The rightward flow of Orthodoxy is attributed to the influence of culturally conservative educational institutions, the tolerance in American society of ethnic diversity, and a partial rejection of secular values, as well as the influence of militantly Orthodox immigrants from Europe.

Likewise in the Syrian community, men and women are educated Judaically, which has an impact on their parents. The observance of religious traditions of the Syrian community overall may be increasing, but the change is not as drastic as it has been in the Ashkenazic Orthodox community. In the Syrian community, "*ḥaredi*" leadership has come from rabbis trained in Ashkenazic yeshivas or from immigrant rabbis from Israel who belonged to the militantly conservative branch of Sephardic rabbis there (see chapters 6 and 8). The trend toward more stringent observance is not solely a reaction to the Ashkenazic *ḥaredim,* but also reflects a Ḥalebi strain of militant conservatism. As in Israel (see chapter 6), some older members of the community see this "black hat" trend as a threat to the way of life that they have developed in Brooklyn.[28]

In the late 1990s, synagogues provide more classes for learning classical texts and fewer social gatherings than in the past. The use of the synagogue for theatrical productions, common in the 1950s and 1960s, is no longer practiced. Some in the community have commented that the increase in Judaic classes at the largest Syrian synagogues (Shaʿare Zion, Ahi Ezer, Bet Torah) has resulted from the influence of the more "religious" institutions, such as Ateret Torah. Many of the older members of the community, men in their seventies and eighties, express concern that the active young men in the synagogue prefer stricter religious practices. The moderate approach to religion in life is being challenged.

The more militant approach to religious observance represents resistance to various aspects of Syrian communal and religious life and to the general American milieu, particularly what has been called "materialism." There is no doubt that the Syrian Jewish community is a very affluent one and that to some extent it has gloried in and enjoyed its wealth. Some ambivalence does exist with regard to this, however, as when one girl admonished another girl who was boasting about her earrings that she should be thankful to her parents for these expensive objects.[29]

The *ḥaredi* approach of Ateret Toṛah and the earlier secular revolt are not the only reactions to such spiritual problems. Some Syrians have joined Ashkenazic groups that serve their needs. One of the larger synagogues has also opened itself to meetings and services for a smaller group, which resembles the groups known as *ḥavurot* in Conservative and Reform synagogues, at least in providing a more intimate setting for religious expression.

There is increasing awareness that drug abuse and addiction to gambling affect a significant number of men and women in the community, as they affect Americans in general. There have been rumors of affairs between women and their male tennis coaches. This has led to a rabbinic ban on women taking tennis lessons from male coaches, which has been obeyed. This is an indication of rabbinic authority. Another approach to such problems has been to set up support groups, especially dealing with drug abuse, at the Sephardic Community Center. Still another way to address such issues has been the appeal for greater observance of Jewish tradition.[30]

The need for specialization in certain synagogue functions, such as Torah reading and leading prayers, is growing since few lay members of the community are capable of serving in these capacities. As a result, cantors of Middle Eastern backgrounds from Israel were brought into Brooklyn during the 1990s and retrained as cantors for the Brooklyn Syrian congregations. Earlier precedents for this include the work of Eliezer al-Beg, a native of Baghdad and trained in Jerusalem who was cantor at Ahi-Ezer in the 1950s and 1960s.[31]

The decree against marriages between Jews and converts to Judaism is a mark of Syrian Jewry in the United States. The decree has been promulgated several times since 1935. This policy is consistent with the background of "militant conservatism" of Aleppan rabbis, although it deviates from Jewish laws, which treat sincerely motivated converts as members of the communities in most respects. In 1988, Sutton claimed that between 1935 and 1987 the number of such marriages with Gentiles and converts averaged three per year, but in 1987 the number rose to fifteen and thus a reaffirmation of the ban was called for. As pointed out in chapter 9, the full impact of this proclamation is felt in the Brooklyn and Deal communities. It has much less force outside of these communities.[32] Some members of the community in America and abroad realize the limits of this decree. Yet other members still send copies of the ban to individuals who appear to be having relationships with Gentiles as a warning of consequences, even if these individuals live in Manhattan, Boston, or Buffalo.

There is a difference between refusal to accept adult converts and acceptance of *gerim qetanim* (young child converts). The Sephardic Rabbinical Council makes a distinction between adult conversions, which are not accepted, and *ger qatan* (child convert; singular of *gerim qetanim*). The latter pertains to a child adopted by a member of the community. After the child is adopted the parents bring the child to the rabbinic council for conversion. The child grows up in the community and is accepted.

Efforts at "Cultural" as Well as "Ethnic" Persistence

In certain sectors of life, efforts are made to preserve the cultural heritage of a Middle Eastern Jewry. This is particularly true with regard to the synagogue liturgy. The number of prayer books specifically reproducing Aleppan liturgical practice has increased in the last fifteen years. The desire of communities to have their community practices reflected in printed form is a direct expression of their identity. While the Aleppan liturgical text does not vary greatly from the Spanish-Portuguese liturgy used by most Sephardim in the United States and Britain, Syrians have recorded their own specific practices. The specific points in the liturgy that they highlight with musical elaboration differ from other Sephardic practices, and thus Syrian prayer books reflect their liturgical performance practices. An example follows for those familiar with the traditional morning service. Syrian cantors begin chanting the morning service with the prayer *nishmat kol ḥai* (the soul of every living thing). Two portions following this text and immediately preceding the *qaddish* (the prayer that in this case marks the boundary between the preliminary prayers and the main morning service), the prayers *shavʿat ʿaniyyim* and *Kel ha-hodaʾot,* receive musical elaboration with congregational singing. To facilitate this liturgical performance practice, these texts are indented in Syrian-printed prayer books.[33]

In addition to the use of *maqāmāt* (Arabic musical modes) in synagogue services, certain Arabic-style songs continue to be used in the synagogue and at ceremonies marking circumcisions, weddings, and bar mitzvahs, which will be discussed in the following. These *pizmonim,* originally composed by Syrian cantors who put Hebrew texts to preexisting Arabic music, are similar to the *baqashot* that are sung in Israeli synagogues (see chapter 6).[34]

Another example of cultural persistence lies in the area of cuisine. Cookbooks and articles in various newspapers help keep such traditions alive, as does the memory of particular dishes associated with certain holidays and seasons. This aspect is, however, as subject to change as any other. Thus the European *hamantashen* (triangular pastries generally eaten on the holiday of Purim) are now included in Syrian cookbooks, while some typical Syrian holiday dishes are omitted from the Syrian cookbook *Deal Delights.*[35]

With regard to Passover, there are some special nuances, since the Ashkenazic and Syrian-Sephardic views of what is permitted and prohibited differ. Ashkenazim extend the prohibition on eating bread and grains to include a category of foods called *qitniyot,* which includes legumes and rice. Syrian Sephardim permit these foods, especially rice. The maintenance of this difference thus forms an important boundary between Ashkenazic and Syrian-Sephardic Jewry.[36]

Seasons and *Simḥot/Ḥaflas*

The insularity of the Syrian community can be seen in the strong social ties of family and close friends. Vacations are taken with these family friends for both short getaways and longer and more exotic travel. Those who remain in the community keep this constant companionship, whether they travel to far-off places or remain in the New York City area. To those who wish to escape this, it may be stifling, but it also reinforces communal ties.[37]

Summer is a special season of enjoyment. Many who go to Deal as a center for summer activities lead a more leisurely life. Much of the activity is on the beach, including swimming on the Sabbath. Many of the rabbis are critical of this period of relaxation in their sermons. Perhaps the relaxation of the summer provides a balance to the religious and social intensity of Brooklyn. Some congregations in Brooklyn have less formal services during the summer: fewer congregants are in attendance, no rabbis are present, and there are no sermons. The services are held in a more intimate setting. It should be noted that the newly "ultra-Orthodox" segment of the community rejects such laxity and some of these people no longer vacation in Deal.[38]

Social occasions often center around joyous celebrations. With close ties to extended families often living nearby in Brooklyn, *simḥot* (happy occasions, usually rites of passage) are primary social opportunities for members of the community. *Brīt mīlahs* (ritual circumcisions), birth welcomings for girls, bar mitzvahs, engagement parties, weddings, and anniversary celebrations are commonly held throughout the year. Some members of the community remark that *simḥot* are constant in the community. Thus, planning, preparing, and participating in joyous celebrations is an ongoing activity. Much of this activity is organized by the women of the family. Such events also bring together relatives who observe Judaism in a wide variety of ways, from lax to stringent.

The music at these celebrations, like the food, reflects the cultural identity of the community. During a *brīt mīlah* several men may join to sing *pizmonim*. For a bar mitzvah, the celebration on a non-Sabbath day in or outside the synagogue typically caters to the tastes of young teenagers. A disc jockey plays a variety of music, including Top 40, Israeli, and occasionally Middle Eastern music. Weddings and anniversary parties feature live musicians playing a similar repertoire as at a bar mitzvah, in addition to ballroom dance music. Some weddings may include two bands, the second playing Middle Eastern music exclusively. Typically this occurs at the end of the evening. Private parties (*ḥafla* in Arabic) commonly include the use of Arabic musicians to play Middle Eastern music.

Rabbinical response to Arabic musicians varies. The primary objection is from rabbis of Ashkenazic descent who oppose the employment of non-Jewish musicians. Nevertheless, many in the community have a strong preference for Arabic music, which developed from their days in Aleppo and has been perpetuated in Brooklyn.[39]

The Sephardic Community Center as a Communal Arena

The Sephardic Community Center on Ocean Parkway is the culmination of a project that was originally begun in the 1940s in Bensonhurst. It is like other Jewish community centers in the United States. It has a gymnasium and sponsors athletic activities. It also has programs for age groups from the youngest to the elderly, including self-help groups. It sponsors "mild" cultural activities. In the mid-1980s, it was the host for the Sephardic Archives, which spurred interest in the history of the Syrian Sephardic community in Flatbush. In the 1980s, the Archives sponsored various cultural programs, including exhibits, concerts, lecture series, and conferences. In connection with these activities, research on a number of topics, including Syrian Jewish music and immigrant life, was begun.[40] In 1999, the Archives were still housed in the Sephardic Cultural Center, but it has not been as active.

The center, however, is subject to the community at large and to the rabbis in particular. For instance, in the early 1980s, center officials wanted to present the full mini-series of *Michel Ezra Safra and Sons,* which was the saga of an Aleppan family which had appeared on Israeli television. Plans were made to bring the author of the novel on which the series was based, Amnon Shamosh, to the center. This program, however, was squashed because of rabbinic opposition to sponsorship of an author who described sex explicitly in his work (although such portrayals are quite restrained in Shamosh's writing). Perhaps the opposition also viewed him suspiciously because he was an active member of a secular socialist kibbutz. Still, the existence of the Sephardic Community Center shows both the acculturation of Syrian Sephardim to American culture and their continued ethnic separation.

One way to understand the Syrian community in Brooklyn and Deal is to see it as similar to the increasingly Orthodox enclaves in the New York metropolitan area. The increasing orthopraxy of these enclaves has reinforced similar tendencies among Syrians. The Syrian Sephardic style may be seen as a variation of what is found among other Orthodox Jews. Other characteristics of these enclaves are the high cost of maintaining an Orthodox way of life and the affluence found in many, although not all, of these communities. Syrian Jews are upper-middle-class consumers and they maintain a "comfortable" lifestyle that has kept pace with suburban American standards. Thus, in addition to local synagogues and schools for the community, a separate culture has emerged that preserves social boundaries within a limited geographic area of a city and for a specific population.

Writing about and by Syrian Jews

Writings about Syrian Jews in New York City since the 1920s come from diverse sources, including newspapers and magazines. Articles in the *New York Times* deal with a variety of topics. Some articles present Syrian Jewry as another part of the diverse and colorful population of the city and metropolitan area. Such articles have dealt with holiday customs, especially holiday foods; the summer resorts of different New Yorkers including Syrian Jews in Deal: and Joseph Sutton as an author of books. Obituaries of community notables are descriptive, although those of the late Rabbi Jacob Kassin also conveyed an image of the community. News articles dealing with "Crazy Eddie's" travails did not mention the community, but articles about the controversy surrounding Rabbi Hecht and about the arrival of Syrian Jewish immigrants did cast light on the community, the former in an equivocal manner. In general, the community's image as portrayed by the press is of a somewhat exotic, close-knit enclave.[41]

The Anglo-Jewish press is similar in its treatment of the community. Some writers, most notably the columnist Ben G. Frank, were particularly intrigued by the community's apparent resistance to assimilation.[42] In fact, this was one of the main points made by Sutton in both *Magic Carpet: Aleppo-in-Flatbush* and *Aleppo Chronicles*. He expresses this in the subtitle to the latter work: "The Story of the Unique Sephardeem of the Ancient Near East—In Their Own Words."

Stanley Sultan's novel, *Rabbi: The Year of Waning*,[43] is one of the lengthiest pictures of the community by a former resident. The novel is set in Bensonhurst-Sea Beach in 1948 (this locale, according to the author, is purposefully fictionalized; he has moved the community a few blocks from its center eastward). The author is a professor of English at Clark University, specializing in Irish literature. The book revolves around two figures, Rabbi Jacob Djubal and his grandson Jason. At the outset of the novel, the rabbi is persuaded on Passover eve to go to stay with his son and daughter-in-law and remove himself from the Lower East Side from Passover until the High Holy Days (or perhaps permanently). Jason, who is about sixteen, is caught between his Jewish background (both Levantine and "Yiddish," in the novel's vocabulary) and the sexual and social tensions that American teenagers face.

The rabbi is also puzzled by the marital problems of his congregants Daniel and Beulah, who are related to him as well as being congregants on the Lower East Side. The author portrays the struggle between tradition and American society, although the Levantine/Arabic Jews of Sea Beach seem more secure in their religious culture than most. They are faced with acculturation to the ways of their Americanized "Yiddish" neighbors. To the latter, they are exotic and their origins are mysterious. Jason's friends occasionally call him "Hindu." For the most part, Syria is not clearly defined as their point of origin. The author generally describes the religious practices and their meaning fairly accurately.

The novel portrays a community dedicated to commerce. While the people are outwardly religiously observant, their commercial interests prevail over religious ones. Jason, the young protagonist of the novel, is disillusioned with both in this period of his life. He will leave the community and its ways behind him.

Like Jack Marshall, the poet (see chapter 9) and Dan Hedaya, the actor, Sultan can be seen as an exile from the community. However, decades after he left Brooklyn, he continues to grapple with the issues that caused him to leave, and he uses this material in his fiction.

The Israeli kibbutz writer of Aleppan origin, Amnon Shamosh, also has set several stories in Brooklyn. He generally portrays the New York Syrians as having achieved a kind of modus vivendi with modern society. In several stories, he evaluates their family life and religious observance in a positive (albeit ironic) light, and contrasts it with the rejection of more traditional family and religious values by other Jews (American Ashkenazim, kibbutzniks). For instance, in one story the Ashkenazic Phil Stein has to decline his Syrian friend's invitation for dinner because Phil does not know his wife's plans, and he is estranged from her. Another story is even more ambivalent. In it, an American Syrian psychiatrist justifies an apparently superstitious practice. When a bride meets a woman who has recently given birth, they must exchange jewelry, lest the bride be barren. In these stories, Shamosh suggests that modern Jewish society has gone too far in the direction of individualism and that it can learn something from the more conservative Middle Eastern Jews who have found a way to synthesize modernity with traditionalism.[44]

Several Syrian groups in Brooklyn are active in publicizing the community through electronic media. A new web site is http://www.bsz.org, which is run by B'nei Sha'are Zion. They are the younger members of the large synagogue on Ocean Parkway. This web site shows the community as its members want it to be portrayed. Among other elements, it summarizes the history of Syrian Jewry, announces community events, and presents *pizmonim.* The Events section includes synagogue information, *minyān* schedules, and a Torah study session.

One element that has been neglected in most previous outside presentations is the place of music in community activities. While the music of Ladino-speaking Sephardim has achieved some popularity, the more Arabic-style music of Syrian Jews has not achieved the same kind of popularity. This reflects a cultural difference. Middle Eastern music is much less successful in reaching a wide public in the United States than "early (classical) music" or European Mediterranean music of the Sephardim. Here the web sites suggest that the Syrians desire to share their music with others.

The Place of the New York Syrian Community in American Jewry

The Syrian enclave in the New York metropolitan area is part of a greater whole and reflects the diversification that has been taking place in American Jewry as a whole, especially in the Orthodox-traditionalizing sectors. The Syrian community in Brooklyn and Deal is very much part of these sectors. It is connected by schools, rabbis, and lay individuals. The publication of the monthly family magazine *IMAGE* shows this. The personal and other advertisements display these ties. In fact, the Personals look as if they are part of a package for the entire metropolitan area, not something specifically Syrian.

Certainly in Brooklyn the Jews who stayed when whites in general fled to the suburbs have tended to be more Orthodox than those who left. The Jewish groups most visible on Ocean Parkway and in surrounding neighborhoods besides the Syrian Jews are Orthodox Ashkenazim and new (mostly non-Orthodox) immigrants from the Soviet Union. The presence of the former, in particular, thus influences the direction of the Syrian Jews, even though Orthodox Ashkenazim are not role models for many Syrians who have confidence in their own traditions. Others, such as the Ateret Torah group, see themselves as Jews first and only secondarily as Syrian Sephardim.

Conclusions

This chapter describes how one ethnic community has persisted and flourished in the face of great pressures to disperse and merge with other groups. The affluence of the group, the members' need to remain together because of strong cultural preferences, their occupational specialization (though diminished), and the group's proximity to ultra-Orthodox enclaves have helped the group to perpetuate its communal cohesion. The phenomenon of an affluent ethnic community is unusual, since ethnic enclaves are usually associated with poverty rather than affluence. Nevertheless there is some fraying, as indicated by those who leave, the assimilation of out-of-towners and others, emulation of Ashkenazic Orthodox Jews, continued intermarriage with Ashkenazim, and the relationship of affluence to such phenomena as alcohol and drug abuse.

It is also hard to know how the community will continue to distinguish itself as the connection with the Aleppan and Syrian past becomes more tenuous. Certain forms of music have been maintained as separate cultural forms (particularly in the liturgy and the *pizmonim* sung at life cycle celebrations), and also some types of cuisine. The interest in maintaining cultural separation is mixed. Certain ultra-Orthodox rabbis, for instance, show little interest in the specifically Aleppan heritage. Other rabbis, however, publish books on Aleppan customs and such practices, and prayer books containing such customs continue to be printed and used. Still, as the community comes to the end of the twentieth century, it maintains itself as a separate enclave within Brooklyn and Deal.

CHAPTER 11

A GLOBAL COMMUNITY: CONCLUSIONS

We have now followed Aleppan Jewry from Ottoman Syria to Europe, Israel, and the Americas.

NUMBERS AND STRUCTURAL SEPARATION

The different communities vary greatly in terms of the size of the Aleppan grouping, the larger Jewish community, and the general community as a whole. Estimates give a rough picture of the settings. Aleppo at the end of the nineteenth century was a city of 100,000 or so. Its population included between six thousand and seven thousand Jews. Jews of various origins had immigrated there and eventually been absorbed into an Arabic-speaking Jewish community with a fairly stable structure.

In Cairo and Alexandria, Syrian Jews were part of a larger Jewish community, which was part of a still larger European and "Levantine" population in a largely Muslim Arab country. It is hard to know how many of these Jews were Aleppans. By 1940, Jews numbered eighty thousand in an Egyptian population of about forty million. Syrian Jews were absorbed into the larger Jewish and European-Levantine aggregates, but not into the larger majority population. The emigration and expulsion of many Jews after 1956 was a sign of this lack of assimilation into the Egyptian population.[1]

At the height of the cotton trade, about five hundred Sephardim of various origins lived in Manchester. The Syrians numbered c. 170. This was in a city with a population of half a million and with approximately thirty-five thousand Jews, most of whom were Ashkenazim. The Sephardic Jews were concentrated by occupation and their residences were segregated from those of the Ashkenazim. In the twentieth century, they were not absorbed by the other Jews so much as the Jews in general were absorbed by British society as a whole. The British educational system and the society in general have a strong conformist streak. Those who have lived in Britain for very long usually become full participants in British society. Yet several Sephardic congregations have survived in Manchester.

In Latin America, there is a division between large and small communities. We might divide the region between Mexico, São Paulo and Rio de Janeiro, and Buenos Aires on the one hand and smaller communities like Guatemala City and Barranquilla on the other. In the former, as we indicated in chapter 7, there are thousands of Jews, while in the latter Jews are counted in the tens and hundreds. The Jewish situation in such countries as Mexico and Guatemala is comparable to that of the Jews in Egypt. To the extent that Jews in these countries became assimilated, they were absorbed into the population of European descent, rather than into the Indian population. As in Egypt, many of the more affluent immigrants from Europe and the Middle East in these countries continued to see themselves as sojourners who were in these lands only temporarily.

Argentina, of course, is a country that has absorbed European immigrants, but it also has a strong xenophobic tradition. This tradition has made it difficult for Jews in particular to feel completely secure. In fact, those Jews who were politically involved and took their citizenship most seriously were under certain dictatorships the least secure, and some were forced into exile.

In Israel, the Aleppans are part of a much larger Jewish population, as they are in the United States. In Palestine/Israel, the basic division was between Jews and non-Jewish Arabs, later transformed into Israelis and Palestinians. There the Ḥalebim have a strong identification with the rest of the Jewish population. The Jewish population is divided between Sephardim and Ashkenazim, which are divided again on the basis of country of origin.

In Jerusalem, the Ḥalebim in 1960 constituted a little more than 1 percent of the Jewish population, or about three to four thousand people. The size of the Ḥalebi origin group was comparable to that of the Jewish population in Panama. In fact, Panama and Israel each had total populations of one to two million in that period. Yet the distinctiveness that marks these Jewish communities is lost in a setting where Aleppans are just another Middle Eastern Jewish grouping that speaks Arabic. Thus, in Israel they tend to be absorbed.

The situation is very different in the United States. There is a big difference between the estimated twenty to forty thousand Aleppans in the New York-New Jersey area and the rest of the Aleppan Jews. The former have maintained a fairly stable enclave in Brooklyn and Deal, New Jersey. In Brooklyn and Deal, the Syrian Jews, who are predominantly Aleppan, have built strong, separate institutions that parallel those in the rest of the very large Jewish community of this metropolitan area.

Numbers help explain the strong separate communities in New York, Mexico, and Buenos Aires, but only in part. Other Jewish groups, including both the Ladino-speaking Sephardim and the German Jews, had equivalent numbers. They also built separate synagogues and other institutions, yet their communities did not survive with such strength.[2]

The Occupational Structure

The occupations that Aleppan Jews have engaged in, both in Syria and elsewhere, have generally been commercial vocations. In Syria, these occupations stretched from itinerant peddlers and craftsmen in villages to international merchants representing foreign concerns. In Egypt and the Americas, peddling was the entry-level position for most Syrian males, as well as for other Jewish and Arabic-speaking immigrants. To some extent in Egypt, Manchester, and Milan, Syrian Jews representing family firms entered the economy as shipping merchants selling textiles.

The Aleppan peddlers in the United States quickly became specialized in particular commodities. While Aleppan Jews did not have a monopoly on these commodities, such specialization helped unify the community, since wholesalers and retailers shared common interests and were dependent on each other. Key commodities from the 1920s onward in the United States were household linens and infantwear. Later, imported electronics became another specialty. In Latin America, many Syrian Jews were textile merchants and factory owners.

The line of trade they shared also kept active bonds alive between Aleppans in the different countries. In fact, as noted in chapter 4, cotton traders from Latin America settled in Manchester, while Manchester families sent scions to Latin American countries.

While Syrian Jews have entered a variety of professions over the years, the fact that many were specialized, whether in galleries and tourist bazaars, infantwear and bargain-discount stores, or electronics, and the fact that they could do much of their business with other members of the community, helped to maintain a common interest among the members of the Syrian community and between communities.

Leaving the kinds of occupations in which the Syrian Jews were concentrated might mean leaving the community or breaking up Syrian structures. Some who entered professions such as law, accounting, or medicine served the businessmen in the Syrian Jewish community, but others did not. Leaving commerce was seen by most as rebellion from the community.

Thus, as noted in various theories explaining the success of intermediary minorities, cohesion is connected to having a common occupation or line of business. The reverse was also true. Among Syrian Jews, cohesion was also connected to a long-enduring preference for going into business over pursuing higher education. Valuing the former and being rewarded for it may have helped promote ethnic separation, while attaining higher education has been more conducive to structural assimilation. It should be noted that in Israel, Manchester, and among the "out-of-towners" in the United States, occupational and commercial specialization has broken down.

Familism and Identificational Separatism

Up to recent times, Aleppan Jews were either self-employed or were employed by family firms. The distinction between the two was not always clear, since a man might start a business with a gift from his wife's family when he got married or he might become involved in receiving goods on consignment from a relative or co-ethnic.

Such investment in a son-in-law's business was combined with the conviction held by many Aleppan Jews that commerce was the best path to wealth and the good life. Throughout my fieldwork, especially in the diaspora, I have been told that this was the case. Even in recent years, several physicians of Syrian origin have told me that their families felt that going into medicine (which most Americans have seen as a path to affluence) was a mistake. The most radical rejection of a business career was by those who chose physical labor and other noncommercial occupations over commerce, such as the poet, Jack Marshall, who became a merchant seaman, a cannery worker, and then a house painter, or novelist Amnon Shamosh, who has lived on a kibbutz for nearly half a century.

The businesses of most Aleppans have been international in character. This was especially true of the export and import of cotton and woolen goods through Manchester and Bradford in the late nineteenth and early twentieth centuries. This was also the case with regard to trade in electronic goods and photographic equipment in the mid- and late twentieth century. Commercial contacts with kin and co-ethnics helped maintain contact between international communities. Other fields, such as the banks of the Safra family, also involved such international contacts.[3]

Where there are sufficient numbers of Syrian Jews, as in New York, involvement in such multinational business is not necessary in order to maintain contact with one's fellow Aleppans. Still, this kind of multinational business has played an important role in encouraging the separation of the Aleppan community.

Frequent migration also encourages maintenance of family and kin ties over great distances and strengthens ethnic group organization. Thus emigrants from Syria, Israel, Egypt, and Latin America in the New York City area have added to the resilience of that ethnic enclave. All of this fits well with other studies of intermediary minorities, such as Overseas Chinese communities or various mercantile Indian castes, where group solidarity is reinforced by dispersal.[4]

Aleppan Men and Women

Although both men and women have been considered throughout this volume, little direct attention has been given to gender concerns, especially in the later chapters. While a substantial number of my own interviews, as well as those conducted by Joseph Sutton and other sources, have been with women, the distinctive accommodations of women and men have not been fully articulated.

Some aspects are clear. In the early phases of immigration, Syrian men generally emigrated first, with women following later. The need to escape conscription during the period from 1909 to 1918 added to this trend. Women were also seen as more vulnerable than men. For the most part, women worked within a family context, regardless of country of residence. Poorer women worked as domestic servants in Syria and Palestine. Some poor women in Syria became dancers and singers. Women also helped in their husbands' shops, especially in the immigrant phase, when shopkeepers were too poor to hire help or when male relatives were unavailable. In those cases where peddling and shopkeeping were combined, women often managed the stores while their husbands were on the road. In her 1929 study in Brooklyn, Lillian Herling wrote that the four Syrian women working in factories were all widows. One finds that in Manchester and other communities, women would go out to work when their families faced hard times, as during the Depression of the 1930s.

Once Aleppan Jews attained a comfortable middle-class way of life, whether in Syria, the Middle East, or elsewhere, married women did not leave the home for employment. In this they were like their non-Syrian counterparts in these places. Household management and leisure activities such as card-playing were the pastimes that appear most prominently in the literature.

Outside employment of women is especially prevalent among those who are less affluent. The economic downturn during the Great Depression and the mobilization during World War II forced or encouraged less affluent Manchester Sephardic women to work in offices or in the military. In the austere Israeli economy of the 1950s and 1960s, many families needed two incomes. Especially among the nonreligious, it was not uncommon for women to work outside the home. This was also the case for some less affluent Syrian families in New York, where women worked before marriage.

In both Israel and the United States, increased schooling has resulted in greater extradomestic employment and communal activity (as noted in chapter 10). While the New York community as a whole is affluent, it is located where living costs are high, and for many, cash flow is a constant problem. In the New York area, this has resulted in many women seeking employment and running new enterprises.

Yael Zerubavel and Dianne Esses, in their study of Syrian Jewish women, point out that women's voices have not generally been heard publicly in the community. Interviews that elicited their life histories have helped break this silence. Yet women are important in preservation of the Syrian Jewish tradition. Even the memory of ethnic foods is part of the tradition that women convey and which remains strong in the memories of their children.[5] The neglect of the women's side of the story is found in other communities as well. For instance, the emphasis on rabbinic texts and stories about rabbis' holy deeds found among the Orthodox again excludes women.

As implied in the preceding paragraphs, all men and women were expected to marry. In the late Ottoman period and on into the twentieth century, women expected to marry at an earlier age than men. In immigrant communities, women often married men much older than they were and who were generally established in business. During the height of immigration from Syria to the United States in the 1920s, proxy marriages were performed for some.[6] For a long time, marriage gifts and dowries were common, and this practice may continue in some places. These practices fit very well with the lives of women as they are described in this section above.

Exposure to outside influences made both men and women within the Aleppan communities at times perceive the life within the community as constricted. Rebellion against this constriction has been most clearly described for New York, but it appears elsewhere as well, though it is obviously less marked where community structures have been weakened, as in Israel or Manchester. The perception of constriction is, however, different for men and women. Occupational considerations play an important role for men, while women's concerns are more often related to the expectation that a young woman must be a beautiful, wealthy bride.

Maintenance of Separate Cultures and Organizations

For the most part, Aleppan Jews have not been conspicuously different from their neighbors. They have readily adopted the language and clothing of their neighbors, and while keeping some ethnic dishes, they have adapted to the cuisines of the lands where they live as well. There is also increasing dependence on food purchased outside of the home, especially where women work gainfully.

This is not to deny the importance of a particular Aleppan taste, which lingers in people's memories and is associated with their home. One lawyer in Jerusalem told me about the unique Aleppan type of kibbe (a bulgar wheat dumpling) that he remembered. American authors Jack Marshall and Stanley Sultan used the names of particular Syrian cakes as titles for pieces that they had written.[7]

One realm that has been a cultural reserve has been music, particularly the synagogue liturgy and the *pizmonim* and *baqashot* (songs and hymns sung in an Arab musical style). Individual Syrian Jews have a wide variety of musical tastes, comparable to those of their neighbors. In the larger communities and in Israel, however, there are singers who preserve the special songs.[8] The special songs—the *pizmonim,* which is the term used most in New York, and the *baqashot,* which is the variety referred to in Israel—help preserve a special Syrian Jewish realm, since they are Arabic-style songs in Hebrew. They also provide the Syrian Jews with a bridge (even more than the food) to the Arab side of their heritage.

With regard to separate organizations in the diaspora, Aleppan Jews have been notable in organizing separate synagogues in the different places where they have resided. This was true in Manchester in the nineteenth century and in Cairo, New York City, Chicago, and Mexico in the twentieth century. On the other hand, such separate institutions did not always survive, due to the small size of the communities. Small out-of-town congregations in Chicago and Atlantic City disappeared and separate Syrian organizations in Manchester merged. Such separatism is not unique to Aleppan Jews, but it may reflect their own sense of a unique identity. In addition, when the environmental culture has been inhospitable to such separatism, as in Israel, separatism has been attenuated.

Intercommunity Ties

Ties between different communities have played an important role in maintaining both the separate community and the separate identity of Aleppan Jews. While the Israeli Ḥalebim have taken an assimilatory approach, they have maintained certain institutions with their brethren abroad in mind (see chapter 6). The maintenance of such ties has been especially marked in Latin America, where for a long time Jews had a sense that they were only sojourners waiting to move on. The "out-of-towners" in various ways renew their sense of a separate Aleppan identity through their ties with Brooklyn and Deal. Those out-of-towners who vacation in Deal or in Florida condominiums where there are many Syrians do this quite seriously. Such ties are also quite marked among the rabbis, some of whom go to Israel every summer.

The Rabbinic Network and Militant Conservatism

As noted throughout the book, first in the 1860s and then after 1900, Aleppan rabbis were known for their militant conservatism and resistance to efforts to "modernize" Judaism. This was first marked in the 1860s by the burning of a book by an Orthodox rabbi in Livorno who sought to reconcile philosophy with the Torah. This strain of militancy has been quite strong among Aleppan rabbis throughout the world.

Some of the Aleppo rabbis who settled in Jerusalem in the 1880s associated themselves with Ashkenazi *ḥaredi* rabbis. They then advised rabbis back in Aleppo on such issues as the propriety of a B'nai B'rith lodge, which they opposed. They provided a religious justification for opposition to Zionist youth movements in Aleppo.

Rabbis trained in Aleppo and Jerusalem went forth to serve Aleppan and other Jewish communities in the Americas. Most of these rabbis came from Aleppan rabbinic families, and they maintained their ties with Jerusalem after 1948. While some of these rabbis were not of Syrian origin, most had been trained at the Porat Yosef Yeshiva in Jerusalem, which was led for many years by the Aleppan Rabbi Ezra ʿAtiyeh. Rabbi Jacob Kassin, who was the spiritual leader of the Aleppan community in Brooklyn, came from Jerusalem, and Rabbi Mordekhai Atiyeh, who served Mexico City, retired to Jerusalem.

Rabbi Shaul Setton Dabbah and his successor, Rabbi Yitzḥaq Shehebar, followed a pattern of opposition to deviation from Orthodox practice in line with militant conservatism, and supported the anti-Zionist Agudat Yisrael, as noted previously. Rabbi Setton Dabbah, like his Jerusalem counterparts, had consulted with an Ashkenazic Orthodox colleague when he promulgated the ban on marriage with converts.

It should be stressed that not all of the rabbis were uniformly conservative in their opposition to accommodation, nor were the conservative rabbis uniformly opposed to accommodation, any more than they had been in Aleppo. This comes out clearly when looking at changes over time in the community in New York City (chapters 8 and 10). Even Rabbi Setton-Dabbah, who initiated the ban on marriage with converts in Argentina, was originally inclined to approve such marriages. In some communities, the rabbinic style has been more accommodationist than elsewhere, as in Manchester, England, or in Cairo in the 1940s.

As pointed out throughout the book, this strain of militancy persists. In Brooklyn, a group close in orientation to the Ashkenazic *ḥaredim* is led by a Jerusalem-born rabbi. Several Ashkenazic Orthodox rabbis have served the community in Brooklyn, the most prominent of whom, Rabbi Abraham Hecht, came out of the Lubavicher Hasidic group.

The Ḥalebi rabbis also continue to maintain contact with one another. Several Aleppan rabbis who serve congregations in the Americas maintain second homes in Jerusalem and visit these homes during long vacations. It is also common for them to send their children to study in yeshivot in Israel and even to seek spouses for their children among the children of other rabbis. Thus, in a variety of ways the rabbis have maintained a particular orientation and social network.

A question more difficult to answer is what the impact of such "militant conservatism" has been on Aleppan communities. Among Jews of various origins, Syrian Jews, especially Aleppans, are generally more religiously observant and intermarry less than either Sephardim or Ashkenazim (excepting Ḥasidim and Ashkenazic *ḥaredim*). They also have a reputation for keeping apart from other Jews, whether in Manchester in the 1870s or New York in the twentieth century. Nevertheless, Aleppan families remain close and tolerate a wide range of observance of tradition as well as laxity in religious practice.

Throughout this volume, the vulnerability of Aleppan Jews to assimilatory trends and pressures has been described. Certainly many have prospered and have learned to enjoy the riches and pleasures that money can buy. The rabbis have not had much influence on the business conduct or on the hedonism of Aleppan Jews. It is not clear that the Aleppan laity has followed the political leadership of the rabbis either. Yet the laity is respectful and proud of its rabbis. They respect the rabbis' connection with the divine and seek their blessing. In any case, the Ḥalebi rabbis have sufficient authority that they do sway the laity, even if they cannot control every aspect of their lives. This is true for the larger communities, especially where some or all of the rabbis are Aleppan. It is not as characteristic of communities like Manchester, which today lacks an Aleppan rabbi. Still, the rabbinate and the fund-raising efforts of Aleppan Israeli institutions have played an important role in maintaining the transnational character of the community.

Images of Aleppan Jews

In the chapters in this book, different and yet often consistent images of Aleppan Jews have been presented. One image applied to Aleppan Jews has been the stereotype of the middleman, whether Jewish or Middle Eastern, as parsimonious, greedy, and often unscrupulous in business. Such groups are often seen as clannish. While some such images are found in hostile sources, group members will also use them. For instance, Amnon Shamosh uses this stereotype in his portrait of Michel Ezra Safra. An alternative image of Ḥalebim is provided by Bryan Burrough in his description of Edmond Safra in his conflict with American Express. In his view, Ḥalebi Jews are seen as seasoned, worldly businessmen, discreet, and demanding of trustworthiness. He also points to their religious observance and tenacious attachment to tradition. Incidentally, the accusations against Edmond Safra recall the libel suit conducted by Abram Besso in Manchester more than a century ago (see chapter 4).[9] Not all members of the Syrian communities were business successes, however, as Jack Marshall notes in a poem that refers to his father's threadbare store in New Jersey.[10]

The latter traits attributed to Aleppan Jews are also found in the writings of authors of Aleppan origin themselves. This is, of course, the case with regard to such a rabbinic author as Ḥakhām David Laniado, whose compendium includes a biographical dictionary of Aleppan rabbis and a collection of rabbinic exempla.[11]

In the works of secular authors, the situation is more complex. The title character in American Stanley Sultan's novel, *Rabbi: A Tale of the Waning Year,* is a saintly rabbi who tries to uphold the moral and religious tradition in the face of worldly corruption and rebellious disbelief. This rabbi is contrasted with another, younger rabbi, who is willing to countenance an imposter who happens to be a wealthy contributor to his synagogue.[12]

The poet Jack Marshall does not contend with Aleppan rabbis directly, but he includes religious themes in his poetry. His references are eclectic, but in some poems he has addressed his anomalous identity as an "Arab-Jew" and interpreted the Orthodox circumlocutions for the deity, as was noted in chapter 9.[13]

Religious tradition for the Israeli novelist and poet Amnon Shamosh is a source to be plumbed. With the exception of one story in which a rabbi helps reconcile a Muslim couple, rabbis do not play an important part in his corpus of stories and novels. Ḥalebi religiosity as portrayed in his work is the laity's observance of and sometimes superstitious respect for magical practices. At the same time, he uses the religiosity of the Syrians in New York as a way of criticizing the failures of secular Israeli society in some realms. He suggests that the Ḥalebim have succeeded in maintaining their own Jewishness better than have members of the kibbutzim and other secular Jews.[14]

Unlike Sultan, Marshall, or Shamosh, Joseph Sutton has remained a member of a very conservative community. He also does not write poetry or fiction. While occasionally critical, he is generally respectful of the rabbinic spiritual leaders of the community. His criticism of the religious and secular leadership is muted, but it is present.[15]

In dealing with images, it should be noted that self-descriptions have implications. The use of the term *Sephardic,* as in Sephardic Community Center, or the association of Eastern Mediterranean Jews in Manchester or Chicago with the Portuguese Marranos, have ramifications. They imply that these Jews from the often-denigrated Arab "Orient" are to be associated with a more upscale past of Spanish nobility. Contrariwise, those, such as Jack Marshall, who stress the "arabism" of these Jews are not afraid of downscale associations. These uses of group names have implications for individual self-identity and for stereotyping by selves and others.

The image of the Ḥalebi or Aleppan Jew will, however, undergo changes, now that there are no more Jews in Aleppo and those born to the immigrants are aging. Even in the most resilient and cohesive communities, such as New York and Mexico, Jews of Aleppan origin are mingling with people of other descents. Still, the survival of this community into the twenty-first century is in itself a remarkable achievement, whatever the future will bring.

Implications for Research

In this book, I have surveyed one community's dispersion throughout much of the world. Most of the chapters have dealt with Aleppans in one city, one country, or one region at a time. In this final chapter, I have drawn together the accounts to compare the different communities and to identify connections between them. Some of this was prefigured in earlier chapters, especially the ones on Manchester and on Jerusalem in the 1990s.

The value of looking at an ethnic community in several dimensions is that the uniqueness of a particular community is in part a function of its relations with co-ethnics living in other places, as well as of its relations with co-residents belonging to other groups. One of the pluses of the diasporic discourse is that it focuses our attention on the former, while most conventional sociology is only concerned with the latter. This is shown in the account of the Ḥalebis in Israel, who appear to be on the road to assimilation within Israeli society, but who maintain institutions sustained from abroad.

The Aleppan Jewish experience shows how a particular ethnic group has succeeded in certain contexts in maintaining its separate organization and identity, while it has not been able to do so to the same extent elsewhere. The experience also shows how the various branches of the community interact. While the Israeli Ḥalebim have not sought to keep their separate organizations, they have maintained ties with other Aleppans and have used these ties to maintain certain organizations in a very different context. The case shows the interrelatedness of a complex set of factors.

The Aleppan case has particular relevance to the nexus between economic specialization and ethnic persistence. The New York Syrian Jews have been particularly successful in keeping a viable ethnic entity alive. In part, this success is connected to the business success of members of the community and their ability to persuade their offspring to continue in businesses like those of their parents. This bears comparison with other "intermediary minorities."

Implications for Jewish Assimilation and Survival

The Aleppan example plays an important role in internal Jewish discussions of whether Jewry will survive as a viable entity in North America and elsewhere in the Diaspora. The Aleppan Jews form an entity that has stemmed the tide of intermarriage and that has maintained itself over a long period of time. Generally Zionists have argued that Jewry cannot survive in the Diaspora, both because of anti-Semitism and because of assimilatory forces. Intermarriage is both symbolic and symptomatic of this phenomenon, since it results in a diluted Jewish identity and may lead to conversion to other religions. Orthodox Jews have argued that only those who remain true to the Torah and who build a wall of separation between themselves and their neighbors can continue as Jews.[16]

The Syrian Jews, especially those in the United States, have been used as an example of a people who both live and flourish in the general economy and also find a way to insulate themselves sufficiently from the society at large to preserve their communal structure and their identity.[17] This description is similar to Edward Spicer's model of minority "persistent peoples" (also known as "persistent cultural systems"). These peoples, including the Navajo, Irish, Welsh, Jews, and Maya, maintain a stance of resistance to the dominant culture.

Each of the groups, according to Spicer, maintains a core culture. This core includes a set of values and some political organization to foster its policy of resistance. While holding on to their symbols of identity, each group shows flexibility in other aspects of the group culture. The flexibility in many aspects of culture does not necessarily lessen the resistance to structural and identificational assimilation. For instance, Jews have changed their mother tongue frequently, while retaining Hebrew as a language of prayer and study. In the case of Syrian Jews, both the rabbis and lay leaders exercise authority over the community, both formally and informally. In applying Spicer's model, we should realize that as a series of generalizations, it is static.[18]

Most Jews, especially those who are not Orthodox, have not shown a particularly stubborn opposition to the dominant cultures of the countries in which they have found themselves. As noted previously, the situation of Syrian Jews is mixed, but there are strong enclaves that have manifested such opposition. The ban in Argentina and the United States on marriage to converts is a manifestation of this.

As the case of the alienated and the exiled in the New York-New Jersey community shows, a heavy price must be paid for insulation. Those who are unhappy in a particular community will reject many of the community's values if that is the only way out. In chapter 10, allusion was made to the appearance of a drug problem in the New York community. This might be seen as a product of affluence, but we know such problems appear among the poor, too. Such addictions exist among Hasidic Jews as well as among Syrians and the general population. The same is true of most other problems, including child and spouse abuse, marital instability, suicide, and mental illness.

There is not necessarily a sharp polar choice between the yeshiva world and abandoning Judaism. It has not been since the Enlightenment. There is no single Syrian Jewish pathway to ethnic persistence, in fact, and these adaptations depend on a particular social and economic set of factors. The

Syrian ways cannot easily be translated into formulae for success for other Jews.

Just as the example of Syrian Jews cannot be used as a model for Jewish survivalists, it cannot provide comfort for those who see in the study of diasporas alternatives to exclusivist nation-states. James Clifford, in his review of the literature on diasporas, found strong evidence for a *diasporist* anti-Zionism "in pre-Holocaust Ashkenazic history, as well as in some critiques of Zionism by some non-Ashkneazic critics of contemporary Israeli society." Clifford and other "diasporists" like him who see diasporas as open communities should take a second look, not only at the situations of medieval Ashkenazic and Sephardic Jewries, but also at a community like that of the Aleppan Jews.[19] These communities were no more open than modern nation-states. Relations between the majority religious community and the minorities were uneasy and strained even in the best of times. Both nationalism (including Zionism) and diasporic accommodations have been adaptations to particular circumstances. Neither is a panacea.

What the case of Aleppan Jews can teach is that while we can find cultural accommodation side by side with ethnic persistence, human beings must pay the price for the adaptations they make. These adaptations are not always dichotomous in terms of rejecting the culture around us or accepting it uncritically. Still, the examples of the Aleppan communities provide us with a panorama of Jews who fit neither the Hasidic ghetto nor unhinged assimilationism.

Notes

Chapter 1

1. Victor D. Sanua, "A Jewish Childhood in Cairo," in *Fields of Offerings: Studies in Honor of Raphael Patai,* V. D. Sanua, ed.(Cranbury, N.J.: Associated Universities Presses, 1983), 283–84.

2. Emilio Picciotto, *Genealogia della Famiglia Picciotto* (Milan: private publication, 1985); H. J. Cohen, "Picciotto," *Encyclopedia Judaica* (Jerusalem: Keter, 1971), 13:498. Mr. Maurice de Picciotto of Los Angeles has compiled a list of documents on this family in a privately distributed paper, "Famille Picciotto, 1787–1908."

3. W. P. Zenner, *Minorities in the Middle: a Cross-Cultural Analysis* (Albany N.Y.: State University of New York Press, 1991).

4. On stranger/sojourner theory, see ibid., 15–17; also see Paul Siu, "The Sojourner," *American Journal of Sociology* 58 (1952): 34–44.

5. Raoul Naroll, "On Ethnic Unit Classification," *Current Anthropology* 5 (1964): 283–312; W. P. Zenner, "Jewish Communities as Cultural Units," in *Perspectives on Ethnicity,* Regina E. Holloman and Serghei Arutiunov, eds. (The Hague: Mouton, 1980), 327–38.

6. Milton M. Gordon, *Assimilation in American Life* (New York: Oxford University Press, 1964); also see Gershon Shaffir, *Immigrants and Nationalists* (Albany, N.Y.: State University of New York Press, 1995), 7–14.

7. The main documents of the culture contact approach and the "anticolonialist critique" can be found in Paul Bohannon and Fred Plog, *Beyond the Frontier* (Garden City, N.Y:: Natural History Press, 1970). These include the two Social Science Research Council Memoranda on Acculturation in 1938 and 1954.

8. Barbara Kirshenblatt-Gimblett, "Spaces of Dispersal," *Cultural Anthropology* 9

(1994): 339–44. Also see James Clifford, "Diasporas," *Cultural Anthropology* 9 (1994): 302–38, which provides a good survey of the "diasporic literature." A Marxist diasporic treatment is found in Linda Basch, Nina Glick Schiller, and Cristina Szanton Blanc, *Nations Unbound: Transnational Projects, Postcolonial Predicaments, and Deterritorialized Nation-States* (Basel: Gordon and Breach, 1995). Their title gives a good idea of their viewpoint.

9. W. P. Zenner, "Essentialism and Nominalism in Urban Anthropology," *City and Society [Annual Review]*, 1 (1994): 53–66.

10. W. P. Zenner, "The Trans-National Web of Syrian Jewish Relations," in *Urban Life: Readings in Urban Anthropology,* 3d ed., G. Gmelch and W. P. Zenner, eds. (Prospect Heights, Ill.: Waveland Press, 1996), 459–72. See Basch et al., *Nations Unbound,* 7, 27.

11. W. P. Zenner, *Minorities in the Middle,* passim.

12. W. P. Zenner, "Trans-National Web."

13. W. P. Zenner, "Middleman Minorities in the Syrian Mosaic: Trade, Conflict and Image Management," *Sociological Perspectives* 30 (1987): 400–421.

Chapter 2

1. H. Klengel and J. D. Hawking, *Real-Lexikon des Assyriologie* (Berlin: de Gruyter, 1932), 50–53.

2. Moshe Rofe, "Agadah u-shmah Tedef," *Darkhei Ere"ṣ* (Publication of the World Center for Aleppo Jews" Traditional Culture, No.2, 1987), 23–25. Yitzhaq Ben-Zvi, *She'ar Yashuv* (Jerusalem: Ben-Zvi Institute, 1966/67), 484–90. Robert Lyons, a photographer, photographed the Tedef shrine in 1995 (see note 4, following).

3. Glanville Downey, *A History of Antioch in Syria from Seleucus to the Arab Conquest* (Princeton, N.J.: Princeton University Press, 1961); *Antioch in the Age of Theodosius the Great* (Norman: University of Oklahoma Press, 1962), 13–15,30,122–23). On the legend of the mother and her seven sons, see Micha Joseph Bin-Gorion, *MiMekor Yisrael: Selected Classical Jewish Folktales,* edited by Dan Ben-Amos (Bloomington: Indiana University Press, 1990), 70–72. As of 1986, Antioch, now Antakya, still had a Jewish community, as well as having an Orthodox Christian majority. See Henry Kamm, "In Ancient Antioch, Modern Hostilities Smolder," *New York Times,* May 27, 1986, p.2.

4. Alexander Dothan (Lutsky), "On the History of the Ancient Synagogue in Aleppo," *Sefunot* 1 (1956): 25–61. Information on the current state of synagogues came from the exhibit *Silent Sacred Spaces: The Synagogues of Syria,* which showed photographs taken by Robert Lyons (Syracuse University, 1996). S. D. Goitein, *A Mediterranean Society* (Berkeley: University of California Press, 1967), 1: 17, 20, notes that for the period between 900 and 1250, we have little material on the Jews of Aleppo. Unlike its counterpart in Cairo, Aleppo's synagogue did not preserve much material from the "classic Islamic period" (eighth to thirteenth centuries). In the materials that he used from the Cairo Geniza, there is comparatively little material on Aleppo or Damascus, though many people have names that indicate their Syrian origins.

5. Amnon Shamosh, *Ha-Keter: Sipuro shel Keter Aram Ṣōbā* (Jerusalem: Ben-Zvi Institute, 1987).

6. This section is a shortened version of what I have written previously on Jews in Late Ottoman Syria. It overlaps with my two articles, "Syrian Jews and Their Non-Jewish Neighbors in Late Ottoman Times," and "Jews in Late Ottoman Syria: Community, Family and Religion," in *Jews among Muslims,* S. Deshen and W. P. Zenner, eds. (Houndmills, England: Macmillan; New York: New York University Press, 1996), 161–86. For full source citations also see W. P. Zenner, "Jews in Late Ottoman Syria," in *Jewish Societies in the Middle East,* S. Deshen and W. P. Zenner, eds. (Lanham, Md.: University Press of America, 1982), 155–210. For an overview of the Aleppan rabbinic literature, see Yaron Harel, *Sifre Are"ṣ: Ha-Sifrut Ha-Toranit shel Ḥakhmei Aram Ṣōvā* (Jerusalem: Ben-Zvi Institute, 1996). For general background on Ottoman Aleppo, see Abraham Marcus, *The Middle East on the Eve of Modernity: Aleppo in the Eighteenth Century* (New York: Columbia University Press, 1989); Bruce Masters, *The Origins of Western Economic Dominance in the Middle East, Mercantilism and the Islamic Economy in Aleppo, 1600–1750* (New York: New York University Press, 1988); and Heinz Gaube and Eugen Wirth, *Aleppo: Historische und geographische Beitrage zur bauliche Gestaltung, zur soziale Organisation und wirtschaftliche Dynamik einer vorderasiatische Fernhandelsmetropole* (Wiesbaden: Reichert, 1984). On Jews in the nineteenth century, see Yaron Harel, "Changes in Syrian Jewry, 1840–1880" (Ph.D. diss., Bar Ilan University, Ramat Gan, 1992). For the sake of brevity, references in this chapter will be kept to a minimum, concentrating on material not cited in previous articles.

7. Thomas Philipp, "French Merchants and Jews in the Ottoman Empire during the Eighteenth Century," in *Jews of the Ottoman Empire,* Avigdor Levy, ed. (Princeton, N.J.: Darwin Press, 1994), 315–26); Renzo Toaff, *La Nazione Ebrea a Livorno e a Pisa,* 1591–1700 (Firenze: L. Olsehki Editore, 1990).

8. Kemal Karpat, "Ottoman Population Records and the Census of 1881/2–1893," *International Journal of Middle Eastern Studies* 9 (1978): 237–74; Justin McCarthy, "Jewish Population in the Late Ottoman Empire," in *Jews of the Ottoman Empire,* Avigdor Levy, ed. (Princeton, N.J.: Darwin Press, 1994), 375–97; Zvi Zohar, "Qehilot She-ba-Suriya, 1880–1918: Peraqim Ba-Demografiya, Kalkalah, u-Mosdot Ha-Qehillah Be-Shilhe Ha-Shilton Ha-Otomani," *Peʿamim* 44 (1990): 80–109. McCarthy corrects some of these official figures for undercounting of Jews. Figures for 1908 were supplied to me by Prof. Bruce Masters. On the geographic distribution of Jews and other religious groups in Aleppo, see Gaube and Wirth, *Aleppo,* 195–208, 427–41.

9. On general attitudes toward religion, see Marcus, *The Middle East,* 222–25. On music, see Mark Kligman, "Modes of Prayer: Arabic Maqāmāt in the Sabbath Morning Liturgical Music of the Syrian Jews in Brooklyn" (Ph.D. diss., New York University, 1997).

10. See Rofe, "Agadah."

11. Haim Gerber, *State Society and Law in Islam: Ottoman Law in Comparative Perspective* (Albany: State University of New York Press, 1994), passim; Najwa Al-Qattan, "The Damascene Jewish Community in the Latter Decades of the Eighteenth Century: Aspects of Socio-Economic Life Based on the Registers of the *Shari'a* Courts," in *The Syrian Lands in the Eighteenth and Nineteenth Century,* Thomas Philipp, ed. Berliner Islamstudien, vol. 5 (Stuttgart: Franz Steiner, 1992), 197–216.

12. Albert Hourani, personal communication.

13. See Philipp, "French Merchants"; Harel, "Changes"; Yaron Harel, "Maʿamadam u-Tadmitam shel B'nai Picciotto Bi-ʿEinei Ha-Moshavah Ha-Tzarfatit Bi-Ḥalebi, 1784–1850," *Michael* 14 (1997): 161–86.

14. For a comprehensive account of the Damascus affair, see Jonathan Frankel, *The Damascus Affair: "Ritual Murder," Politics, and the Jews in 1840* (Cambridge: Cambridge University Press, 1996), especially 17–64;, W. P. Zenner, "Middleman Minorities in the Syrian Mosaic: Trade, Conflict and Image Management," *Sociological Perspectives* 30 (1987): 400–421; Harel, "Changes," 254–72; Yaron Harel, "Jewish-Christian Relations in Aleppo as Background for the Jewish Response to the Events of October 1850," *International Journal of Middle Eastern Studies* 30 (1998): 77–96; Goitein, *A Mediterranean Society,* 198.

15. Harel, "Changes," 273–82.

16. On the Middle Ages, see Goitein, *A Mediterranean Society,* 100–101. On the division of labor, also see Carleton Coon, *Caravan* (New York: Henry Holt, 1951), 1–9. On competition for contracts between Jews and others, see the story in David Laniado, *La-Qedoshim Asher Ba-Are"ṣ* (Jerusalem: privately published, 1980), 191, retold in Zenner, "Syrian Jews and Their Non-Jewish Neighbors." This story, set in the eighteenth century, is similar to the case of thirteen Jewish copper brokers who lost their jobs when the government sold the copper monopoly to a new contractor. See Marcus, *The Middle East,* 171.

17. Marcus, *The Middle East,* 159. In general, his book presents a good picture of everyday life.

18. J. A. D. Sutton, *Magic Carpet: Aleppo-in-Flatbush* (Brooklyn, N.Y.: Thayer-Jacoby, 1979), 249–50. Also see lists of occupations given by Al-Qattan (1992).

19. Harel, "Changes," 30–31, 47–63.

20. Marcus, *The Middle East,* 159.

21. Based on interviews in Jerusalem.

22. See Norman Stillman, *The Jews of Arab Lands in Modern Times* (Philadelphia: Jewish Publication Society, 1991), 222.

23. On these rabbinic reactions to "modernity," see Zvi Zohar, "Shamranut Loḥemet: Qavim Le-Manhigutam Ha-Ḥevratit-Datit shel Ḥakhmei Ḥaleb Be-ʿEt Ha-Ḥadashah" (Activist conservatives: The socio-religious policy of Aleppo's rabbis 1865–1945) *Peʿamim* 53 (1993): 57–78; idem, "A Maskil in Aleppo: 'The Torah of Israel and the People of Israel' by Rabbi Yitzhaq Dayan," in *New Horizons in Sephardic Studies,* Yedidah Stillman and George Zucker, eds. (Albany: State University of New York Press, 1993), 93–107; and Yaron Harel, "Tesisah Ruḥanit Ba-Mizraḥ—Yesodah shel Qehillah Reformit Bi-Ḥaleb Bi-Shnat 1862" (Spiritual agitation in the East: Founding of a Reform congregation in Aleppo in 1862), *Hebrew Union College Annual* (1993): xix–xxxv. On the "accommodationism" of the late nineteenth century and the influence of Jerusalem Orthodox rabbis on Aleppo, see Yaron Harel, "*Hashpaʿat Rabbanei Ha-ʿEdah Ha-Ḥaredit ʿal Ḥakhmei Ha-Ḥalebim ve-ha-Bukharim Bi-Yerushalayim* (unpublished paper, 1998).

24. Harel, "Changes," 380–83.

25. This is indicated in the photographs and other documents, such as wedding invitations used in issues of *Darkhei Ere"ṣ,* the periodical publication of the World Center for Aleppo Jews' Traditional Culture, 1985–1990, volumes 1–6.

26. The story of a Jew who saves his life by showing the *ṣīṣīt* during an anti-Christian massacre is found in A. R. Malachi, Ha-yehudim be-Hitkommemut ha-Druzim. *Ḥorev* 1 (1934/35): 105–16, which deals with the Druze-Christian conflict in Lebanon in 1860.

Chapter 3

1. For further description of Syrian Jews during the Mandatory period, see Norman Stillman, *The Jews of Arab Lands in Modern Times* (Philadelphia: Jewish Publication Society, 1991), 263–81, 291–94, 329–30, 371–75; also Irit Abramsky-Bligh, "Yehudei Suriya Taḥat Shilton Vichy," *Peʿamim* 28 (1986): 131–50. Also see the photographs in various issues of *Darkhei Ere"ṣ*, published by the World Center for Aleppo Jews Traditional Culture (Tel Aviv) since 1988.

2. This term was used by Judith Goldstein in "Jewish-Muslim Relations in Remnant Community," a paper delivered at the annual meeting of the Association for Jewish Studies, Boston, December 1977. Another study of such a community is Andre Levy, "Jews among Muslims: Perceptions and Reactions to the End of Casablancan Jewish History" (Ph.D. diss., Hebrew University, Jerusalem, 1995).

3. William E. Schmidt, "Persecution Ended; Syrian Jews Stage an Exodus," *New York Times*, January 15, 1994, A4; Larry Yudelson, "The Exodus from Syria Is Completed," *(Albany) Jewish World*, October 20, 1994, p. 7. Most national and international articles in the *Jewish World* and other local Jewish papers are syndicated by the Jewish Telegraphic Agency (JTA).

4. For example, see the description of a Hong Kong community in James L. Watson, *Emigration and the Chinese Lineage* (Berkeley: University of California Press, 1975).

5. Mark Tessler and Linda Hawkins, "The Political Culture of Jews in Tunisia and Morocco," *International Journal of Middle Eastern Studies* 11 (1980): 56–86.

6. Tabitha Petran, *Syria* (New York: Praeger, 1972), 200, 204 n.19; Marion Woolfson, *Prophets in Babylon* (London: Faber and Faber, 1980), 173–77, 209–12, 229–49); National Association of Arab Americans (N.A.A.A.), "On Syrian Jews," Washington, D.C., 1978. (Obtained through the embassy of the Syrian Arab Republic.)

7. See Saul S. Friedman, *Without Future: The Plight of Syrian Jews* (New York: Praeger, 1989) as an example of this approach. While, as a scholar, I am quite critical of this viewpoint, it has fueled much of the fervor that helped in the successful efforts to free Syrian Jewry from the restrictions on their emigration. I do not diminish the suffering described in these works or the sincerity of those who worked on behalf of Syrian Jews. He also documents efforts of North American Jews, especially those of Judy Feld Carr, to rescue Syrian Jews. Since Friedman wrote before the Syrian government began to allow open emigration in 1992, he was circumspect about these efforts, which included discreet assistance to families in need and payment of bribes to help emigrés. On Carr, see Bill Gladstone, "Canadian Grandmother Reveals Her Role in Rescue of Syrian Jews," the *Jewish World*, December 12, 1996, p. 24.

8. See Richard Antoun and Donald Quataert, *Syria: Society, Culture and Polity* (Albany: State University of New York Press, 1991); Darrow Gary Zenlund, "Post-

Colonial Aleppo, Syria: Struggles in Representation and Identity," (Ph.D. diss., University of Texas-Austin, 1991). (Ann Arbor: University Microfilms, 1991.)

9. Joseph A. D. Sutton, *Aleppo Chronicles: The Story of the Unique Sephardeem of the Ancient Near East—In Their Own Words* (Brooklyn, N.Y.: Thayer-Jacoby, 1988).

10. See Abramsky-Bligh, "Vichy," 131–50.

11. See H. J. Lowenberg, "Palestine and the Middle East: Syria and Lebanon," *American Jewish Yearbook* (American Jewish Committee, New York) 50 (1948–49): 441–42; David Z. Laniado, *La-Qedoshim Asher Ba-Are"ṣ* (Jerusalem, privately published, 1980); Joseph B. Schechtman, *On Wings of Eagles* (New York: Yoseloff, 1961), 148–66; Sutton, *Aleppo Chronicles,* 195, 206–10, 237–38.

12. Petran, *Syria,* passim; Itamar Rabinovitch, *Syria Under the Baath,* (New York: Halsted, 1972), passim. Hanna Batatu, "Some Observations on the Social Roots of Syria's Ruling Military Elite: The Causes of Its Dominance," *Middle East Journal* 35 (1981): 331–44, has interpreted the Syrian Muslim Brotherhood as representative of a declining Sunni urban elite.

13. Mordecai Kosover, "Syria," *American Jewish Yearbook* 51 (1952): 419–20.

14. Walter Z. Lacqeuer and Naqdimon Rogel, "The Middle East: Syria," *American Jewish Yearbook* 57 (1956): 518–20.

15. Ibid. For this period also see Don Peretz, "Syria," *American Jewish Yearbook* 58 (1957): 403–4.

16. Philip Baram, "The Arab Middle East," *American Jewish Yearbook* 67 (1966): 421–22. During this period, in 1965, the Syrians captured and executed Eli Cohen, an Israeli spy. As far as is known, there was no contact between Cohen and the local Jewish community. Baram does not attribute any exacerbation of the situation of the Jewish community to this incident.

17. See Sutton, *Aleppo Chronicles,* 230.

18. Joseph A. D. Sutton, *Magic Carpet: Aleppo-in-Flatbush* (Brooklyn, N.Y.: Thayer-Jacoby, 1979), 247.

19. On the situation at that time, see the news releases of the Committee of Concern on the Plight of Syrian Jews, November 18, 1971, January 1972, March 2, 1972; Marvine Howe, "Jewish Leader in Syria Hopeful, Sees an 'Exaggeration' of Plight," *New York Times,* February 4, 1972, 8; Friedman, *Without Future,* 51–58.

20. N.A.A.A., "On Syrian Jews," 1978; *Sixty Minutes,* broadcasts of February 16, 1975, March 21, 1976; Michael Morton, "Syrian Jews No Longer Harassed," *Jerusalem Post,* April 29, 1977, 4; George E. Gruen, "The Current Situation of Syrian Jews," Testimony before Special Subcommittee on Investigations, Committee on International Relations, U.S. House of Representatives, June 25, 1975 (Reprinted by American Jewish Committee); David Hirst, "Syrian Jews Seek New Identity," *Guardian,* February 27, 1975, 4; John J. O'Connor, "CBS' 60 Minutes Returns to Syrian Jews," *New York Times,* March 23, 1976.

21. Sutton, *Magic Carpet,* 244–46; Bernard Gwertzman, "Syrian Proxy-Marriage Plan Lets Jewish Women Emigrate to U.S.," *New York Times,* July 31, 1977, 1, 34; Murray Schumach, "3 'Proxy' Brides from Syria to Wed New Suitors in Brooklyn Rites," *New York Times,* January 23, 1978, 27, 49. The Assad period was described in reasonably favorable terms by recent Syrian emigrants interviewed by Efrat Tahar-Kedem, "Psychological, Sociological, and Cultural Views of the Refugee Phenomenon

in the Immigration and Absorption of Syrian-Origin Women during 1992–1997," Paper presented at the Conference on The Jewish Immigration from the Muslim Countries, Haifa University, June 1998.

22. Sutton, *Aleppo Chronicles,* 224–25.

23. Ibid., 229.

24. The Syrian-born writer Amnon Shamosh has written a story, "Seder Nashim" (The Order of Women) (in *Maʿayan Ḥatum* [The sealed fountain] [Tel Aviv: Ha-Kibbutz Ha-Meʾuḥad, 1984], 7–14), portraying the poignancy of this situation for many Jewish women in Syria.

25. Batatu, "Some Observations"; Zenlund, "Post-Colonial Aleppo," esp. 162–67; Samir Al-Khalil [Makiya Kanan], *Republic of Fear* (Berkeley: University of California Press, 1989), passim.

26. Friedman, *Without Future,* 25–26.

27. Sutton, *Aleppo Chronicles,* 222–23.

28. Ibid., 227–28.

29. Thomas Friedman, "Syria Giving Jews Freedom to Leave," *New York Times,* April 28, 1992, A1, A10. Mary B. W. Tabor, "Exodus to a Brooklyn Neighborhood Slows to a Trickle," *New York Times,* January 21, 1993, B1, B3. The situation in 1995 was reported by the photographer, Robert Lyons.

Chapter 4

1. On the growth of Beirut, see Leila Fawaz, *Merchants and Migrants in Nineteenth Century Beirut* (Cambridge, Mass.: Harvard University Press, 1983), esp. 47, 51–52, 86. On the growth of Lebanese Jewry during the 1950s, see Joseph B. Schechtman, *On Wings of Eagles* (New York: Yoseloff, 1961), 167–83; and Hayyim J. Cohen, *The Jews of the Middle East 1860–1972* (Jerusalem: Israel Universities Press, 1973), 44, 78–80, 101, 140, 141.

2. On the history of Jews in modern Egypt, see Jacob M. Landau, *Jews in Nineteenth Century Egypt* (New York: New York University Press, 1969); and Gudrun Kremer, *The Jews in Modern Egypt* (Seattle: University of Washington Press, 1989). Syrian Jews are mentioned here and there, but there is no full account of the Syrian Jewish migration in these or other books on the subject. On converts with Aleppan surnames, see Norman Stillman, *The Jews of Arab Lands in Modern Times* (Philadelphia: Jewish Publication Society, 1991), 245–47. On communists and leftists, see Joel Beinin, *Was the Red Flag Flying There? Marxist Politics and the Arab-Israeli Conflict in Egypt and Israel, 1948–1965* (Berkeley: University of California Press, 1990), especially 55–56, 105, 106; and idem, *The Dispersion of Egyptian Jews: Culture, Politics and Formation of a Modern Diaspora* (Berkeley: University of California Press, 1998), 135, 139, 140–41, 144, 158. Also see Joseph A. D. Sutton, *Aleppo Chronicles: The Story of the Unique Sephardeem of the Ancient Near East—In Their Own Words* (Brooklyn: Thayer-Jacoby, 1988), 267–74, 288–94; Yaʾakov Choeka and Hayyim Sabato, *Minḥat Aharon: Meʾasef Torani Le-Zikhrom shel Ha-Rav Aharon Choeka* (Jerusalem: private printing, 1989–90), 15–32. On the "Second Exodus," see Andre Aciman, *Out of Egypt* (New York: Farrar-Straus, Giroux, 1994), passim. Also see Beinin, *Dispersion,* passim.

3. On nineteenth-century Baghdad, see Shlomo Deshen, "Baghdad Jewry in

Late Ottoman Times: The Emergence of Social Classes and Secularization," *Association for Jewish Studies Review* 19 (1994): 19–44. On an Aleppan in India, see Sutton, *Aleppo Chronicles,* 496–502. The Japanese anthropologist Izumi Sato is engaged in a study of the Kobe community. See I. Sato, "A History of the Kobe Jewish Community in Memory," paper presented at the 96th annual meeting of the American Anthopological Association, Washington, D.C., November 21, 1997. On Marseilles, see M. L. Bierbrier, "East Meets West: The Altaras Family from Syria to Marseilles," Proceedings of the Fifth International Seminar on Jewish Genealogy, Paris, 1998, 89–96. The data on Milan is based on observations made during brief visits to Milan in 1961 and 1992 and on interviews.

4. Maurice Samuel, *The Gentleman and the Jew* (New York: Knopf, 1950), 10; Chaim Raphael, "The Manchester Connection," *Commentary* 82 (September 1986): 48–53.

5. N. J. Frangopulo, "Foreign Communities in Manchester," *Manchester Review* 10 (1965): 189–206; idem, *Tradition in Action: The Historical Evolution of the Greater Manchester County,* (East Ardsley: Wakefield Publications, 1977), chapter 8, 113–33; Eric Glasgow, "The Greeks in Manchester," *Greek Gazette,* November 1974, 5; B.Jenazian, "Armenians in Manchester—A Commercial Community," in *Sevan,* 1953 (a mimeographed publication, copy available at Manchester Central Library); Bill Williams, *The Making of Manchester Jewry, 1740–1875* (Manchester: Manchester University Press, 1976), 81–88, 260, 319–24, 334; Fred Halliday, "The *Millet of Manchester:* Arab Merchants and Cotton Trade," *British Journal of Middle Eastern Studies* 19 (1992): 159–76.

6. D. C. M. Platt, "Further Objections to an 'Imperialism of Free Trade,' " *Economic History Review* 26 (1973): 77–91.

7. Sutton, *Aleppo Chronicles,* 58, 426.

8. Albert Hourani, *A History of the Arab Peoples* (Cambridge, Mass.: Harvard University Press, 1991), 276. See Williams, *Making of Manchester,* 83, 320–22; Halliday, *Millet,* passim.

9. H. M. Nahmad, n.d. (copies of unpublished notes and files copied for the author by (Mrs.) Mary Nahmad of Oxford.) Fadlo Hourani was the Lebanese consul in Manchester in 1948 and the father of historian Albert Hourani. Mr. Basil Jeuda (personal communication) estimates that there were about 200 Sephardic households, 175 in South Manchester, around 1930, which he sees as the peak of the Sephardic presence. About one-third of these were Syrian. Using the Shipping Merchants Directory, the cotton trade had peaked before World War I and was well into decline by 1930.

10. Williams, *Making of Manchester,* 319–24; Lucien Gubbay and Abraham Levy, *The Sephardim: Their Glorious Tradition from the Babylonian Exile to The Present Day* (London: Carnell, 1992), 207–8. A paper has just appeared on the beginning of the Aleppan colony in Manchester, including the first rabbi and shoḥeṭ. Yaron Harel, "The First Jews from Aleppo in Manchester: New Documentary Evidence," *Association for Jewish Studies Review* 23 (1998): 191–202. Harel sees the appointment of rabbis in the "new diaspora" following the pattern of rabbinic leadership in Aleppo's hinterland (e.g., Antakya and Killiz).

11. The Withington congregation celebrated its ninetieth anniversary in 1994.

see Rosemary Eshel and Basil Jeuda, *Withington Congregation of Spanish and Portuguese Jews,* (Manchester, 1994, brochure and exhibit catalogue). Movement of Sephardic Jews is traceable using the city directories (*Kelly's Directories for Manchester, Salford,* etc.).

12. City directories, 1886–l965, available at Manchester Central Library (within that is the Trades Directory and Slater's Directory of Shipping, etc.,.Merchants).

13. Trades Directory, 1912, 2016.

14. Nahmad, n.d.; also see Halliday, *Millet,* passim.

15. "Kinder," "The Levanters and Their Doings," *The Spy* (Manchester, 1892): September 17, September 24, November 12, November 26, December 3. Available at Manchester Central Library. For the context of the *Spy* and its founder, Henry Yeo, see Bill Williams, "The Anti-Semitism of Tolerance: Middle Class Manchester and the Jews, 1870–1900," in *City, Class and Culture: Studies of Social Policy and Cultural Production in Victorian Manchester,* Alan J. Kidd and K. W. Roberts, eds. (Manchester: Manchester University Press, 1985), 74–102 (esp. 83–90, 99). Also see Halliday, *Millet,* who discusses how another paper, the *Manchester City News,* dealt with these cases and how some correspondents to the daily press praised the contributions of Middle Eastern merchants.

16. See Halliday, *Millet,* on social relations. Louis Golding, *Magnolia Street* (London: Gollancz, 1932); also see Samuel, *Gentleman,* 9–17.

17. *Jewish Yearbook,* 5663 (1903), Who's Who section.

18. Manchester Jewish Museum, Protocols J164, J217. The notes on my respondents, such as "Ralph Ades", were variously transcribed in 1958 and 1959, as well as in 1988. Also see Lydia Collins, "1917 Petition of Baghdad Merchants at Manchester," *The Scribe* (published by the Exilarch foundation, London), no.56 (1993, 7–8, which details restrictions placed on Ottoman Jews and Muslims during World War I. Also see Halliday, *Millet.*

19. Sutton, *Aleppo Chronicles,* 425–33.

20. See John Davis Investment Column, "The Rise of David Alliance," *The Observer,* July 26, 1987, 35.

21. On Manchester today, see Gubbay and Levy, *The Sephardim,* 1992, 208. Information on the merger is from correspondence with Lydia Collins. For a general description of present-day Manchester, which, however, contains little on the Jews, see Ian Taylor, Karen Evans, and Penny Fraser, *A Tale of Two Cities: Global Change, Local Feeling and Everyday Life in the North of England: A Study of Manchester and Sheffield* (London: Routledge, 1996).

22. Abner Cohen, *Two Dimensional Man,* (Berkeley and Los Angeles: University of California Press, 1974).

23. W. P. Zenner, "The Transnational Web of Syrian Jewish Relations," in *Urban Life: Readings in Urban Anthropology,* 3d ed., G. Gmelch and W. P. Zenner, eds. (Prospect Heights, Ill.: Waveland Press, 1996), 459–72.

Chapter 5

1. Immanuel Bensinger, "Syria," *Jewish Encyclopedia* (New York: Funk and Wagnalls, 1905), 9:646–48.

2. For an overview of the Jewish communities in Ottoman Palestine, see Yitzhak

Ben-Zvi, "Eretz Yisrael under Ottoman Rule, 1517–1917," in *The Jews: Their History, Culture and Religion,* L. Finkelstein, ed. (Philadelphia: Jewish Publication Society, 1960), 1:602–89; Raphael Patai, *Israel between East and West* (Philadelphia: Jewish Publication Society, 1953), 56–58, 79–83; Jeff Halper, *Between Redemption and Revival: The Jewish Yishuv in Jerusalem in the Nineteenth Century* (Boulder Colo.: Westview, 1991), esp. 179–93, 210–11.

3. Patai, *Israel between East and West,* 82.

4. Zvi Zohar, "Qehillot Yisrael she-ba Suriya," esp. 86–87.

5. Most of these accounts of the interaction between Syrian and European Jews were from oral interviews. Also see Yaron Harel, "*Hashpa'at Rabanei Ha 'Edah HaḤaredit 'al Ḥakhmei Ha-Ḥalebim ve-Ha-Bukharim Bi-Yerushalayim,*" 1998.

6. Joseph Schechtman, *On the Wings of Eagles* (New York: Yoseloff, 1961), 165.

7. See David Gurevich, *The Jewish Population of Jerusalem* (Jerusalem: Jewish Agency, 1940), tables 19 and 20. Urfalis from the Urfa area of south-central Turkey are considered separately from Ḥalebis by Gurevich, Schmelz, and the people of Jerusalem themselves. For a summary of this material see W. P. Zenner, *Syrian Jewish Identification in Israel* (Ann Arbor: University Microfilms International, 1965), 108–11. Much of this material was supplied by the late Oscar Schmelz, who gave me access to materials from his 1958 census of Jerusalem. The Aleppan majority is also indicated by the existence in 1960 of one Damascus-endowed and eight Ḥalebi synagogues in Jerusalem.

8. See Zionist Archives and Ben Zvi Institute, files on Syria.

9. Schechtman, *On Wings,* 52, 165.

10. Nechemia Meyers, "Another Opinion: Syrian Immigrants Await Brethren," *(Albany) Jewish World,* May 5, 1992, 3.

11. Avraham Abbas, "On the History of the HeḤalutz Movement in Syria and Lebanon," *Shevet ve-Am* 3 (1958): 113–23. On the Shamosh family migration, see Amnon Shamosh, "A Family in Aleppo," (Jerusalem: Center for Programming, Department of Development and Services, World Zionist Organization, 1979). Also see Shamosh's oral biography in Joseph A. D. Sutton, *Aleppo Chronicles: The Story of the Unique Sephardeem of the Ancient Near East—In Their Own Words* (Brooklyn: Thayer-Jacoby, 1988), 454–63.

12. On Middle Eastern Jews in late Mandatory Palestine, see S. N. Eisenstadt, *The Absorption of Immigrants* (London: Routledge and Kegan Paul, 1954), 90–104; Patai, *Israel between East and West.* Also see Zenner, *Syrian Jewish Identification,* 99–139.

13. On Raphael Shlomo Ben Meir Laniado, see David Laniado, *La-Qedoshim asher ba-Are"ṣ,* 82, No. 265; On Ezra 'Atiyeh, ibid., 539–40, No. 419. On the connection of Ḥalebim with the Jerusalem *ḥaredim,* see Z. Zohar, " 'The Torah of Israel and the People of Israel' by Rabbi Yitzhak Dayyan," in *New Horizons in Sephardic Studies,* Yedida K. Stillman and George K. Zucker, eds. (Albany: State University of New York Press, 1993), 93–108; see also Y. Harel, *Hashpa'at.*

14. Amnon Shamosh, "A Family"; Sutton, *Aleppo Chronicles,* 454–63.

Chapter 6

1. The results of this study were reported in my doctoral dissertation, Walter P. Zenner, *Syrian Jewish Identification in Israel* (Ann Arbor, Mich.: University Microfilms International, 1966), esp. 208–88.

2. See Walter Weiker, *The Unseen Israelis: The Jews of Turkey in Israel* (Lanham, Md.: University Press of America, 1988); and idem, "Ethnicity among Turkish Jews in Haifa," *Israel Social Science Research* 10 (1995): 23–42. Also see Guy Haskell, *From Sofia to Jaffa* (Detroit: Wayne State University Press, 1994). Whether or not a particular origin group was seen as problematic varied with the times. When most of the Jews of Baghdad arrived in Israel in 1950, they were settled in transition camps called *ma'abarot* and they were seen as a group needing special attention. Twenty years later they were perceived in a very different way.

3. See Weiker, *Unseen Israelis* and "Ethnicity among Turkish Jews." Weiker's definition of "Turkish Jews" differs somewhat from my usage of "Syrian Jews." He means specifically immigrants from the Republic of Turkey, especially those who immigrated between 1948 and the present. His questions specifically relate Turkish identity to identification with Turkish national culture. This is more explicit in his work than their relationship to the Judeo-Spanish heritage, although he asks about that as well. Since Syrian Jews as I define them include families who left Syria under Ottoman as well as Mandatory and Republican rule, my orientation regarding Syrian Jews is different.

4. Raphael Cohen-Almagor, "Cultural Pluralism and the Israeli Nation-Building Ideology," *International Journal of Middle Eastern Studies* 27 (1995): 461–84.

5. Walter P. Zenner, "Ambivalence and Self-Image among Oriental Jews in Israel," *Jewish Journal of Sociology* 5 (1963): 214–23; idem, "Syrian Jewish Identification," 176–207, 289–327; idem, "Sephardic Communal Organizations in Israel," *Middle East Journal* 21 (1967): 173–86; idem, "Saints and Piecemeal Supernaturalism among the Jerusalem Sephardim," *Anthropological Quarterly* 38 (1965): 201–17.

6. Michael Romann and Alex Weingrod, *Living Together Separately: Arabs and Jews in Contemporary Jerusalem* (Princeton, N.J.: Princeton University Press, 1993).

7. Nancie L. Gonzalez, *Dollar, Dove, and Eagle: One Hundred Years of Palestinian Migration to Honduras* (Ann Arbor: University of Michigan Press, 1992), 57–60.

8. Jeff Halper, "Modern Jerusalem: Policies, Peoples, Planning," in *Critical Essays in Israeli Society, Religion and Government,* K. Avruch and W. P. Zenner, eds. (Albany: State University of New York Press, 1997), pp. 93–111.

9. For further description of the Levis and other families, see Zenner, "Syrian Jewish Identification," 247–88.

10. W. P. Zenner, "Raful Leaves School," *Reconstructionist* 28, no. 15 (1962): 21–24. On schools, also see Jeff Halper, *Ethnicity and Education: The Schooling of Afro-Asian Jewish Children in a Jerusalem Locality* (Ann Arbor, Mich.: University Microfilms International, 1978). Halper did his work in Naḥala'ot in the early 1970s.

11. See W. P. Zenner, "Jews in Late Ottoman Syria," in *Jews among Muslims,* Shlomo Deshen and Walter P. Zenner, eds. (Houndsmill: Macmillan, 1996), 177–81, for a description.

12. Cf. W. P. Zenner, "Syrian Jewish Identification," 383–90.

13. Tamar Katriel, *Communal Webs: Communication and Culture in Contemporary Israel* (Albany: State University of New York Press, 1987), 35–49.

14. Zenner, "Ambivalence and Self-Image," passim.

15. Amnon Shamosh, *Michel Ezra Safra u-Vanav*(Ramat Gan: Massada, 1978). The television series was produced in 1990.

While this book has been translated into Spanish, an English translation has not as yet been published.

16. There are exceptions to this, such as one of the protagonists of the novel *Arazim* (Tel Aviv: Massada, 1990), who visits his mother in a poor section of Aleppo.

17. Walter P. Zenner, "The Trans-National Web of Syrian Jewish Relations," in *Urban Life: Readings in Urban Anthropology,* George Gmelch and W. P. Zenner, eds., 3d ed. (Prospect Heights, Ill.: Waveland Press, 1996), 467–69; David Laniado, *La-Qedoshim asher Ba-Are"ṣ* (Jerusalem:private publication, 1980), 136–38.

18. Zenner, "Sephardic Communal Organizations," 176–77.

19. Amnon Shamosh, *Ha-Keter: Sipuro shel Keter Aram Ṣōbāh* (HaKeter: The story of the Aleppo Codex) (Jerusalem: Ben Zvi Institute, 1987), 76, 82–88, 152–54, 161–63.

20. For a laudatory biography of Rabbi Yomtov Yedid and Menaḥem Yedid's communal activities, see Yomtov Yedid and Menaḥem Yedid, *Ner Yomtov* (Jerusalem: Yeshivat Simḥat Yom Tov, 1992), 16–33. For these illustrations, see *Darkhei Ere"ṣ* (Journal of the World Center for Aleppo Jews Traditional Culture), 2–6 (1987–90), passim.

21. On *baqashot,* see W. P. Zenner, "Censorship and Syncretism: Some Social Anthropological Approaches to the Study of Middle Eastern Jews," in *Studies in Jewish Folklore,* F. Talmage, ed. (Cambridge Mass.: Association for Jewish Studies, 1980), 377–94. Also see Ruth Katz, "Mannerism and Cultural Change: An Ethnomusicological Example," *Current Anthropology* ll (1970): 465–75. *Baqashot* overlap but are not identical to the songs called *pizmonim* (see chapter 10).

22. On SHAS, see Aaron Willis, "Sephardic Torah Guardians: Ritual and the Politics of Piety," Ph.D. diss., Princeton University (Ann Arbor, Mich.: University Microfilms International, 1993). On *Qol Sinai,* see Zenner, "Sephardic Communal Organizations," 184–85. SHAS is seen as a party refusing "to accept Mizraḥi [Middle Eastern Jewish] identity as a deformed, lacking version of an Ashkenazi, Euro-centric model of the Israeli self." see Pnina Motzafi-Haller, "A Mizraḥi Call for a More Democratic Israel," *Tikkun* 13, no.2 (March/April 1998): 50–52. As I have indicated by my reference to garb, so also with the style of talmudic learning. SHAS itself represents a Europeanized version of Sephardic Judaism. Also on these issues, see Norman Stillman, *Sephardic Religious Responses to Modernity* (Luxembourg: Harwood Academic Publishers, 1995), 76–86.

23. Laniado, *La-Qedoshim Asher Ba-Are"ṣ*. For further analysis of this and related works, see W. P. Zenner, "Remembering the Sages of Aram Ṣōbā," in *Israeli Society, Politics and Religion,* Kevin Avruch and Walter P. Zenner, eds. (Albany: State University of New York Press, 1997), 137–51.

24. For reviews and surveys of Shamosh's writing, see Walter P. Zenner, "Aleppo and the Kibbutz in the Fiction of Amnon Shamosh," *Shofar* 6, no. 3 (spring 1988): 25–35; idem, "Espionage and Cultural Mediation," in *Critical Essays on Israeli Social Issues and Scholarship,* Russell Stone and W. P. Zenner,eds. (Albany: State University of New York Press, 1994), 31–42; Avraham Marthan, "An Authentic Human Voice: The Poetry of Amnon Shamosh," in *Critical Essays on Israeli Social Issues and Scholarship,* Russell Stone and Walter P. Zenner, eds. (Albany: State University of New York Press, 1994), 43–61. For English translations of Shamosh's fiction, see his *My*

Sister, the Bride and Other Stories (Ramat Gan: Massada, 1979). During the late 1970s and early 1980s, translations of Shamosh's short stories and poetry appeared in such Anglo-Jewish publications as *Midstream, Moment,* and the *Jewish Spectator.*

Chapter 7

1. Paul Siu, "The Sojourner," *American Journal of Sociology* 58 (1952): 34–44. In the context of middleman minority see Edna Bonacich, "A Theory of Middleman Minorities," *American Sociological Review* 38 (1973): 583–94; W. P. Zenner, *Minorities in the Middle: A Cross-Cultural Analysis* (Albany: State University of New York Press, 1991), 15–17.

2. Victor Mirelman, *Jewish Buenos Aires, 1880–1930* (Detroit: Wayne State University Press, 1990), 26; Judith Laikin Elkin, *The Jews of the Latin American Republics* (Chapel Hill: University of North Carolina Press, 1980), 168; Daniel J. Elazar, *The Other Jews: The Sephardim Today* (New York: Basic Books, 1989), 145. The tables come from Sergio DellaPergola, "Demographic Trends of Latin American Jewry," in *The Jewish Presence in Latin America,* Judith Laikin Elkin and Gilbert W. Merkx, eds. (Boston: Allen and Unwin, 1987), 85–133, esp. 90–91.

3. See Martin Cohen, *The Martyr* (Philadelphia: Jewish Publication Society of America, 1973); Matilde Gini de Barnatan, "Cryptojews in Rio de Plata in the Seventeenth Century," in *New Horizons in Sephardic Studies,* Yedida K. Stillman and George K. Zucker, eds. (Albany: State University of New York Press, 1993), 137–47; also see Eva Alexandra Uchemany, "The Periodization of the History of New Christians and Crypto-Jews in Spanish America," in *New Horizons in Sephardic Studies,* Yedida K. Stillman and George K. Zucker, eds. (Albany: State University of New York Press, 1993), 109–36.

4. Corinne A. Krause, *The Jews in Mexico: A History with Special Emphasis on the Period from 1857 to 1930* (Ann Arbor, Mich.: University Microfilms International, 1971); Haim Avni, *Argentina and the Jews* (Tuscaloosa: University of Alabama Press, 1991), 1–44; Elkin, *Jews of the Latin American Republics,* 3–53.

5. Elkin, *Jews of the Latin American Republics,* 54–75, 125–55.

6. Victor Mirelman, "Sephardic Immigration to Argentina Prior to the Nazi Period," in *The Jewish Presence in Latin America,* Judith L. Elkin and Gilbert Merkx, eds. (Boston: Allen and Unwin, 1987), 24–25.

7. Mirelman, Jewish Buenos Aires; Ignacio Klich and Jeffrey Lesser, "The *Turco* Immigrants in Latin America," special issue, *The Americas* 53(1996): 1–152.

8. For a general consideration of this immigration, see Ignacio Klich, "*Criollos* and Arabic Speakers in Argentina: An Uneasy *Pas de Deux,* 1888–1914," in *The Lebanese in the World,* Albert Hourani and Nadim Shehadi, eds. (London: I.B. Tauris, 1992), 243–84; Klich and Lesser, "*Turco* Immigrants," passim; Jeffrey Lesser, "From Pedlars to Proprietors: Lebanese, Syrian and Jewish Immigrants in Brazil," in *The Lebanese in the World,* Albert Hourani and Nadim Shehadi, eds. (London: I.B. Tauris, 1992), 393–410; Ignacio Klich, "Arabes, judios y arabes judios en la Argentina de la primera mitad del novecientos," *Estudios interdisciplinarios de America Latina y Caribe* (July–December 1995), 109–43. On anti-Arab prejudice in contemporary Argentina, see Ignacio Klich, "Argentina," in *Survey of Jewish Affairs, 1991*, William Frankel and

Antony Lerman, eds. (Oxford: Blackwell and London: Institute of Jewish Affairs, 1991), 216–31.

9. Gabriel Garcia Marquez, *A Chronicle of a Death Foretold* (New York: Knopf, 1982), 10, 93–94; also see Nancie L. Gonzalez, *Dollar, Dove and Eagle: One Hundred Years of Palestinian Migration to Honduras* (Ann Arbor: University of Michigan Press, 1992), 138, 169. Also see the references in note 8. For a general consideration of stereotypes of middleman minorities, see Zenner, *Minorities,* 46–60.

10. The Buenos Aires newspaper is cited by Mirelman, *Jewish Buenos Aires,* 25.

11. For Rivas, see Krause, *Jews in Mexico,* 104.

12. Susan Gilson Miller, "Kippur on the Amazon: Jewish Emigration from Northern Morocco in the Late Nineteenth Century," in *Sephardi and Middle Eastern Jewries: History and Culture in the Modern Era,* Harvey E. Goldberg, ed. (Bloomington: Indiana University Press, 1996), 190–209.

13. Krause, *Jews in Mexico,* 103; see Liz Hamui de Halabe, *Los Judios de Alepo en Mexico* (Mexico: Maguen David, 1989), 115–24. One of the pictures shown in Hamui de Halabe's book shows an Aleppan immigrant with a rifle during the Mexican Revolution, while another shows a peddler, dressed in a suit and tie, while a Mexican peasant carries his backpack (127, 129).

14. Joseph A. D.Sutton, *Aleppo Chronicles: The Story of the Unique Sephardeem of the Ancient Near East—In Their Own Words* (Brooklyn: Thayer-Jacoby, 1988), 240–44. For more on the Ashkenazi family in the United States, also see chapter 9 of this book.

15. Krause, *Jews in Mexico,* 106–10, 155. For a description of the Monte Sinai Synagogue and other Jewish sites in Mexico City, see June Carolyn Erlick, "Eloquent Corners of Jewish Heritage," *New York Times,* January 19, 1997, 5: 16.

16. Margalit Bejereno, "Ha-Sefaradim Ki-Ḥalutzei Ha-Hagira Ha-Yehudit La-Kuba u-Terumatam Le-Ḥayyim Ha-Yehudim Ba-Kuba," in *Society and Community, Proceedings of the 2nd International Conference for Research of the Sephardic and Oriental Heritage,* A. Haim, ed.(Jerusalem: Misgav Yerushalayim, 1991), 113–31. Also see her comparison of the Sephardim (primarily Ladino-speakers) in M. Bejarano, "L'Integration des Sephardes en Amerique Latine: Le cas des communautes de Buenos Aires et la Havane," in *Memoires Juives D'Espagne et du Portugal,* E. Benbassa, ed. (Jerusalem: Hebrew University Abraham Harman Institute for Contemporary Jewry, 1996), 207–19.

17. Celia Stopnicka Rosenthal, "The Jews of Barranquilla," *Jewish Social Studies* 18 (1956): 262–74.

18. Mirelman, *Jewish Buenos Aires,* 35–45.

19. Ibid., 84–85, 98–99, 102–9, 121–31, 154.

20. Sutton, *Aleppo Chronicles,* 147, 210–11, 494.

21. Ibid., 241.

22. Mirelman, *Jewish Buenos Aires,* 98–99; Sutton *Aleppo Chronicles,* 145–46.

23. Sutton, *Aleppo Chronicles,* 211–14.

24. Sergio DellaPergola, Georges Sabagh, Mehdi Bezorgmehr, Claudia der-Martirosian, and Susana Lerner, "Hierarchic Levels of Subethnicity: Near Eastern Jews in the United States, France, and Mexico," *Sociological Papers* (Bar Ilan University Institute for Community Studies), 6, no.2 (June 1996): 1–42. Isaac Dabbah and David

Betesh present a less sanguine view of interreligious marriage in Mexico City; see Sutton, *Aleppo Chronicles,* 438–41. The richness and density of Aleppan Jewish activity is suggested in Hamui de Halabe, *Los Judios de Alepo,* 149–323. What appears in a celebratory volume must, of course, be examined critically, but this work does show the activities of several organizations over a half century.

25. Bryan Burrough, *Vendetta: American Express and the Smearing of Edmond Safra* (New York: Harper Collins, 1992), 36–37.

26. Burrough, *Vendetta,* 108.

27. Sutton, *Aleppo Chronicles,* 210–11, 215.

28. Rosenthal, "Jews of Barranquilla," passim.

29. Susan Birnbaum, "Shopkeepers in Panama Are Major Victims," *(Albany) Jewish World* and Jewish Telegraphic Agency, December 28, 1989, 1, 10.

30. Paul Lewis, "Two Delegates Vying to Be the Voice of the New Government," *New York Times,* December 29,1989, A12. Shortly after the invasion, David Betesh, a Panamanian businessman was interviewed by National Public Radio (All Things Considered, December 23, 1989). Betesh and Abadi are common surnames among Aleppan Jews.

31. David Pitt, "United States Troops Seize Israeli Regarded as Top Noriega Advisor," *New York Times,* December 29, 1989, A1, A12; Birnbaum, "Shopkeepers."

32. On recent activity in Mexico, see Hamui de Halabe, *Los Judios de Alepo,* 313–21; Sutton, *Aleppo Chronicles,* 213–14, 438–40.

33. Mirelman, *Jewish Buenos Aires,* 126, 128, 154–55; Moshe Zemer, "The Rabbinic Ban on Conversion in Argentina," *Judaism* 37 (1988): 84–93. Zemer generally evaluates the ban as ineffective, but the ban was extended to New York. See Sutton, *Aleppo Chronicles,* 84–84d. Most leaders there believe it has been effective, but this may be as much because of the general cohesion in the community as for any other reason.

34. Mirelman, *Jewish Buenos Aires,* 154–55, 126, 128.

35. Sutton, *Aleppo Chronicles,* 144–48.

36. Daniel C. Levy, "Jewish Education in Latin America," in *The Jewish Presence in Latin America,* Judith Elkin and Gilbert Merkx, eds. (Boston: Allen and Unwin, 1987), 157–84, esp. 179. On schools and youth movements among Aleppans in Mexico, see Hamui de Halabe, *Los Judios de Alepo,* 219–89.

37. DellaPergola et al., "Hierarchical Levels," 17–21, 31–32.

38. See Klich and Lesser, "*Turco* Immigrants," 5–8.

Chapter 8

1. For other studies of this community in this period, see Victor D. Sanua, "A Study of the Adjustment of Sephardi Jews in the New York Metropolitan Area," *Jewish Journal of Sociology* 9 (1967): 25–33; Joseph A. D. Sutton, *Magic Carpet: Aleppo-in-Flatbush* (Brooklyn: Thayer-Jacoby, 1979); idem, *Aleppo Chronicles: The Story of the Unique Sephardeem of the Ancient Near East—In Their Own Words* (Brooklyn: Thayer-Jacoby, 1988); Faye Ginsburg, "Power, Purity and Pollution: Menstrual Rituals in Judaism," paper presented at the Annual Meeting of the Northeastern Anthropological Association, Saratoga Springs, March 29, 1981; Sephardic Archives, "The Spirit of Aleppo: Syrian Jewish Immigrant Life in New York, 1890–1939" (Brooklyn: Se-

phardic Community Center, 1986) (exhibit catalog); Yael Zerubavel and Dianne Esses, "Reconstructions of the Past: Syrian Jewish Women and the Maintenance of Tradition," *Journal of American Folklore* 100 (October–December 1987): 528–39.

2. Lucius C. Miller, "A Study of the Syrian Population of Greater New York, New York" (n.d., c. 1903); Ralph A. Felton, "A Sociological Study of the Syrians in Greater New York" (Master's thesis, Columbia University, 1912); Philip M. Kayal and Joseph M. Kayal, *The Syrian-Lebanese in America* (Boston: Twayne, 1975), 84–90, 94–105. On the immigration of two families, see Robert Chira, *From Aleppo to America: The Story of Two Families* (New York: Rivercross, 1994), 25–58.

3. See Miller, "Syrian Population"; Sutton, *Magic Carpet,* 3–46, 62–79. The residential patterns of Syrian Jews generally and Aleppans in particular vary from place to place and period to period. In Jerusalem, Ḥalebim were first of all residents of neighborhoods with other Sephardi and Middle Eastern Jews. In Aleppo, Jews lived side by side with Muslims, but not with Christians. In Manchester, affluent Sephardim and some Ashkenazim lived in the south, while most East European immigrants lived in the north. It is unclear why the Sephardic immigrants who had lived in a tiny mini-ghetto on the Lower East Side went separate ways when they moved to Brooklyn and the Bronx.

4. See Sanua, "Adjustment"; Sutton *Magic Carpet,*46; Youssef M. Ibrahim, "Egyptian Jews in Brooklyn Take Hope at Sadat's Peace Initiatives," *New York Times,* December 12, 1977, 35. 5. See Sanua, "Adjustment."

6. Philip Hitti, *Syrians in America* (New York: Dutton, 1924), passim; Kayal and Kayal, *Syrian-Lebanese,* 84–90; Lillian Herling, "A Study in Retardation with Special Regard to the Status of the Syrians" (Master's thesis, Columbia University, 1929).

7. Herling, "A Study."

8. Sutton, *Magic Carpet,* 63–64; also, a Syrian Christian informant.

9. See Thomas F. Brady, "Gunman and Policeman Die in Times Square Area Battle." *New York Times,* March 1, 1970, 1, 24; Carter B. Horsley, "Inroads by Tourist Trade Shops Troubling Fifth Avenue," *New York Times,* April 20, 1975, section 8, pp. 1, 12; W. P. Zenner, "Arabic-Speaking Immigrants in North America as Middleman Minorities," *Ethnic and Racial Studies* 5 (1982): 457–77, esp. 463–65; Sutton, *Magic Carpet,* 10–19, 62–73.

10. Michael Kaufman, "Candy Store Alumni Honor the 'Boss.' " *New York Times,* January 24, 1970, 36.

11. Hayyim J. Cohen, "Sephardic Jews in the United States: Marriage with Ashkenazim and Non-Jews," *Dispersion and Unity* 13/14 (1971–72): 151–60.

12. Herling, "A Study"; Michael Steinhardt, "A Minority within a Minority" (Bachelor Honor Thesis, University of Pennsylvania, 1960).

13. Clare Boothe (Luce), *The Women* (New York: Random House, 1937), passim.

14. See Zerubavel and Esses, "Reconstructions," for a discussion of Syrian Jewish women's status, roles, and discourse.

15. Ben G. Frank, "Our Syrian Jewish Community," *American Examiner,* September 14, 1968, 29–30; idem, "Homogeneity of Syrian Jews Here Noted in Summer Synagogue," *(Schenectady) Jewish World,* September 16, 1971, 4; Howard Eisenberg, "Those Splendid Syrians Weekend in Deal," *Jewish Living* (September–October 1979):

36–40; Sutton, *Magic Carpet,* 44–45; Lionel Koppman, "A Dream Grows in Brooklyn: First Syrian JCC is Born of Joint Jewish Community Efforts," *Jewish Welfare Board Circle* 36, no.5 (1979): 9–11. Koppman wrote a version of the history that omitted mention of the earlier abortive Magen David Community Center.

16. *Community Bulletins,* Magen David Yeshiva, Brooklyn, 1959, no. 3–9.

17. W. P. Zenner, "Sephardic Communal Organizations in Israel," *Middle East Journal* 21 (1967): 173–86.

18. Frank, "Our Syrian Jewish Community"; David da Sola Pool, *Annual Report* (New York: Union of Sephardic Congregations, 1935), passim.

19. Ginsburg, "Power, Purity and Pollution."

20. W. P. Zenner, "Saints and Piecemeal Supernaturalism among the Jerusalem Sephardim," *Anthropological Quarterly* 38 (1965): 201–17.

21. Claudia Roden, *The Book of Middle Eastern Food* (New York: Knopf, 1972); Raymond Sokolov, "Jews Whose Tradition Includes Stuffed Grape Leaves at the Seder, *New York Times,* April 12, 1973, 54; Sisterhood of Deal, *Deal Delights* (Deal, N.J.: Synagogue of Deal, 1980). For a fuller discussion of Aleppan cooking, see C. Roden, *The Book of Jewish Food* (New York: Knopf, 1997).

22. On schooling in the 1920s, see Lillian Herling, "A Study"; Sutton, *Magic Carpet,* 101–3. Also see Morris Gross, *Learning Readiness in Two Jewish Settings* (New York: Center for Urban Education, 1967).

23. For other portraits of the varieties of ethnic experience in Brooklyn, see Sutton, *Magic Carpet,* 109–35.

24. Lawrence Plotnik, "The Sephardim of New Lots," *Commentary* 25 (1958): 28–35.

25. See W. P. Zenner, "Common Ethnicity and Separate Identities: Interaction between Jewish Immigrant Groups," in *Cross-Cultural Adaptations,* Y. Y. Kim and W. B. Gudykunst, eds. (Newbury Park, Calif.: Sage, 1988), 267–85.

26. Sanua, "Adjustment"; Ibrahim, "Egyptian Jews."

27. Joseph Ashear, "Manufacturer and an Activist in Jewish Affairs" (obituary), *New York Times,* January 4, 1979, 19.

28. Steinhardt, "A Minority."

29. Herling, "A Study."

Chapter 9

1. The accounts here were mainly collected by me, but I will also utilize accounts found in Joseph A. D. Sutton, *Aleppo Chronicles: The Story of the Unique Sephardeem of the Ancient Near East—In Their Own Words* (Brooklyn: Thayer-Jacoby, 19878). The accounts that Sutton collected are generally by individuals who have moved to Brooklyn or Deal, while most of my accounts are by those who are still "out-of-towners."

2. Sutton, *Aleppo Chronicles,* 240–48; also see for this period, ibid., 324–25. For the Ashkenazi family in Mexico, see chapter 7 of this book.

3. See John J. McEneny, *Albany: Capital City on the Hudson* (Woodland Hills, Calif.: Windsor, 1981), 210. Also interview with Barbara Freed.

4. see Sutton, *Aleppo Chronicles,* 266, 278–79, 378, 396–97; the other cases are from Zenner field notes.

5. Sutton, *Aleppo Chronicles,* 266.

6. Ibid., 378.

7. Ibid., 278–79.

8. On Los Angeles, see ibid., 74; On Montreal, see ibid., 353–54. More work needs to be done on the Californian and Canadian Aleppan communities.

9. R. W. Apple, "Haddad-Farbstein Campaign Draws Attention to Syrian Jews," *New York Times,* June 1, 1964, 21.

10. Sutton, *Aleppo Chronicles,* 370.

11. This section is based on W. P. Zenner, "Chicago's Sephardim: A Historical Exploration," *American Jewish History* 79 (1989–90): 221–41, esp. 228–29.

12. For further discussion of these anecdotes, see W. P. Zenner, "Common Ethnicity and Separate Identities: Interaction between Jewish Immigrant Groups," in *Cross-Cultural Adaptations,* Y. Y. Kim and W. B. Gudykunst, eds. (Newbury Park, Calif.: Sage, 1988), 267–85.

13. A new pattern that was noted in the Chicago case is that of founding new Sephardic *minyānim.* While most of these new *minyanim* are in the New York metropolitan area, new such prayer groups have been founded elsewhere, including Minneapolis and Boston. Syrian Jews, whether married to Ashkenazic women or not, have been important catalysts in several of these.

14. Jack Marshall, biographical sketch and poems in *Grape Leaves,* Gregory Orfalea and Sharif Elmusa, eds. (Salt Lake City: University of Utah Press, 1988), 176–91. Also see Jack Marshall, *Sesame* (Minneapolis: Coffee House Press, 1993), esp. 23–36, and biographical sketch on jacket; Diane Matza, ed., *Sephardic American Voices: Two Hundred Years of a Literary Legacy* (Hanover, N.H.: University Press of New England, 1997), 164–67. On Stanley Sultan, see ibid., 121–27, 177–220. The paradox of being simultaneously Arab and Jew also appears in a younger author, Herbert Hadad, whose father was Aleppan and who was raised in New England: see ibid., 65–67, 308–13.

15. Sutton, *Aleppo Chronicles,* 396–406.

16. Daniel I. Silverberg, *To Honor Tradition: The Shift towards Religious Conservatism in the Syrian Jewish Community of Brooklyn* (Bachelor Honor Thesis, Harvard University, Committee on the Study of Religion, 1997), 13.

Chapter 10

1. The Egyptian, Lebanese, and Israeli Sephardim live in close proximity to older Syrian Jews, but they have separate synagogues. Many are of Aleppan descent. They tend to use the same schools. Rabbi Shimon Alouf, rabbi of Ahavah Ve-Aḥvah (the Egyptian synagogue), taught at the Magen David Yeshiva, a large Syrian day school, which closed in September 1999.

2. Sutton uses the term "social homogeneity" coupled with "religious insularity" to describe the community *(Aleppo Chronicles: The Story of the Unique Sephardeem of the Ancient Near East—In Their Own Words* [Brooklyn: Thayer-Jacoby, 1988], 73). Our analysis is grounded in the description of the different dimensions of the assimilatory process by Milton M. Gordon *(Assimilation in American Life* [New York: Oxford University Press, 1964], 18–83). We view the Syrian Jews as an "eth-class"—that is,

an ethnic group that occupies a particular position in the class structure of the United States.

3. On the importance of Deal for mate selection and the Deal Casino, see Sutton, *Aleppo Chronicles,* 75–76, 413. Also see Elizabeth Bumiller, "It's a Summer Thing: Like-Minded New Yorkers Flock Together," *New York Times,* May 26,1996, 27, 30. Joseph A. D.Sutton, *Magic Carpet: Aleppo-in-Flatbush* (Brooklyn: Thayer-Jacoby, 1979), 108, has a brief description of the social clubs that played an important role in the community, both in Brooklyn and in Deal.

4. One part-Aleppan who moved to the suburbs is the poet Linda Ashear, who grew up in Brooklyn but now lives in Westchester County. She writes that she has no Sephardic friends in her new home. See Diane Matza, ed., *Sephardic-American Voices: Two Hundred Years of a Literary Legacy* (Hanover, N.H.: University Press of New England, 1997), 159–60. On Yvonne Tabboush, see Sutton, *Aleppo Chronicles,* 425–33.

5. On Kings Highway businesses, see Sutton, *Aleppo Chronicles,* 78–79.

6. Robert Chira, personal communication. See chapter 9 for more on William Haddad.

7. Sutton, *Aleppo Chronicles,* 394–95.

8. Advertisement, *IMAGE* (March 1996), 24.

9. For example, Joseph Abe Sultan, M.D., who went to Yale; see Sutton, *Aleppo Chronicles,* 406–14. Also see ibid., 100–103.

10. See *IMAGE,* March 1996, October 1997, among other issues.

11. On the top businesses, see *Crain's New York Business,* November 25, 1995, 30–48. Such lists quickly become outdated. Also see Sutton, *Aleppo Chronicles,* 103–5.

On the *Crazy Eddie* episode, see, among other accounts, Sutton, *Aleppo Chronicles,* 104; and stories in the *New York Times,* from Stephen Labaton, "What is Crazy Eddie Really Up to," *New York Times,* June 14, 1984, F1, F25; to "Crazy Eddie Sentencing Is Weighed," *New York Times,* March 23, 1994; and Lisa W. Foderaro, "Crazy Eddie's Returning, Minus 2 Jailed Founders," *New York Times,* January 20, 1998, B1, B8. On "The Wiz," see David Ornstein, "Competitor Likely to Replace Wiz, *Albany Times-Union,* December 18, 1997, E1, E5; Lisa W. Foderaro, "Wiz Store Closings Are Across Northeast," *New York Times,* December 18, 1997, B10.

12. Sutton, *Aleppo Chronicles,* 104; Bryan Burrough, *Vendetta: American Express and the Smearing of Edmond Safra* (New York: Harper Collins, 1992); Saul Hansell, "Republic Breaks with Tradition," *New York Times,* November 24, 1993, D1.

13. An unusual newer immigrant was Joseph Galapo, an Egyptian-born New York City policeman who was killed while carrying out a "routine drug arrest" in 1988. His funeral service was held at the Magen David Congregation in Brooklyn. See David E. Pitt, "Man Charged in Shooting of Officer by His Partner," *New York Times,* August 18, 1988, B1, B4.

14. Bernard Weinraub, "Dan Hedaya is Fading out of Anonymity," *New York Times,* November 14, 1995, C23, C17.

15. Sutton, *Aleppo Chronicles,* 394–95.

16. Ibid., 404–14.

17. Ibid., The February 1996 issue of *IMAGE* contains an article in which a

woman advertises herself; see Stephanie Franco, "Let's Get Acquainted ," *IMAGE,* February 1996, 20. Also see advertisements in other issues of this "neighborhood family" magazine.

18. Shoshana Macktez Landow, "Responding to the Challenge of American Society, A Continuous Process of Adaptation and Resistance: The Uniquely Successful Syrian-Jewish Community of Brooklyn," (Junior Paper in Anthropology, Princeton University, spring 1990), 37–39.

19. See the newsletter of the Historical Society of Jews from Egypt, called "*The Second Exodus*," first issued in December 1995. Also see Victor D. Sanua, "A Jewish Childhood in Cairo," in *Fields of Offerings: Studies in Honor of Raphael Patai,* V. D. Sanua, ed. (Cranbury, N.J.: Associated University Presses, 1983), 283–295.

20. Historical preservation activities in 1998 revolved around two separate groups. One was the "Historical Society," centered in Congregation Ahavah ve-Aḥvah. The other center was Professor Victor D. Sanua, who organized a conference on Jews from Egypt held at Columbia University in December 1997. He received assistance from *IMAGE* magazine. Recent immigrants from Syria are mainly Damascenes. Unlike their American cousins, they are still Arabic-speakers. They have received aid from the New York Association for New Americans. They continue to form a subgroup in the community. See Gloria Zicht, "The Immigration of Syrian Jews to New York 1992–1994: An Agency's Adaptation to a Different Culture," *Journal of Jewish Communal Service* 72 (1996): 256–62.

21. Wolfgang Saxon, "Jacob Kassin, 94, Chief Rabbi of Brooklyn's Syrian Sephardim," *New York Times,* January 9, 1994, D-20; Rabbi Jacob S. Kassin, "Autobiography," *IMAGE,* January 1995, 6–7; Eliezer al-Beg, *Me-Aram Naharayim ʿad Yerushalayim* (New York: private publication, 1961); Sutton, *Aleppo Chronicles,* 81. The January 1995 issue of *IMAGE* contained eulogies of Rabbi Kassin. Also see David Herszenhor, "Sephardic Jews Shift Leadership, Father to Son," *New York Times,* December 25, 1994, sect. 13 (city), p. 7; and Deena Yellin, "A Legacy Continues," *Jewish Week,* February 24, 1995, 16–17.

22. See Larry Yudelson, "Halakhic Exponents Maintain Assassination of Leaders Viable," *Jewish World,* July 6, 1995, 7; Joe Sexton, "An Assassin's Shot Reverberates at a Synagogue in Brooklyn," *New York Times,* November 17, 1995, B1, B2; idem, "How a Rabbi's Rhetoric Did, or Didn't, Justify Assassination," *New York Times,* December 3, 1995, 51. See also Cynthia Mann, "Hecht Suspended, Israel Rally Set for Manhattan," *Jewish World,* December 7, 1995, 3. On the Ashkenazic influence on Sephardic religious circles in Israel, see chapters 5 and 6. Also see Norman A. Stillman, *Sephardic Religious Responses to Modernity* (Luxembourg: Harwood Academic Publishers, 1995), 65–86.

23. Sutton, *Aleppo Chronicles,* 98. Also see Daniel I. Silverberg, "To Honor Tradition: The Shift towards Religious Conservatism in the Syrian Jewish Community in Brooklyn" (honors thesis, Harvard University, Committee on the Study of Religion, 1997).

24. Daniel J. Elazar, *The Other Jews: The Separdim Today* (New York: Basic Books, 1989), 171.

25. Yellin, "Legacy." On Rabbi Kassin, see note 21.

26. It should be stressed that while modern Orthodox synagogues are "Ameri-

canized," this does not apply to the ultra-Orthodox. On traditional folk religion, see W. P. Zenner, "Saints and Piecemeal Supernaturalism among the Jerusalem Sephardim," *Anthropological Quarterly* 38 (1965): 201–17. Also see Sutton, *Aleppo Chronicles,* 99.

27. See Samuel Heilman and Steven Cohen, *Cosmopolitans and Parochials: Modern Orthodox Jews in America* (Chicago: University of Chicago Press, 1989), 180–93; also see Jenna W. Joselit, *New York's "Jewish" Jews* (Philadelphia: Jewish Publication Society, 1990), 147–53.

28. As noted in chapter 8, an ultra-Orthodox group had emerged in the 1950s, but it was small and marginalized. In fact, Rabbi Jose Faur, the leader of this particular group, later taught Talmud at the Conservative Jewish Theological Seminary. In the 1960s, a new group began to emerge under different leadership. In addition, Orthodox Judaism generally in the United States since 1950 has become more conservative and less willing to accommodate itself to contemporary culture. Rabbi Yosef Harari-Raful, who is the head of the Ateret Torah Yeshiva, is the leader of this ultra-Orthodox segment of the Syrian community today. His approach differs sharply from Faur's 1958 approach in several ways. Faur is a "Sephardic nationalist," who has striven to emphasize the superiority of Sephardim over Ashkenazim, while Harari-Raful is close to the Ashkeanzic yeshiva style. Faur introduced his followers to general intellectual trends, while Harari-Raful does not. Faur in 1958 challenged accommodation, but he did not represent the militant conservatism that Harari-Raful adheres to. Daniel Silverberg, "To Honor Tradition," sees the change that Harari-Raful has led as one whereby the former observance and toleration of lax observance are part of a customary traditionalism, which is now giving way to a more text-oriented and self-conscious orthodoxy.

On Faur, see Sutton, *Aleppo Chronicles,* 91–92. Faur by the 1980s had become a model for some right-wing Conservative rabbis who sought to formulate an independent traditionalist position on the lines of the Livorno rabbis Elijah Ben-Amozegh, whose work had been burnt in Aleppo in the 1860s, and Sabato Morais, founder of the Jewish Theological Seminary of America.

29. Landow, "Responding to the Challenge," 34–35.

30. See Sutton, *Aleppo Chronicles,* 294–95, for one woman's perception of the contemporary (1980s) community, including comments on "ultra-Orthodoxy" and drug use.

31. See Mark Kligman, "Modes of Prayer: Arabic *Maqamat* in the Sabbath Morning Liturgical Music of the Syrian Jews in Brooklyn" (Ph.D. Diss., New York University, 1997).

32. Sutton, *Aleppo Chronicles,*84–85.

33. Kligman, "Modes," chapters 4, 5, and 7.

34. See Kay Kaufman Shelemay, *Let Jasmine Rain Down: Song and Remembrance among Syrian Jews in the Americas* (Chicago: University of Chicago Press, 1998).

35. See Sisterhood of Deal, *Deal Delights* (Deal, N.J.: Synagogue of Deal, 1980). Also see Joan Nathan, "Syria in Brooklyn: The Special Tastes of Rosh ha-Shanah," *New York Times,* September 12, 1990, C3; and Peter Hellman, "Aleppo on the Hudson: The Savory Traditions of Syrian Jewish Cooking Endure in a New York Kitchen," *Saveur* 23 (Dec. 1997): 88–98. Grace Sason gives recipes for certain traditional

dishes, including various varieties of kibbe, in her *Kosher Syrian Cooking* (Brooklyn: privately published, 1988), 54–62.

36. On Syrian and Egyptian Passover, see Lorna J. Sass, "A Passover Feast Rich in Memories and Cuisine," *New York Times,* April 15, 1981, C1, C6; "Fewer Brand Names on Passover Doesn't Mean Less," *Jewish World,* April 13, 1989, 4.

37. See Landow, "Responding to the Challenge," who makes this point in her thesis.

38. See Bumiller, "It's a Summer Thing."

39. See Shelemay, *Let Jasmine Rain Down.* With regard to rabbinical response to the use of Arabic music, see Rabbi Ovadia Yosef, *Sefer She'elot u-teshuvot Yehaveh Da'at* (Jerusalem, 1978), vol.2, #5:24–28.

40. The following are publications that resulted from Archives activity: *The Victory Bulletin* (Brooklyn: Sephardic Community Center, 1984); Marianne Sanua, "From the Pages of the *Victory Bulletin:* The Syrian Jews of Brooklyn during World War II," in *YIVO Annual* (Evanston, Ill.: Northwestern University Press, 1990), 19:283–330; *The Spirit of Aleppo: Syrian Jewish Immigrant Life in New York, 1890–1939* (Brooklyn: Sephardic Community Center, 1986); Yael Zerubavel and Dianne Esses, "Reconstructions of the Past: Syrian Jewish Women and the Maintenance of Tradition," *Journal of American Folklore* 100 (1987): 528–39; Kay Kaufman Shelemay, "Together in the Field: Team Research among Syrian Jews in Brooklyn, New York," *Ethnomusicology* 32, no. 3 (1988): 369–84; Kay Kaufman Shelemay and Sarah Weiss, *Pizmon: Syrian Jewish Religious and Social Song* (Hohokus, N.J.: Meadowlark, a division of Shanachie Records Corp., 1986).

41. On Sutton see William E. Farrell, "About New York: At 74, He Eagerly Chronicles Brooklyn's Syrian Jews," *New York Times,* November 12, 1980, B3. Notable obituaries are the following: "Joseph Ashear, 82, Manufacturer and Activist in Jewish Affairs," *New York Times,* Jan. 4, 1979; Wolfgang Saxon, "Jacob Kassin, 94, Chief Rabbi of Brooklyn's Syrian Sephardim," *New York Times,* December 9, 1994; Wolfgang Saxon, "Joseph Ades, 95, Businessman Who Financed Schools and Causes," *New York Times,* December 18, 1996, B13. For other *New York Times* articles, check through above endnotes and those for chapter 8. For an article on the 1995 Harlem incident, see Philip Kasinitz and Bruce Haynes, "The Burning of Freddy's: Black-Jewish Conflict in Harlem," *CommonQuest: The Magazine of Black-Jewish Relations* 1, no. 2 (1996): 25–34. Joseph Sutton does refer to the image of Syrian Jewish businessmen in a rather apologetic vein. See Sutton, *Magic Carpet,* 67–68. This aspect of the Syrian Jewish image is discussed in chapter 11.

42. See Ben G. Frank,"Our Syrian Jewish Community," *American Examiner,* September 14, 1968, 29–30; idem, "Homogeneity of Syrian Jews Here Noted in Summer Synagogue," *Jewish World,* September 16, 1971, 4; idem, "Where Mideast Meets West," *Chicago Sentinel,* December 14, 1972. All of these articles were syndicated by the Jewish Telegraphic Agency, which serves the Anglo-Jewish press.

43. Stanley Sultan, *Rabbi: A Tale of the Waning Year* (West Whateley, Mass.: American Novelists' Cooperative, 1977).

44. See Amnon Shamosh, "Ha-Hevdel Ha-Qatan" (The small difference), in *Iti Me-Levanon* (Tel Aviv: Ha-Kibbutz Ha-Me'uḥad, 1981), 47–56; idem, "Barbara Gindi Nikhneset La-Ḥupa" (Barbara Gindi gets married), 31–39; idem, "Shnei Max 'Ab-

bady" (The two Max Abbadys), in *Ma'ayan Ḥatum* (Tel Aviv: Ha-Kibbutz Ha-Me'u-ḥad, 1984), 15–30. For a more critical view of Syrian Jews in the United States being buffeted by the forces of American culture, see his *Michel Ezra Safra u-Vanav* (Michel Ezra Safra and sons) (Ramat Gan: Massada, 1978), 266–67. Also see Walter P. Zenner, "Aleppo and the Kibbutz: The Fiction of Amnon Shamosh," *Shofar,* 6, no. 3 (spring 1988): 25–35.

Chapter 11

1. Most of the figures in this section can be found in the earlier chapters of this book pertaining to each of these areas.

2. See Steven M Lowenstein, *Frankfurt on the Hudson: The German Jewish Community of Washington Heights, 1933–1983, Its Structure and Culture* (Detroit: Wayne State University Press, 1989).

3. Bryan Burrough, *Vendetta: American Express and the Smearing of Edmond Safra* (New York: Harper Collins, 1992), 29–56.

4. For this line of reasoning, see W. P. Zenner, "The Jewish Diaspora and the Middleman Adaptation," In *Diaspora: Exile and the Jewish Condition,* Étan Levine, ed. (New York: Jason Aronson, 1983), 141–56; idem, "The Trans-National Web of Syrian-Jewish Relations," in *Urban Life: Readings in Urban Anthropology,* 3d ed., George Gmelch and W. P. Zenner, eds. (Prospect Heights, Ill.: Waveland Press, 1996), 459–72. Also see W. P. Zenner, *Minorities in the Middle: A Cross-Cultural Analysis* (Albany: State University of New York Press, 1991), 74–80, 89–93.

5. On women's occupations in Brooklyn during the 1920s, see Lillian Herling, "A Study in [school] Retardation with Special Regard to the Syrians" (master's thesis, Columbia University, 1929), 19. Also see Yael Zerubavel and Dianne Esses, "Reconstructions of the Past: Syrian Jewish Women and the Maintenance of Tradition," *Journal of American Folklore* 100 (October–December 1987): 528–39.

6. See Robert Chira, *From Aleppo to America: The Story of Two Families* (New York: Rivercross, 1994), 35. Also note the proxy marriages for women from Syria in the 1970s, as discussed in Bernard Gwertzman, "Syrian Proxy-Marriage Lets Syrian Women Emigrate to U.S.," *New York Times,* July 31, 1977, 1, 34.

7. The 1980 edition of *Deal Delights* (Deal, N.J.: Synagogue of Deal) omits the very typical Aleppan dish of *kibbe ḥamḍa.* See Jack Marshall, *Sesame* (Minneapolis: Coffee House Press, 1993), esp. 23–36), which refers to a Syrian cookie made with sesame seeds and which he associates with his mother. See Stanley Sultan, "Ba'lawa," *West Branch* (fall 1997): 28–33.

8. See chapter 10, notes 31 and 34.

9. With regard to Shamosh's writing, see Amnon Shamosh, *Michel Ezra Safra u-Vanav* (Ramat Gan: Massada, 1978). Also see W. P. Zenner, "Aleppo and the Kibbutz: The Fiction of Amnon Shamosh," *Shofar* 6, no. 3 (1988): 25–35; and W. P. Zenner, "Espionage and Cultural Mediation," in *Critical Essays on Israeli Social Issues and Scholarship,* Russell Stone and W. P. Zenner, eds. (Albany: State University of New York Press, 1994), 31–42; also see Avraham Marthan, "An Authentic Human Voice: The Poetry of Amnon Shamosh,"in *Critical Essays,* Russell Stone and W. P. Zenner, eds., 43–61; Burrough, *Vendetta,* 27–56.

10. Marshall, *Sesame,* 80.

11. David Laniado, *La-Qedoshim asher Ba-Are"ṣ* (Jerusalem, 1980). For an interpretation of this work and works derived from it, see W. P. Zenner, "Remembering the Sages of Aram Soba (Aleppo)," in *Critical Essays on Israeli Society, Religion and Government,* Kevin Avruch and W. P. Zenner, eds. (Albany: State University of New York Press, 1997), 137–51.

12. Stanley Sultan, *Rabbi: A Tale of the Waning Year* (West Whateley, Mass.: American Novelists' Cooperative, 1977).

13. Marshall, *Sesame,* 46–48.

14. Amnon Shamosh, "Barbara Gindy Nikhneset La-Ḥupāh" (Barbara Gindy gets married), in *Iti Me-Levanon* (Tel Aviv: Ha-Kibbutz Ha-Me'uḥad, 1981), 31–39; and Amnon Shamosh, "Shnei Max ʿAbbady" (the two Max Abbadys), in *Maʿayan Ḥatum* (Tel Aviv: Ha-Kibbutz Ha-Me'uḥad, 1984), 15–30. Also see W. P. Zenner, "Aleppo and the Kibbutz." On the blood libel, see Amnon Shamosh, "The Purim of Aram Zobah," *Jewish Spectator* 44, no. 1 (1979): 35–38; Compare his treatment of this event with that of Laniado, *La-Qedoshim,* 195. Shamosh omits any reference to the role of a rabbi, while the rabbi is the hero of Laniado's version. A rabbi plays an important role in another Shamosh story; see Shamosh, "Crumbs," *Present Tense* 9, no. 1 (November 1981): 55.

15. Joseph A. D. Sutton, *Magic Carpet: Aleppo-in-Flatbush* (Brooklyn: Thayer-Jacoby, 1979), 74–103; and idem, *Aleppo Chronicles: The Story of the Unique Sephardeem of the Ancient Near East—In Their Own Words* (Brooklyn: Thayer-Jacoby, 1988), 80–100. In an appendix to the former work, Sutton gives us a précis of Laniado's biographical dictionary.

16. For a recent account of this debate from a more or less Zionist or Orthodox viewpoint, see Steven Bayme, "Whither American Jewry?" *Contemporary Jewry* 17 (1996): 148–54. Bayme's viewpoint, which is currently in ascendancy, has been called the "survivalist" viewpoint. It stresses "in-reach" educational efforts aimed at committed Jews. It is opposed to the "transformist" approach of those who believe that despite intermarriage, American Jewry will survive. Also, the survivalists feel that most efforts at outreach toward those on the periphery of the Jewish community are futile. One might add that despite lip service, most Jewish cultural and educational efforts, whether by Orthodox or non-Orthodox, Zionist or non-Zionist Jews in the post–World War II era, have been "in-reach" efforts. Only the Lubavicher Hasidim have conducted sustained outreach efforts, and these have had mixed results.

17. See note 42 in chapter 10. Also see Sutton, *Magic Carpet,* esp. ix–xiii.

18. Edward Spicer, *The Yaquis: A Cultural History* (Tucson: University of Arizona Press, 1980), 333–62. This is probably his definitive statement on this subject.

19. James Clifford, "Diasporas," *Cultural Anthropology* 9 (1994): 302–38.

References

This list of references consists of works cited in the endnotes of each chapter. Works that will not be cited consist of articles in such publications as newspapers, popular magazines, yearbooks, pamphlets, standard reference works, and unpublished academic papers.

Abramsky-Bligh, Irit. 1986. "Yehudei Suriya Taḥat Shilton Vichy." *Peʿamim* 28:131–50.

Abu-Lughod, Janet L. 1987. "The Islamic City: Historic Myth, Islamic Essence, and Contemporary Relevance." *International Journal of Middle Eastern Studies* 19:155–76.

Aciman, André. 1994. *Out of Egypt*. New York: Farrar-Straus, Giroux.

Al-Khalil, Samir (Kanan Makiya). 1989. *Republic of Fear*. Berkeley: University of California Press.

Al-Qattan, Najwa. 1992. "The Damascene Jewish Community in the Latter Decades of the Eighteenth Century: Aspects of Socio- Economic Life Based on the Registers of the *Sharīʿa* Courts." In *The Syrian Lands in the 18th and 19th Century*. Thomas Philipp, ed., 197–216. Stuttgart: Franz Steiner, Berliner Islamstudien, vol. 5.

Antoun, Richard, and Donald Quataert. 1991. *Syria: Society, Culture and Polity*. Albany: State University of New York Press.

Basch, Linda, Nina Glick Schiller, and Cristina Szanton Blanc. 1995. *Nations Unbound: Transnational Projects, Post-Colonial Predicaments, and Deterritorialized Nation-States*. Basel: Gordon and Breach.

Batatu, Hanna. 1981. "Some Observations on the Social Roots of Syria's Ruling Military Elite: The Causes of Its Dominance." *Middle East Journal* 35:331–44.

Bayme. Steven. 1996. "Whither American Jewry?" *Contemporary Jewry* 17: 148–54.

Beinin, Joel. 1990. *Was the Red Flag Flying There? Marxist Politics and the Arab-Israeli Conflict in Egypt and Israel, 1948–1965.* Berkeley: University of California Press.

———. 1998. *The Dispersion of Egyptian Jews: Culture, Politics and Formation of a Modern Diaspora.* Berkeley: University of California Press.

Bejereno, Margalit. 1991. "Ha-Sefardim Ki-Ḥalutzei Ha-Hagira Ha-Yehudit La-Kuba u-Terumatam Le-Ḥayyim Ha-Yehudim Ba-Kuba." In *Society and Community, Proceedings of the 2nd International Conference for Research of the Sephardi and Oriental Heritage,* A. Haim, ed., 113–33. Jerusalem: Misgav Yerushalayim.

———. 1996. "L'integration des Sephardes en Amerique Latine: La cas des communautés de Buenos Aires et la Havane." In *Mémoires Juives D'Espagne et du Portugal,* E. Benbassa, ed., 207–19. Jerusalem: Hebrew University Abraham Harman Institute for Contemporary Jewry.

Bensinger, Immanuel. 1905. "Syria." Jewish Encyclopedia. New York: Funk & Wagnalls. 11:646–648.

Ben-Zvi, Yitzhak. 1960. "Eretz Yisrael under Ottoman Rule, 1517–1917." In *The Jews: Their History, Culture and Religion,* Louis Finkelstein, ed., 1:601–89. Philadelphia: Jewish Publication Society.

———. 1966/67. *She'ar Yashuv.* Jerusalem: Ben Zvi Institute.

Bin-Gorion, Micha Joseph. In *MiMekor Yisrael: Selected Classical Jewish Folktales.* Edited by Dan Ben-Amos. Bloomington: Indiana University Press. 70–72.

Bohannan, Paul, and Fred Plog. 1970. *Beyond the Frontier.* Garden City, N.Y.: Natural History Press.

Bonacich, Edna. 1973. "A Theory of Middleman Minorities." *American Sociological Review* 38:583–94.

Burrough, Bryan. 1992. *Vendetta: American Express and the Smearing of Edmond Safra.* New York: Harper Collins.

Chira, Robert. 1994. *From Aleppo to America: The Story of Two Families.* New York: Rivercross.

Choeka, Ya'akov, and Ḥayyim Sabato. 1989–90. *Minḥat Aharon: Me'asef Torani Le-Zikhron shel Ha-Rav Aharon Choeka.* Jerusalem: private publication.

Clifford, James. 1994. "Diasporas." *Cultural Anthropology* 9:302–38.

Cohen, Abner. 1974. *Two-Dimensional Man.* Berkeley: University of California Press.

Cohen, Hayyim J. 1971. "Picciotto." *Encyclopedia Judaica,* 13:498.

———. 1973. "Sephardic Jews in the United States: Marriage with Ashkenazim and Non-Jews." *Dispersion and Unity* 13/14:151–60.

———. 1973. *The Jews of the Middle East 1860–1972.* Jerusalem: Israel Universities Press.

Cohen, Martin. 1973. *The Martyr.* Philadelphia: Jewish Publication Society of America.

Cohen-Almagor, Raphael. 1995. "Cultural Pluralism and the Israeli Nation-Building Ideology." *International Journal of Middle Eastern Studies* 27:461–84.

Coon, Carleton. 1951. *Caravan.* New York: Henry Holt.

DellaPergola, Sergio. 1987. "Demographic Trends of Latin American Jewry." In *The Jewish Presence in Latin America,* Judith L. Elkin and Gilbert W. Merkx, eds. Boston: Allen and Unwin. 85–113.

DellaPergola, Sergio, Georges Sabagh, Mehdi Bezorgmehr, Claudia der-Martirosian, and Susana Lerner. 1996. "Hierarchic Levels of Subethnicity: Near Eastern Jews in the United States, France, and Mexico." *Sociological Papers* (Bar Ilan University Institute for Community Studies) 6, no. 2 (June). 1–42.

Deshen, Shlomo. 1994. "Baghdad Jewry in Late Ottoman Times: The Emergence of Social Classes and Secularization." *Association for Jewish Studies Review* 19:19–44.

Deshen, Shlomo, and Walter P. Zenner. 1982. *Jewish Societies in the Middle East.* Lanham, Md.: University Press of America.

———. 1996. *Jews among Muslims: Communities in the Precolonial Middle East.* New York: New York University Press and Houndmills: Macmillan.

Dothan [Lutzky], Alexander. 1956. "On the History of the Ancient Synagogue in Aleppo," *Sefunot* 1:25–61.

Downey, Glanville. 1961. *A History of Antioch in Syria from the Seleucids to the Arab Conquest.* Princeton, N.J.: Princeton University Press.

———. 1962. *Antioch in the Age of Theodosius the Great.* Norman: University of Oklahoma Press.

Eisenstadt, Shmuel N. 1954. *The Absorption of Immigrants.* London: Routledge and Kegan Paul.

Elazar, Daniel J. 1989. *The Other Jews: The Sephardim Today.* New York: Basic Books.

Elkin, Judith Laikin. 1980. *The Jews of the Latin American Republics.* Chapel Hill: University of North Carolina Press.

Fawaz, Leila. 1983. *Merchants and Migrants in Nineteenth Century Beirut.* Cambridge, Mass.: Harvard University Press.

Frangopulo, N. J. 1965. "Foreign Communities in Manchester." *Manchester Review* 10:189–206.

———. 1977. *Tradition in Action: The Historical Evolution of the Greater Manchester County.* East Ardsley: Wakefield Publications.

Frankel, Jonathan. 1997. *The Damascus Affair: "Ritual Murder," Politics, and the Jews in 1840.* Cambridge: Cambridge University Press.

Fredman, Ruth Gruber. 1981. "Cosmopolitans at Home: The Sephardic Jews of Washington, D.C." *Anthropological Quarterly* 54:61–67.

Friedman, Saul S. 1989. *Without Future: The Plight of Syrian Jews.* New York: Praeger.

García Márquez, Gabriel. 1982. *A Chronicle of a Death Foretold.* New York: Knopf.

Gaube, Heinz, and Eugen Wirth. 1984. *Aleppo: Historische und geographische Beitrage zur bauliche Gestaltung, zur soziale Organisation und wirtschaftliche Dynamik einer vorderasiatische Fernhandelsmetropole.* Wiesbaden: Reichert.

Gerber, Haim. 1994. *State, Society and Law in Islam: Ottoman Law in Comparative Perspective.* Albany: State University of New York Press.

Gini de Barnatan, Matilde. 1993. "Cryptojews in Rio de Plata in the Seventeenth Century." In *New Horizons in Sephardic Studies,* Yedida K. Stillman and George K. Zucker, eds., 137–47. Albany: State University of New York Press.

Goitein, Shlomo D. 1971. *A Mediterranean Society.* Vol. 1. Berkeley: University of California Press.

Goldberg, Harvey E. 1990. *Jewish Life in Muslim Libya: Rivals and Relatives.* Chicago: University of Chicago Press.

Golding, Louis. 1932. *Magnolia Street.* London: Gollancz.

Gonzalez, Nancie L. 1992. *Dollar, Dove and Eagle: One Hundred Years of Palestinian Migration to Honduras.* Ann Arbor: University of Michigan Press.

Gordon, Milton M. 1964. *Assimilation in American Life.* New York: Oxford University Press.

Gross, Morris. 1967. *Learning Readiness in Two Jewish Settings.* New York: Center for Urban Education.

Gubbay, Lucien, and Abraham Levy. 1992. *The Sephardim: Their Glorious Tradition from the Babylonian Exile to the Present Day.* London: Carnell.

Gurevich, David. 1940. *The Jewish Population of Jerusalem.* Jerusalem: Jewish Agency.

Halliday, Fred. 1992. "The *Millet* of Manchester: Arab Merchants and Cotton Trade." *British Journal of Middle East Studies* 19:159–76.

Halper, Jeff. 1978. *Ethnicity and Education: The Schooling of Afro-Asian Jewish Children in a Jerusalem Locality.* Ann Arbor, Mich.: University Microfilms.

———. 1991. *Between Redemption and Revival: The Jewish Yishuv in Jerusalem in the Nineteenth Century.* Boulder Colo.: Westview Press.

———. 1997. "Modern Jerusalem: Policies, Peoples, Planning." In *Critical Essays in Israeli Society, Religion and Government,* Kevin Avruch and Walter P. Zenner, eds. Albany: State University of New York Press.

Hamui de Halabe, Liz. 1989. *Los Judios de Alepo en Mexico.* Mexico: Maguen David.

———. 1997. *Identidad Colectiva: Rasgos Culturales de los Immigrantes Judeo-Alepinos en Mexico.* Mexico: JGH Editores Ciencia y Cultura Latinoamericana.

Harel, Yaron. 1992. "Changes in Syrian Jewry, 1840–1880." Ph.D. diss., Bar Ilan University, Ramat Gan.

———. 1993. "Tesisah Ruḥanit Ba-Mizraḥ—Yesodah shel Qehillah Reformit Bi-Ḥaleb Bi-Shnat 1862" (Spiritual agitation in the East: Founding of a Reform congregation in Aleppo in 1862). *Hebrew Union College Annual* 63:xix–xxxv.

———. 1996. *Sifrei Are"ṣ: Ha-Sifrut Ha-Toranit shel Ḥakhmei Aram Ṣōvā.* Jerusalem: Ben Zvi Institute.

———. 1998. "The First Jews from Aleppo in Manchester: New Documentary Evidence." *Association for Jewish Studies Review* 23: 191–202.

———. 1998. "Jewish-Christian Relations in Aleppo as Background for the Jewish Response to the Events of October 1850." *International Journal of Middle Eastern Studies* 30:77–96.

Haskell, Guy. 1994. *From Sofia to Jaffa.* Detroit: Wayne State University Press.

Heilman, Samuel, and Steven Cohen. 1989. *Cosmopolitans and Parochials: Modern Orthodox Jews in America.* Chicago: University of Chicago Press.

Hitti, Philip. 1924. *Syrians in America.* New York: George Doran.

Horowitz, Donald. 1985. *Ethnic Groups in Conflict.* Berkeley and Los Angeles: University of California Press.

Hourani, Albert. 1991. *A History of the Arab Peoples.* Cambridge, Mass.: Harvard University Press.

Joselit, Jenna W. 1990. *New York's "Jewish" Jews.* Philadelphia: Jewish Publication Society.

Karpat, Kemal. 1978. "Ottoman Population Records and Census of 1881/82–1893." *International Journal of Middle Eastern Studies* 9:237–74.

Kasinitz, Philip, and Bruce Haynes. 1996. "The Burning of Freddy's: Black-Jewish Conflict in Harlem," *CommonQuest: The Magazine of Black-Jewish Relations* 1, no. 2: 25–34.

Katriel, Tamar. 1987. *Communal Webs: Communication and Culture in Contemporary Israel.* Albany: State University of New York Press.

Katz, Ruth. 1970. "Mannerism and Cultural Change: An Ethnomusicological Example." *Current Anthropology* 11:465–75.

Kayal, Philip M., and Joseph M. Kayal. 1972. *The Syrian-Lebanese in America.* Boston: Twayne.

Kirshenblatt-Gimblett, Barbara. 1994. "Spaces of Dispersal." *Cultural Anthropology* 9:339–44.

Klich, Ignacio. 1991. "Argentina." In *Survey of Jewish Affairs,* William Frankel and Antony Lerman, eds., 216–31. Oxford: Blackwell and London: Institute of Jewish Affairs.

———. 1992. "*Criollos* and Arabic Speakers in Argentina: An Uneasy *Pas de Deux,* 1888–1914." In *The Lebanese in the World,* Albert Hourani and Nadim Shehadi, eds. London: I.B. Tauris. 243–284.

———. 1995. "Arabes, judios y arabes judios en la Argentina de la primera mitad del novecientos." *Estudios interdiciplinarios de America Latina y Caribe* (July–December): 109–43.

Klich, Ignacio, and Jeff Lesser, ed. 1996. "The *Turco* Immigrants in Latin America" (special issue). *Americas* 53:1–152.

Kligman, Mark. 1997. "Modes of Prayer: Arabic Maqāmāt in the Sabbath Morning Liturgical Music of the Syrian Jews in Brooklyn." Ph.D. diss., New York University.

Krause, Corinne A. 1970. *The Jews in Mexico: A History with Special Emphasis on the Period from 1857 to 1930.* Ann Arbor, Mich.: University Microfilms.

Kremer, Gudrun. 1989. *The Jews in Modern Egypt.* Seattle: University of Washington Press.

Landau, Jacob M. 1969. *Jews in Nineteenth Century Egypt.* New York: New York University Press.

Laniado, David. 1980. *La-Qedoshim Asher Ba-Are"ṣ.* Jerusalem: privately printed.

Lesser, Jeffrey. 1992. "From Pedlars to Proprietors: Lebanese, Syrian, and Jewish Immigrants in Brazil." In *The Lebanese in the World,* Albert Hourani and Nadim Shehadi, eds. London: I.B. Tauris. 393–410.

Levy, Andre. 1995. "Jews among Muslims: Perceptions and Reactions to the End of Casablancan Jewish History." Ph.D. diss., Hebrew University, Jerusalem.

Lowenstein, Steven M. 1989. *Frankfurt on the Hudson: The German Jewish Community of Washington Heights, 1933–1983, Its Structure and Culture.* Detroit: Wayne State University Press.

Lutzky, A. (Dothan). 1940. "The Francos and the Effects of the Capitulations on the Jews of Aleppo" (in Hebrew). *Zion* 6:46–79.

Malachi, A. R. 1934/35. "Ha-Yehudim be-Hitkommemut Ha-Druzim." *Ḥorev* 1:105–16.

Maoz, Moshe. 1968 *Ottoman Reform in Syria and Palestine.* London: Oxford University Press.

Marcus, Abraham. 1989. *The Middle East on the Eve of Modernity: Aleppo in the Eighteenth Century.* New York: Columbia University Press.

Marthan, Avraham. 1994. "An Authentic Human Voice: The Poetry of Amnon Shamosh." In *Critical Essays on Israeli Social Issues and Scholarship,* Russell Stone and Walter P. Zenner, eds., 43–61. Albany: State University of New York Press.

Masters, Bruce. 1988. *The Origins of Western Economic Dominance in the Middle East: Mercantilism and the Islamic Economy in Aleppo, 1600–1750.* New York: New York University Press.

Matza, Diane, ed. 1997. *Sephardic-American Voices: Two Hundred Years of a Literary Legacy.* Hanover, N.H.: University Press of New England.

McCarthy, Justin. 1994. "Jewish Population in the Late Ottoman Empire." In *The Jews of the Ottoman Empire,* Avigdor Levy, ed., 375–88. Princeton, N.J.: Darwin Press.

McEneny, John. 1980. *Albany—Capital City on the Hudson.* Woodland Hills, Calif.: Windsor.

Miller, Susan Gilson. 1996. "Kippur on the Amazon: Jewish Emigration from Northern Morocco in the Late Nineteenth Century." In *Sephardi and Middle Eastern Jewries: History and Culture in the Modern Era,* Harvey E. Goldberg, ed. Bloomington: Indiana University Press. 190–209.

Mirelman, Victor. 1987. "Sephardic Immigration to Argentina Prior to the Nazi Period." In *The Jewish Presence in Latin America,* Judith L. Elkin and Gilbert Merkx, eds., 13–32. Boston: Allen and Unwin.

———. 1990. *Jewish Buenos Aires, 1880–1930.* Detroit: Wayne State University Press.

Naff, Alixa. 1985. *Americans from the Arab World.* Carbondale, Ill.: University of Southern Illinois Press.

Naroll, Raoul. 1964. "On Ethnic Unit Classfication." *Current Anthropology* 5:283–312.

Orfalea, Gregory, and Sherif Elmusa. 1988. *Grape Leaves.* Salt Lake City: University of Utah Press.

Patai, Raphael. 1953. *Israel between East and West.* Philadelphia: Jewish Publication Society.

Petran, Tabitha. 1972. *Syria.* New York: Praeger.

Philipp, Thomas. 1994. "French Merchants and Jews in the Ottoman Empire during the Eighteenth Century." In *Jews of the Ottoman Empire,* Avigdor Levy, ed., 315–26. Princeton, N.J.: Darwin Press.

Picciotto, Emilio. 1985. *Genealogia della Famiglia Picciotto.* Milan: private publication.

Platt, D. C. M. 1973. "Further Objections to an 'Imperialism of Free Trade.' " *Economic History Review* 26:77–91.

Plotnik, Lawrence. 1958. "The Sephardim of New Lots." *Commentary* 25:28–35.

Rabinovitch, Itamar. 1972. *Syria under the Baath.* New York: Halsted.

Raphael, Chaim. 1986. "The Manchester Connection." *Commentary* 82 (September): 48–53.

Roden, Claudia. 1972. *A Book of Middle Eastern Food.* New York: Knopf.

———. 1997. *The Book of Jewish Food.* New York: Knopf.

Romann, Michael, and Alex Weingrod. 1993. *Living Together Separately: Arabs and Jews in Contemporary Jerusalem.* Princeton, N.J.: Princeton University Press.

Rosenthal, Celia Stopnicka. 1956. "The Jews of Barranquilla." *Jewish Social Studies* 18:262–74.

Russell, Alexander. 1794. *The Natural History of Aleppo.* 2d ed. 2 vols. London: n.p.

Samuel, Maurice. 1950. *The Gentleman and the Jew.* New York: Knopf.

Sanua, Marianne. 1990. "From the Pages of the *Victory Bulletin:* The Syrian Jews of Brooklyn during World War II." *YIVO Annual* 19:283–330.

Sanua, Victor D. 1967. "A Study of the Adjustment of Sephardi Jews in the New York Metropolitan Area." *Jewish Journal of Sociology* 9:25–33.

———. 1977. "Contemporary Studies of Sephardi Jews in the United States." In *A Coat of Many Colors,* Abraham D. Lavender, ed., 281–88. Westport, Conn.: Greenwood Press.

———. 1983. "A Jewish Childhood in Cairo." In *Fields of Offerings: Studies in Honor of Raphael Patai,* V. D. Sanua, ed. Cranbury, N.J.: Associated University Presses. 283–95.

Sason, Grace. 1988. *Kosher Syrian Cooking.* Brooklyn: private publication.

Schechtman, Joseph B. 1961. *On Wings of Eagles.* New York: Yoseloff.

Segall, Joseph. 1910. *Travels through Northern Syria.* London: Society for Promoting Christianity Amongst the Jews.

Sephardic Archives. 1984. *The Victory Bulletin.* Brooklyn:Sephardic Community Center.

———. 1986. *The Spirit of Aleppo: Syrian Jewish Immgrant Life in New York, 1890–1939.* Brooklyn: Sephardic Community Center.

Shaffir, Gershon. 1995. *Immigrants and Nationalists.* Albany: State University of New York Press.

Shamosh, Amnon. 1978. *Michel Ezra Safra u-Vanav.* Ramat Gan: Massada.

———. 1979. *My Sister, the Bride and Other Stories.* Ramat Gan: Massada.

———. 1981. *Iti Me-Levanon.* Tel Aviv: Ha-Kibbutz Ha-Me'uhad.

———. 1984. *Ma'ayan Ḥatum* (The sealed fountain). Tel Aviv: Ha-Kibbutz Ha-Me'uhad.

———. 1987. *HaKeter: Sipuro shel Keter Aram Ṣōbāh* (HaKeter: The story of the Aleppo Codex). Jerusalem: Ben Zvi Institute.

———. 1990. *Arazim.* Tel Aviv: Massada.

Shelemay, Kay Kaufman. 1988. "Together in the Field: Team Research among Syrian Jews in Brooklyn, New York," *Ethnomusicology* 32, no. 3: 369–84.

———1998. *Let Jasmine Rain Down: Song and Remembrance among Syrian Jews in the Americas.* Chicago: University of Chicago Press.

Sisterhood of Deal. 1980. *Deal Delights.* Deal, N.J.: Synagogue of Deal.

Siu, Paul. 1952. "The Sojourner." *American Journal of Sociology* 58:34–44.

Stillman, Norman. 1991. *The Jews of Arab Lands in Modern Times.* Philadelphia: Jewish Publication Society.

———. 1995. *Sephardic Religious Responses to Modernity.* Luxembourg: Harwood Academic Publishers.

Sultan, Stanley. 1977. *Rabbi: A Tale of the Waning Year.* West Whateley, Mass.: American Novelists' Cooperative.

Sutton, Joseph A. D. 1979. *Magic Carpet: Aleppo-in-Flatbush.* Brooklyn: Thayer-Jacoby.

———. 1988. *Aleppo Chronicles: The Story of the Unique Sephardeem of the Ancient Near East—In Their Own Words.* Brooklyn: Thayer-Jacoby.

Taylor, Ian, Karen Evans, and Penny Fraser. 1996. *A Tale of Two Cities: Global Change, Local Feeling and Everyday Life in the North of England: A Study of Manchester and Sheffield.* London: Routledge.

Tessler, Mark, and Linda Hawkins. 1980. "The Political Culture of Jews in Tunisia and Morocco." *International Journal of Middle Eastern Studies* 11:56–86.

Toaff, Renzo. 1990. *La Nazione Ebrea a Livorno e a Pisa, 1591–1700.* Firenze: L. Olsehki Editore.

Uchemany, Alexandra. 1993. "The Periodization of the History of New Christians and Crypto-Jews in Spanish America." In *New Horizons in Sephardic Studies,* Yedida K. Stillman and George K. Zucker, eds., 109–36. Albany: State University of New York Press.

Watson, James L. 1975. *Emigration and the Chinese Lineage.* Berkeley: University of California Press.

Weiker, Walter. 1988. *The Unseen Israelis: the Jews of Turkey in Israel.* Lanham, Md.: University Press of America.

———. 1995. "Ethnicity among Turkish Jews in Haifa." *Israel Social Science Research* 10:23–42.

Williams, Bill. 1976. *The Making of Manchester Jewry, 1740–1875.* Manchester: Manchester University Press.

———. 1985. "The Anti-Semitism of Tolerance: Middle Class Manchester and the Jews, 1870–1900." In *City, Class and Culture: Studies of Social Policy and Cultural Production in Victorian Manchester,* Alan J. Kidd and K. W. Roberts, eds. Manchester: Manchester University Press. 74–102.

Willis, Aaron. 1993. "Sephardic Torah Guardians: Ritual and the Politics of Piety." Ph.D. diss., Princeton University. Ann Arbor, Mich.: University Microfilms International, Order #AAC-932-8110.

Woolfson, Marion. 1980. *Prophets in Babylon.* London: Faber and Faber.

Yedid, Yomtov, and Menahem Yedid. 1992. *Ner Yomtov.* Jerusalem: Yeshivat Simḥat Yomtov.

Yosef, Ovadia. 1978. *Sefer She'elot u-teshuvot Yehaveh Da'at.* Jerusalem: privately published.

Zemer, Moshe. 1988. "The Rabbinic Ban on Conversion in Argentina." *Judaism* 37:84–93.

Zenlund, Darrow Gary. 1991. "Post-Colonial Aleppo, Syria: Struggles in Representation and Identity." Ph.D. diss., University of Texas-Austin. Ann Arbor, Mich.: University Microfilms International.

Zenner, Walter P. 1962. "Raful Leaves School." *Reconstructionist* 28, no. 15: 21–24.

———. 1963. "Ambivalence and Self-Image among Oriental Jews in Israel." *Jewish Journal of Sociology* 5:214–23.

———. 1965. "Syrian Jewish Identification in Israel." Ph.D. diss., Columbia University. Ann Arbor, Mich.: University Microfilm Order No. 66–8536.

———. 1965. "Saints and Piecemeal Supernaturalism among the Jerusalem Sephardim." *Anthropological Quarterly* 38:201–17.

———. 1967. "Sephardic Communal Organizations in Israel." *Middle East Journal* 21:173–86.

———. 1970. "Ethnic Stereotyping in Arabic Proverbs." *Journal of American Folklore* 83, no. 350: 417–29.

———. 1972. "Some Aspects of Ethnic Stereotype Content in the Galilee: A Trial Formulation." *Middle Eastern Studies* 8:405–16.

———. 1980 "Jewish Communities as Cultural Units." In *Perspectives on Ethnicity,* Regina E. Holloman and Serghei Arutiunov, eds., 327–38. The Hague: Mouton.

———. 1980. "Censorship and Syncretism: Some Anthropological Approaches to the Study of Middle Eastern Jews." In *Studies in Jewish Folklore,* F. Talmage, ed., 377–94. Cambridge, Mass.: Association for Jewish Studies.

———. 1981. "The Syrian Jews of Metropolitan New York: A Bibliographical Guide." *Jewish Folklore and Ethnology Newsletter* 4:3–4, 6–8.

———. 1982. "The Jews in Late Ottoman Syria." In *Jewish Societies in the Middle East,* S. Deshen and W. P. Zenner, eds., 155–210. Lanham, Md.: University Press of America.

———. 1982. "Arabic-Speaking Immigrants in North America as Middleman Minorities" *Ethnic and Racial Studies* 5:457–77.

———. 1983. "The Jewish Diaspora and the Middleman Adaptation." In *Diaspora: Exile and the Jewish Condition,* Étan Levine, ed. New York: Jason Aronson. 141–56.

———. 1983. "Syrian Jews in New York Twenty Years Ago." In *Fields of Offerings: Papers in Honor of Raphael Patai,* Victor D. Sanua, ed., 173–93. Cranbury, N.J.: Associated Universities Presses.

———. 1987. "Middleman Minorities in the Syrian Mosaic: Trade, Conflict and Image Management." *Sociological Perspectives,* 30:400–421.

———. 1988. "Aleppo and the Kibbutz: The Fiction of Amnon Shamosh." *Shofar* 6, no. 3: 25–35.

———. 1988. "Common Ethnicity and Separate Identities: Interaction among Jewish Immigrant Groups." In *Cross-Cultural Adaptations (International and Intercultural Communications Annual 11),* Y. Y. Kim and W. B. Gudykunst, eds., 267–85. Newbury Park, Calif.: Sage.

———. 1989–90. "Chicago's Sephardim: A Historical Exploration." *American Jewish History* 79:221–41.

———. 1990. "Jewish Retainers as Power Brokers." *Jewish Quarterly Review* 81:127–49.

———. 1991. *Minorities in the Middle: A Cross-Cultural Analysis.* Albany: State University of New York Press.

———. 1993. "Espionage as Cultural Mediation." In *Critical Essays on Israeli Social Issues and Scholarship,* Russell Stone and W. P. Zenner, eds., 31–42. Albany: State University of New York Press.

———. 1994. "Essentialism and Nominalism in Urban Anthropology." *City and Society [Annual Review]* 1:53–66.

———. 1996. "The Trans-National Web of Syrian Jewish Relations." In *Urban Life: Readings in Urban Anthropology,* 3d ed., George Gmelch and W. P. Zenner, eds., 459–72. Prospect Heights, Ill.: Waveland Press.

———. 1996. "The Descendants of Aleppo Jews in Jerusalem." *Israel Affairs* 3:95–110.

———. 1997. "Remembering the Sages of Aram Ṣōbā (Aleppo)." In *Critical Essays on Israeli Society, Religion and Government,* Kevin Avruch and W. P. Zenner, eds., 137–51. Albany: State University of New York Press.

Zenner, Walter, and Shlomo Deshen. 1997. *Jews among Muslims: Communities in the Pre-colonial Middle East.* New York: New York University Press and Houndmills: Macmillan.

Zerubavel, Yael, and Dianne Esses. 1987. "Reconstructions of the Past: Syrian Jewish Women and the Maintenance of Tradition. *Journal of American Folklore* 100: 528–39.

Zicht, Gloria. "The Immigration of Syrian Jews to New York, 1992–1994: An Agency's Adaptation to a Different Culture." *Journal of Jewish Communal Service* 72:256–62.

Zohar, Zvi. 1990. "Qehilot Yisrael she-ba-Suriya, 1880–1918: Peraqim Ba-Demografiya, Kalkalah, u-Mosdot Ha-Qehillah Be-Shilhei Ha-Shilton Ha-Otomani." *Peʿamim* 44:80–109.

———. 1993. "Shamranut Loḥemet: Qavim Le-Manhigutam Ha-Ḥevratit-Datit shel Ḥakhmei Ḥaleb be-ʿEt Ha-Ḥadashah" (Activist Conservatives: The socio-religious policy of Aleppo's rabbis 1865–1945). *Peʿamim* 53:57–78.

———. 1993. " 'The Torah of Israel and the People of Israel' by Rabbi Yitzhak Dayan." In *New Horizons in Sephardic Studies,* Yedidah Stillman and George Zucker, eds., 93–107. Albany: State University of New York Press.

Index

Books in the Raphael Patai Series in Jewish Folklore and Anthropology

The Myth of the Jewish Race, revised edition,
by Raphael Patai and Jennifer Patai, 1989

The Hebrew Goddess, third enlarged edition,
by Raphael Patai, 1990

Robert Graves and the Hebrew Myths: A Collaboration,
by Raphael Patai, 1991

Jewish Musical Traditions,
by Amnon Shiloah, 1992

The Jews of Kurdistan, by Erich Brauer,
completed and edited by Raphael Patai, 1993

Jewish Moroccan Folk Narratives from Israel, by Haya Bar-Itzhak
and Aliza Shenhar, 1993

For Our Soul: The Ethiopian Jews in Israel, by Teshome G. Wagaw, 1993

*Book of Fables: The Yiddish Fable Collection of Reb Moshe Wallich,
Frankfurt am Main, 1697*, translated and edited by Eli Katz, 1994

From Sofia to Jaffa: The Jews of Bulgaria and Israel,
by Guy H. Haskell, 1994

Jadid al-Islam: The Jewish "New Muslims" of Meshhed,
by Raphael Patai, 1998

Saint Veneration among the Jews in Morocco,
by Issachar Ben-Ami, 1998

Arab Folktales from Palestine and Israel,
introduction, translation, and annotation by Raphel Patai, 1998

*Profiles of a Lost World: Memoirs of East European
Jewish Life before World War II*, by Hirsz Abramowicz, translated by
Eva Zeitlin Dobkin, edited by Dina Abramowicz and Jeffrey Shandler, 1999

A Global Community: The Jews from Aleppo, Syria,
by Walter Zenner, 2000